RELUCTANT NEIGHBOR

RELUCTANT NEIGHBOR

Turkey's Role in the Middle East

HENRI J. BARKEY, EDITOR

UNITED STATES INSTITUTE OF PEACE PRESS
WASHINGTON, D.C.

The views expressed in this book are those of the authors alone; they do not necessarily reflect views of the United States Institute of Peace.

United States Institute of Peace
1550 M Street, N.W.
Washington, D.C. 20005

Printed in the United States of America.

The paper used by this publication meets the minimum requirements of American National Standard for Information Sciences—Permanence of Paper for Printed Library Materials, ANSI Z39.48-1984.

Library of Congress Cataloguing in Publication Data
Reluctant Neighbor: Turkey's Role in the Middle East/Henri J. Barkey, ed.
    p. cm.
   ISBN 1-878379-64-X (pbk.: alk. paper)
   1. Middle East—Relations—Turkey. 2. Turkey—Relations—Middle East. 3. East and West. I. Barkey, Henri J.
   DS63.2.T8 R 1996
   327.561—dc21   96-39739
                                                         CIP

CONTENTS

PREFACE

"Turkey after the Cold War is equivalent to Germany during the Cold War—a pivotal state, where diverse strategic interests intersect."

—Richard Holbrooke

As former Assistant Secretary of State Holbrooke indicates, Turkey's long-standing strategic relevance to the United States and the West has been cast in a new light by such recent events as the fall of the Soviet Union, the breakup of Yugoslavia, and the emergence of independent Turkic states in the Transcaucasus and Central Asia. Still, despite their recognition of Turkey's strategic location among regions in flux, scholars and policymakers have tended to neglect the fact that it is also part of the Middle East, long an unstable region. Although any Middle East specialist will acknowledge Turkey's significant role in the history of the region and its distinctive relationships with the Arab states and Israel, it is not often spoken of as an important factor in the peace process or in Western calculations in the Persian Gulf. Nor does one hear much about Turkey's relationships with its immediate neighbors—Syria, Iraq, and Iran—although they have every bit as much potential for upheaval as its relations with Europe and the states of the former Soviet Union.

But Turkey's burgeoning importance in the Middle East can be seen in such instances as Ankara's deepening engagement with the Kurds in northern Iraq, stresses in its relations with Syria over the Kurds and sharing Tigris and Euphrates water, and its controversial military cooperation with Israel.

In June 1994, the United States Institute of Peace convened "A Reluctant Neighbor: Analyzing Turkey's Role in the Middle East," a conference designed to initiate a discussion of these issues and bring together scholars and other experts from Turkey and the Middle East, as well as American and European specialists on the region. The overwhelming response to this conference indicates the growing interest in understanding this dimension of Turkey's foreign policy, and the liveliness of the discussion helped persuade us to develop a book creating a document of the debate on which students and policymakers might draw. The present volume includes chapters developed from papers presented at the conference and subsequently considerably expanded and updated, as well as a new essay by Alan Makovsky designed to complete the overview. Contributors come from Turkey, Syria, Iran, and Iraq, as well as the United States and Britain, bringing to bear varied backgrounds, viewpoints, and disciplines.

I would like to acknowledge the invaluable assistance of Patricia Carley, program officer at the United States Institute of Peace, who worked with me to organize the original conference. I would also like to express my gratitude to Institute President Richard H. Solomon, who supported the conference and book projects throughout their development, as well to Kenneth M. Jensen, who as the Institute's then-director of research and studies was the first to approve of the conference idea. In addition, Priscilla Jensen worked diligently on bringing the manuscript to fruition.

RELUCTANT NEIGHBOR

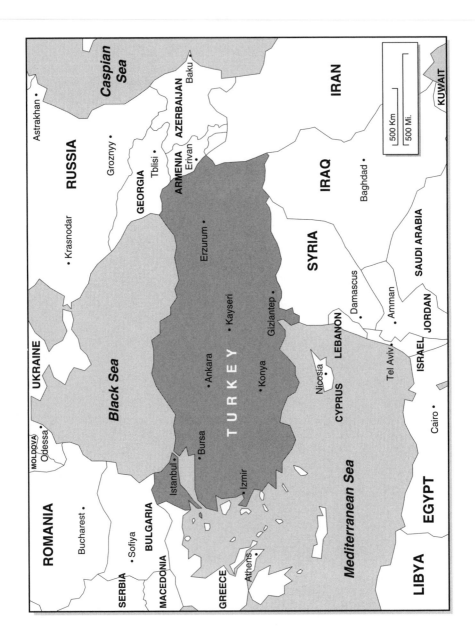

CHAPTER ONE

TURKEY'S PLACE IN THE WORLD

Patricia Carley

Few countries occupy Turkey's exceptional position—literally at the crossroads between the cultures of East and West, overlapping Europe and Asia geographically, economically, politically, and even spiritually, as a Muslim country that aspires to be part of the West. The inherent incongruity has haunted the country for much of its modern history. Turkey's location and seemingly paradoxical aspirations have left it with something like an identity crisis, or at least an identity dilemma, which continues to mark not only the national character but how Turkey views itself and its place in the world.

The contradictions are manifold. Though it is an unequivocally Islamic country, Turkey is only loosely part of the Middle East, and the Turks are neither ethnically nor linguistically Arab. At the same time, its attempts to fit in with the West have been complicated by Western ambivalence toward Islam, among other reasons. Culturally, Turkey stood alone. Until the independence of the Turkic-speaking Central Asian states and Azerbaijan, the Turkish language was not related to the language of any other internationally recognized sovereign state. Turkey, it seemed, simply did not fit anywhere.

To understand Turkey's confounding—and sometimes confused —position in the world, one need look only at how it has been characterized by outside observers, including scholars, strategists, and diplomats. At different times Turkey has been said to belong, all at once, to the Near East, the Middle East, the southern flank, the northern tier, the Balkans, the Islamic world, the West generally, and Western Europe specifically. Added to those categories since the fall of the Soviet Union are the Turkic world and even, loosely defined,

Central Asia. And, in fact, Turkey *does* belong to each of these groups in some way. No wonder the Turks have spent much of their modern history feeling like the "odd country out." It is essential, when considering Turkey's relations with other states in the world, to be mindful of this identity dilemma.

ORIGINS OF TURKEY'S FOREIGN POLICY—THE LEGACY OF ATATÜRK

To understand Turkey's foreign policy it is crucial to grasp the spirit of the founding of the Turkish Republic and the critical role and legacy of Mustafa Kemal Atatürk. It is hardly an exaggeration to say that Turkey would not exist as a modern country without Atatürk's determination to establish a Turkish nation-state and his possession of the military acumen that made it a reality. In 1919, the Ottoman Empire lay in ruins after the devastation of World War I. The empire's dismemberment was made official with the signing of the Treaty of Sèvres in 1920, which stipulated that all its European territory except a small slice around Istanbul (occupied by the British) was to be cut away; all Arab lands removed; the region around Izmir (formerly Smyrna) given to the Greeks; the eastern Anatolian provinces divided between an independent Armenia and a potentially independent Kurdistan; and, finally, large regions of south and southwest Anatolia granted to France and Italy to administer as spheres of influence. The last sultan, though still nominally on the throne in Istanbul, relinquished virtually all his powers to the British. The Straits of Bosporus and the Dardanelles were demilitarized and administered not by the Turks but by a permanent Allied commission in Istanbul, and Anatolia was placed under the control of the Allied Financial Commission. In 1920, the very idea that an independent and sovereign Turkish state might emerge would not have received serious attention.

Yet by 1923, in the wake of Atatürk's startling victories over the French, Italians, British, and Greeks, and after he had regained control of Istanbul, the Allies were forced to sign the Treaty of Lausanne, recognizing the establishment of the Turkish Republic. After the military victory over the occupying powers, Atatürk went on to define the parameters of the Turkish nation-state in virtually all walks of public and political life, including domestic and foreign policy. The new Turkish Republic was to be a modern, Westernized nation, and

Atatürk spent the rest of his life, until his death in 1938, not only setting up the institutions needed to achieve this goal, but molding the mind of the people in that direction.

Atatürk's foreign policy was directed away from the East and from other Turkic and Islamic peoples. From the very start of his military struggle for Turkey, he had firmly eschewed any form of pan-Turkism or pan-Islamism. The pan-Turkism movement in the late nineteenth century in the Ottoman Empire promoted the ultimate unification of the world's Turkic peoples, most of whom, after the Anatolian Turks, lived under Russian control. Atatürk believed that pan-Turkism and other such "foolish ideologies" were ultimately responsible for the humiliating defeat of the Turkish nation at the hands of the Allies. Not only did pan-Turkism represent a quagmire for Turkey, but it was not, Atatürk believed, consonant with the Western concept of the modern nation-state. Similarly, Atatürk had little interest in maintaining historical ties with the rest of the Islamic world. Pan-Islamism was as dangerous for the new state as pan-Turkism.

DOMESTIC CHANGES

Atatürk also instituted a series of domestic reforms to reinforce the new republic's movement away from the Islamic world and toward the West. The most important was the secularization of the government and, to a certain extent, of society—a policy that grew out of Atatürk's conviction that Islam as expounded by the Ottoman sultan was responsible for Turkey's backward economic and social state. Political power was to originate with the Grand National Assembly and was not, for the first time in Turkish history, bound to religious ideology. *Sha'ria* courts were abolished in 1925 and replaced by courts grounded in a civil code, thus denying clerics power over judicial, criminal, and even social matters. By 1928, Islam had been removed as the official religion from the Turkish constitution, and the state assumed many of the functions of the old Islamic institutions.

Another powerful move toward modernization was the reform of the alphabet. For centuries, Ottoman Turkish had been written in Arabic script, though that script was not entirely suited to the Turkish language. In 1928, Atatürk decreed that Turkish would henceforth be written in the Latin alphabet. Furthermore, many non-Turkish words —primarily Arabic and Persian accretions—were to be discarded and replaced by "true" Turkish words (in some cases fabricated). This reform moved the Turkish people one step further not only from their religion (since Arabic is the language of the Prophet), but from their Ottoman history. Today a Turk who wants to read tracts and documents from the Ottoman period must first take the trouble to learn the Arabic script. In fact, as a result of his reforms, the Turkish language has changed to such an extent that a Turk today needs a dictionary to read Atatürk's speeches.

ATATÜRK'S RELATIONS WITH THE SOVIET UNION

Ironically, considering the historic rivalry between the Russian and Ottoman Empires, Turkey's need to secure friendly relations with the Soviet Union was a strong factor behind Atatürk's rejection of pan-Turkist and pan-Islamic ideas. Indeed, ultimately the Soviet Union and Turkey maintained good relations throughout most of their modern history. Atatürk chose this course not because he had any doubts about his country's Western orientation, but because he knew the importance of avoiding unnecessary conflict—or even hostile relationships—on Turkey's borders. Thus it was necessary to establish good relations with Turkey's powerful northern neighbor, with the aim of making Turkey a neutral as well as Western-looking state.

The new regime in Moscow was also mindful of the value of good relations with countries on its border. Grounding the relationship in the March 1921 Treaty of Friendship, which contained a pledge by both sides not to interfere in the affairs of the other, each side agreed to forbid the formation of organizations which could be interpreted as hostile to the other. For example, Atatürk proscribed pan-Turkist organizations and ignored the existence of Turkic peoples of Central Asia and the Caucasus in the Soviet Union, and the Soviet government abandoned its support for underground communist parties in Turkey.

Even during the Cold War years, and despite sometimes unfriendly rhetoric, Turkey maintained civil if not cordial relations with the Soviet Union. The most notable interruption in this state of affairs was in the months immediately after World War II, when Stalin made bellicose demands on the Straits (claiming Moscow's right to joint control) and on regions of eastern Turkey (the area containing the cities of Kars and Ardahan, which the Russians had conceded were part of Turkey in the 1921 friendship treaty). Relations between the two became very tense, ultimately propelling Turkey to abandon its officially neutral stance and join the newly formed North Atlantic Treaty Organization (NATO) alliance.

Stalin's actions were regretted by succeeding Soviet leaders, and within two months of his death in 1953, the territorial demands were unequivocally dropped in the hope of mending relations with the Turks. Though Turkey was by this time squarely a NATO member, the position of mutual "tolerance" between Ankara and Moscow was renewed, despite the even more strident ideological differences. Atatürk's belief that cordial relations with the Soviet Union were more important than ideological divisions or the fate of the USSR's sizable Turkic population remained a central tenet of Turkey's foreign policy.

ATATÜRK AND THE KURDS

The Turkish state's relations with its Kurdish population of some 12 million have been troubled virtually since the beginning of the Turkish Republic. In addition to military victories and radical social reforms, another important legacy of Atatürk was the consolidation of the idea of Turkish ethnicity as the core identity of the Turkish Republic. During the centuries of Ottoman rule, the term "Turk" was most often used as a derogatory epithet to refer to an uncultured peasant. The ruling elites identified themselves as Ottomans or simply as Muslims; the rest of the Turkish population referred to themselves as Muslims or perhaps as residents of a particular village. This remained the case even in the latter part of the nineteenth century as the nationalist movement among the Turks in the Ottoman Empire was developing.

It was Atatürk who made the radical break with the past. He built the Republic of Turkey firmly around the idea of Turkish national identity and language within a fixed territory and rejected the notion of a multinational empire. As part of this process, the term "Turk" was elevated from derogatory epithet to an identity that every Turk could adopt. In the course of those early years, it became a central tenet of the Turkish Republic that within its borders lived the Turkish nation. Atatürk even instituted population exchanges with Greece to "simplify" the ethnic composition of Turkey. The very concept of the new Turkey depended directly on uniformity of nationhood, and the notion that the republic might contain people who belonged to some other nation was extremely threatening.[1] This aspect of Atatürkist thought has changed little through the generations.

The problem was—and remains—that peoples other than Turks found themselves inside the Republic of Turkey, and the largest of these groups is the Kurds. Their very existence became an issue, most notably in 1925 and again in 1937, when the Kurds in the southeastern part of the country rebelled and were brutally suppressed. Since then, the Turkish government has advanced stringent policies designed to promote the integrity of the nation, suppressing any element of Kurdish cultural or linguistic distinctiveness and encouraging the assimilation of the Kurds into the wider Turkish population. The use of Kurdish in any official or public capacity was banned until very recently; indeed, until only a few years ago, the very existence of the Kurdish people in Turkey continued to be officially denied.

The formation in the late 1970s of a radicalized Kurdistan Workers Party (PKK) with a stated aim of increased autonomy for the Kurdish region took the struggle to a new level. By 1984, the PKK was resorting to violent terrorist activities. For the government, these activities signaled the ultimate intention of dismembering Turkey, and, indeed, some PKK elements have demanded independence. The Turkish government has responded militarily to PKK violence, often resulting in the killing of non-PKK Kurdish villagers. In the past ten years, the regional carnage has led to the deaths of thousands of Kurdish and Turkish civilians, as well as Turkish soldiers and Kurdish guerrillas. Journalists and others who have taken up the Kurds' cause have also been killed.

TURKEY LOOKS EAST

Since the end of World War II, Turkey's strategic significance to the United States and to NATO as the only member of the Western alliance to border the Soviet Union has been unquestioned. Turkey also demonstrated its importance to the West by supporting the coalition in the 1991 war against Saddam Hussein, a move that was opposed by many in Turkey. It has been seen as a gateway to such once unfamiliar places as Azerbaijan, Kazakstan, Kyrgyzstan, Turkmenistan, and Uzbekistan, and it is important also with respect to other Muslim countries, with which it has complex and sometimes troubled relations. With the fall of the USSR, its decline in strategic importance in that respect has been countered by increased potential in other areas, namely the Middle East and surrounding countries.

Though Turkey's relations with the countries of the Middle East have been shaped largely by the Western foreign policy orientation established by Atatürk, they have also been colored by the Ottoman past. All of the countries of what is today called the Middle East, except Iran, were once part of the Ottoman Empire. Within the empire, Turks and Arabs lived together for centuries, forming the bulk (together with the Kurds) of the Islamic *umma*, or community of believers. As members of the *umma*, Arabs enjoyed rights and privileges that the non-Muslim *millets*—such minority groups as the Armenians, Greeks, and Jews—did not. Yet the Turks and the Arabs remained distinct groups, separated by language, history, culture, and ethnicity, as well as by the inescapable fact that the Ottoman Turks ruled and the Arabs were their subjects.

By the end of the nineteenth century, sentiments giving rise to nationalist movements elsewhere in the world had permeated the Ottoman Empire, which by that time had lost Greece and Egypt as well as other territories. A small group of intellectuals initiated a movement to promote "Ottoman" identity, aiming to rally different national groups in the empire around the Ottoman ruler. Part of that movement later abandoned the effort at kindling Ottoman identity, branching off instead to form a movement aimed at advancing the goals of the Turkish population. In 1908, these Young Turks, as they became known, succeeded in wresting political power from an increasingly impotent sultan and set up a new regime. In the end, it was events during the relatively short period of Young Turk rule that irretrievably damaged relations between the Turks and the Arabs, by this time themselves agitating for independence from Ottoman rule. The extremist Turkification policies of the Young Turks, in the form of harsh suppression of Arab language and culture, resulted in an angry backlash that resonates even today in Turkey's relations with the Arab world. At the same time, Arab attempts to break away from Ottoman rule drove them to side with the British during World War I —an act still viewed as treachery by the Turks. Though these events happened nearly a century ago, they are still very much on the minds of the Turks and the Arabs as they contemplate a significant change in their relations.

Relations between Turkey and Syria have not been warm for most of this century, clouded by Arab suspicions dating back to the Young Turk era and compounded by a territorial dispute over Alexandretta (or, as the Turks call it, the Hatay region), which was under French mandate when the Turkish Republic was founded. In 1938, a plebiscite determined that the majority of the population was Turkish—a result strongly disputed then and now by the Arabs. After a year of independence, Hatay became part of Turkey in 1939.

During the Cold War, the two countries were positioned on opposing sides—Turkey as a member of NATO and Syria as an ally of the Soviet Union. With the end of the bipolar divide, however, Turkish-Syrian relations have become more focused on regional issues, particularly water. Antagonism between them heightened in the 1970s when the Turks began construction of the Southeastern Anatolia Project, or GAP, the large dam project on the Euphrates River that, when completed in the mid-1980s, restricted the flow of water into Syria. That friction was compounded by Turkish claims that the Syrian government gives safe haven to PKK members—something Syria has never acknowledged, though PKK leader Abdullah Öcalan is now based in Syria.

The presence of Kurds in neighboring countries such as Iraq has only recently become a significant foreign policy issue for Turkey, and even now it is not always a contentious one. During the Iran-Iraq conflict in the 1980s, Turkey and Iraq cooperated on the Kurdish issue, even to the extent that Baghdad allowed the Turks to carry out cross-border actions against PKK supporters who had fled to Iraq. Confrontation with Iraq over the issue began only with the 1991 Gulf War, when Turkey sided with the United States and its allies and supported the embargo against Iraq—an unaccustomed hostile position. Immediately after the war, Saddam attacked the Kurds in northern Iraq and hundreds of thousands fled to Iran and especially to Turkey. The countries allied against Iraq moved in and created a safe haven for the Kurds in northern Iraq, leaving them with de facto autonomy, a situation which for the Turks was discomforting at best. More than once since, Turkey has disconcerted the West by invading northern Iraq ostensibly to attack PKK bases there.

Turkey and Iran have been rivals since the days when each was the center of an empire—Ottoman and Persian. The competition took many forms, including the quest for territory and power and the battle between the two largest sects of Islam—Sunnism and Shi'ism. The rivalry also involved a contest over which would be the dominant culture in the region: the Ottoman Turks long sought acknowledgment of their cultural superiority over the Persians.

Events in this century have changed the course of Turkish-Iranian relations. As each shed its empire and established itself as a nation-state, the rivalry abated almost entirely. Atatürk's inward-looking policies were based on the premise that the modern Turkish nation had few quarrels with its neighbors, including Iran. Relations warmed further when Iran adopted a Western-oriented policy under the shah, and both countries became members of U.S.-backed security organizations such as the Central Treaty Organization (CENTO). However, the 1979 Iranian revolution quickly soured relations between the two. Although economic relations have gradually improved since then, and neither country has made a point of antagonizing the other, Ankara remains cautious about close ties to Tehran and skeptical of Iran's true intentions. Persistent suggestions of Iranian support for Islamic-oriented extremist organizations in Turkey are particularly worrisome for Turkey's secularist leaders.

TURKEY REMAINS UNIQUE

The modern Turkish Republic was built on the foundation of an almost complete break with the Ottoman past, and some of the changes —secularism, for example—remain controversial to some segments of Turkish society. However, Atatürk's reforms shaped the very definition of the republic, especially in regard to how generations of ruling elites have determined its foreign policy and to how it views its place in the world. This orientation may not be unshakable; Turkey's developing relations with the Turkic former republics of the Soviet Union suggest that some of Atatürk's tenets are finally being displaced. What is incontestable is that Atatürk's relevance and legacy endure in Turkey, and it is important to examine any changes in Ankara's foreign policy against the background of this fundamental fact of Turkish life.

Turkey truly is an important link between East and West, a country that has made itself a bridge from empire to modern nation-state, from theocracy to secular Muslim state, and from a system of economic backwardness to relative modernization. But it is precisely because of these radical shifts, accomplished under Atatürk's leadership in a breathtakingly short time, that Turkey has been left with a more complicated and unclear sense of itself than is the case for many other modernizing countries. For this reason, Turkey's identity crisis is likely to continue.

Turkey's place in today's post–Cold War world is in a state of flux. Until the collapse of the Soviet Union, its foreign policy was fairly unequivocal in its Western orientation, built into the very fabric of the country by Atatürk. However, recent developments in the world political system made change inevitable, and the result is likely to be a shift eastward. Turkey will continue to look toward the West; it will not shrink from its commitment to the NATO alliance, and the West will carry on as its main trading partner. Yet the tugs from its neighbors, with whom it has generally enjoyed pragmatically cordial relations, receive increasing attention in Ankara, accompanied by growing frustration that many Western policies—the embargo against Iraq, for example—work against Turkey's interests. How Turkey balances the tensions in its relations with East and West will have significant bearing on its ability to carve out its own unique position, engaged but independent, as the century nears its close.

CHAPTER TWO

THE OTTOMAN TWILIGHT ZONE OF THE MIDDLE EAST

Selim Deringil

The historian Eric Hobsbawm defines an interesting category—the "twilight zone" of historical consciousness. This zone is the intellectual territory where memory and history meet, where the memory of our grandparents overlaps with the history textbooks.[1] Recent works dealing with the politics of the Middle East have emphasized memory, looking at the Ottoman prehistory of the region: "The Eastern Question in its conventional usage . . . provides the key to understanding a political culture that still characterizes the Middle East."[2] Similarly, Ehud Toledano, in a recent work on mid–nineteenth century Egypt, warns against "the danger of the loss of the Ottoman context" in the Balkans and the Middle East.[3]

Recently as well, the Ottoman past has been featured more and more frequently as a leitmotif in the Turkish and foreign press. Robert Kaplan, in a recent article, says that "the former Ottoman Empire and even the former Byzantine world are fusing back together following the aberration of the Cold War. The implications of this tectonic shift are, needless to say, enormous."[4] This point of view regards the end of the Ottoman centuries, the period from say, 1880 to 1920, as the framework for many of the present-day problems of the Middle East.

THE PROBLEM OF PALESTINE

Some of the most momentous issues in today's Middle East may indeed have roots in Ottoman history and politics. The intensification of Jewish immigration to Palestine dates from the 1890s, during the reign of the Ottoman sultan Abdulhamid II and the pogroms in Romania and Russia. This matter has now become the center of an intense debate in Turkey and elsewhere. The Islamic Turkish right claims that the sultan made a heroic effort to prevent the immigration of Jews to the Ottoman province of Syria. Their opponents, on the other hand, contend that he actually encouraged their settlement. As usual, the historical record, based on Ottoman archival documentation, seems much more shaded by nuance. On August 17, 1891, Abdulhamid dictated to his private secretary, "These Jews are renowned for taking over trade and manufacture wherever they settle and for causing the impoverishment of the local people. That is why they are not welcomed anywhere they go. That is also why they are not to settle in Our imperial Domains, and if they present themselves here, they are to be told to go to America."[5]

Judging from this statement and others like it, it is easy to conclude that the sultan was dead set against Jewish immigration to Palestine. But in truth, though he was not particularly keen on the idea, there was very little he could do about it. As more and more Jews began pouring into Istanbul throughout the 1890s, the Ottoman government found that it had very little chance of turning them away. This was precisely the point made by Grand Vizier Kamil Pasa when he pointed out to the sultan that there was no stemming the Jewish tide, and that considerable sums of money were being sent to Jews already in Palestine, "particularly those who are foreign subjects in Jerusalem are regularly receiving funds from Europe, whereas those Jews who are subjects of your imperial Majesty languish in poverty." It was therefore determined that the "Ottoman Jews" should be given seed grain and money on a regular basis.[6]

As the pogroms in Romania and Russia intensified, hundreds of Jews began to arrive in Istanbul, claiming Ottoman subject status on the basis of Ottoman passports, many forged. The municipal authorities in Istanbul were ordered to conduct a census of the refugees and compile a register of those who were genuine Ottoman subjects and those who were "foreign Jews." The Ottoman Jews were to have their fares paid and be given money to start new lives in Izmir and Salonika, whereas the foreign Jews were to be returned to the embassies of their country of provenance. The fact was that the Ottoman Empire had very little diplomatic leverage at this time, so it is highly likely that the "foreign Jews" also stayed.[7]

The issue here seems to have been clearly one of nationality rather than ethnicity. As far as the Ottoman government was concerned, the Jews in Palestine were a danger if they served as a fifth column for foreign interference in the state's affairs. Otherwise, once they were there, it was simply a matter of making the best of the situation and trying to turn it to account. Practical help could ensure their loyalty as citizens and minimize the risk of foreign intervention. When the Baron de Rothschild volunteered a team of "the best doctors in France," which he would send to Palestine at his own expense, he was told politely by the Ottoman government that they "had quite adequate medical facilities to care for our population in Palestine."[8]

On April 15, 1892, on the occasion of the 400th anniversary of the Jewish expulsion from Spain, Jewish community leaders in Bucharest sent a message of gratitude to the sultan via his ambassador: "On this 400th anniversary of our first arrival in Ottoman domains, we the members of the Jewish community of Bucharest would like to express our profound gratitude for the protection and hospitality granted to us by the ancestors of His Imperial Majesty."[9]

By 1898, as the Ninth Zionist Congress drew nigh, the Ottoman government became increasingly worried about the loyalties of Jews in Palestine. In July 1898, the Porte—the office of the Grand Vizier—reported that the primary aim of the Zionist committees was to "create a situation in Palestine whereby the Jews there would constitute an independent state under foreign protection."[10] The attitude of the Ottoman government toward the Jews, immigrant or local, was based primarily on citizenship—what mattered was that the person in question be a loyal Ottoman first and Jewish second. For example, some Jewish notables in Istanbul were decorated for "their commendable efforts toward the establishment of a newspaper in the Jewish language and in Turkish in order to teach the Jewish children their mother tongue, which is Turkish."[11]

THE KURDISH ISSUE

Long-standing problems with the Kurds may also be better understood in the light of history. In a panel discussion on Turkish TV in November 1993, a group of Kurdish "loyal" tribal leaders were invited to comment on the Kurdistan Workers Party (PKK). They were extremely virulent in their attacks on the PKK, referring to them as "not Kurds but Armenians" and telling an audience of millions that many of the PKK members killed had been found to be uncircumcised—a thinly veiled hint that they were not Muslims. The tragic irony of this situation only becomes apparent when one looks back at the Ottoman Empire of the 1890s. The chances are that the Kurdish chiefs on television are the descendants of the *Hamidiye* irregular cavalry forces formed during the reign of Abdulhamid II, the same regiments primarily involved in the Armenian massacres of the 1890s and the mass deportations of 1915 in which hundreds of thousands of Armenians perished.

The Kurds themselves had traditionally been an unruly element in eastern Anatolia. Some historians see the last major Kurdish sheikh, Sheikh Ubaydallah, as the leader of an independence movement under the guise of his short-lived Kurdish League in the early 1880s.[12] Thus the creation of the *Hamidiye* irregular cavalry regiments from the Kurdish tribes was a double-ended policy, to pacify and assimilate the Kurds and to use them as a weapon against the Armenian independence movement. The choices open to the Ottoman government were much the same choices that are available to the Turkish government today: "The Kurds were a potentially dangerous element in the region which needed to be either totally suppressed—an unreasonable policy given the character of the times and the government— or pampered and appeased while kept under loose supervision."[13]

The *Hamidiye* regiments were conceived as an irregular force on the Russian Cossack model, and Ottoman officers were actually sent to St. Petersburg to "learn Cossack-style drill" to use in training the *Hamidiye*.[14] Several cavalry captains returned in 1896, "having completed their training in Petersburg in Cossack-style tactics," which they were now to impart to the *Hamidiye* units in the Ottoman Fourth and Fifth Armies.[15] It was specifically stated that these units would be deployed "against Armenian brigands."[16] Therefore, Armenian historians have been right in pointing out the anti-Armenian priority of the *Hamidiye* regiments: "Though the Kurds had been much more a threat to Ottoman unity than the Armenians in the years past, the sultan backed these fellow Muslims against Christian Armenians whom he saw as a disruptive element linked to his enemies abroad."[17]

Another aspect of the *Hamidiye* regiments was that they were designed as a vehicle for social engineering, as the tribes selected were to have special primary schools established in their regions.[18]

The leading chiefs' sons would also be brought to Istanbul, to be trained in Turkish language and manners in the famous "Tribal School" (*Mekteb-i Asiret*).[19] In addition, for the duration of their service, *Hamidiye* tribesmen and their families were exempt from taxation on their herds and other taxable resources.[20] These privileges are very similar to present-day advantages granted to those Kurdish elements in eastern Anatolia, armed by the state and expected to contribute to the fight against the PKK as "local defense units" (*kolcu*).

Very soon after the formation of the first *Hamidiye* regiments, it became apparent that the degree of state control over them would be problematic. As early as 1887, reports began of unruly behavior among the tribes armed by the state.[21] Yet the scheme went forward, and by 1892 tribes were being recruited in the areas of the Fourth, Fifth, and Sixth Ottoman Armies, in northeastern Anatolia, northern Syria, and north-central Iraq, respectively.[22] It is important to realize that these regiments were not to include only Kurds, but Arab Bedouin and Turcoman nomads.[23] The Commission for the Establishment of the *Hamidiye* Regiments reported regularly during this period that the "bold warriors who have never seen a city or a town and remain in a state of savagery" had given elaborate feasts to honor the envoys of the sultan and to celebrate their inclusion "in this singular honour."[24]

By mid-1892 it had been established that the number of regiments should be increased to one hundred, and that they should include the desert-dwelling Bedouin.[25] Another aspect of what would today be called the "socialization" of these tribes was their periodic rotation to Istanbul to serve as the sultan's imperial guard for one year. It was hoped that this period of service would serve to "improve the demeanor and general conduct" of the tribes.[26] The tribesmen in Istanbul would be given special dress uniforms and each regiment would be given an elaborately embroidered banner to symbolize attachment to the state. By the end of 1892 it was reported that fifty-two regiments had been formed; twenty-one were in the process of formation.[27]

Although Istanbul thought that it could ultimately control these units, as the century drew to a close, it became painfully apparent that this was not the case. Not only did the *Hamidiye* prey on defenseless Armenian villagers, they also ceaselessly fought other Kurds, particularly the Alevis.[28] Increasingly, the reports from the field dealt with their transgressions. On January 16, 1898, three *Hamidiye* officers in the Diyarbekir region were reported to be "illegally collecting taxes, going astray, and oppressing the local population." Orders were sent out for their arrest and court-martial in Diyarbekir.[29] Practically all the eastern villagers reported untoward activity by the *Hamidiye*. On March 2, 1899, it was reported from Erzurum that three *Hamidiye* officers had been involved in plundering villagers and killing peasants;[30] on March 30, it was reported from Erciye that the *Hamidiye* Captain Abdul Aga was actively involved in plunder.[31]

Most of the cases reported deal with transgressions against fellow Muslims; transgressions against Christians were apparently either not reported or not considered transgressions. One of the rare cases where the British Embassy became involved probably involved Armenians. A *Hamidiye* lieutenant colonel, Haci Bey, from the Artus tribe, was reported to have "indulged in brigandage and shed much blood which has gone unpunished." The vilayet of Mosul was ordered to arrest him "and punish him in an exemplary fashion." The people who had been wronged were told that they could bring their complaints to the courts of Cizre and Mardin.[32]

As the century neared its end, Istanbul became increasingly concerned that the *Hamidiye* command was proving more a liability than an asset. The imperial chief of staff continued to report that various *Hamidiye* tribal commanders "did not show the necessary characteristics of command and responsibility." Some had registered as *Hamidiye* commanders despite the fact that "they were too old to mount a horse"; others had been found wanting in morals and responsibility. More seriously, the regular officers and troops who had been attached to the *Hamidiye* units had taken up their bad habits. It was ordered that a register be compiled of "those who had been seen to be of objectionable behaviour" and that they be brought before courts-martial in administrative centers like Van and Erzurum.[33]

Another aspect of the state's policy in the eastern Anatolian provinces was to conduct a census of the population. The Kurdish tribes to be included in the *Hamidiye* regiments were to be provided with Ottoman identity cards, and births and deaths recorded systematically. Although this sounded fine on paper, it was very difficult to put into practice, given the "state of savagery of most of the tribes."[34] Complaints continued to come in, often involving the Porte in disputes with foreign powers, such as the complaint dealing with the "excesses of a *Hamidiye* commander against Russian subjects in Erzurum." This situation was increasingly causing the military authorities to conclude that "those regiments which are not immediately useful should be discharged."[35]

Another way in which the *Hamidiye* were counterproductive was through their tendency to re-create the old system of tribal consolidation. The policy of co-opting the tribes against the formation of powerful local leaders was basic to the whole *Hamidiye* project. Now this danger seemed to be reemerging worse than ever as the tribes were now armed and, to some extent, trained by the state.[36] But the Armenian crisis continued to keep eastern Anatolia on the boil, and by the end of 1903, the Porte shifted to the more flexible policy of summoning the *Hamidiye* regiments to points of trouble only when they were needed, and then discharging them.[37]

The "Young Turks," who deposed Abdulhamid in 1909, continued his Kurdish policies much in the same vein, changing the regiment names from *Hamidiye Alaylari* to *Asiret Alaylari*, "tribal regiments." They continued to grow in the period leading up to the Great War. It is a sublime irony that the military strongman of the Committee of Union and Progress, Mahmut Sevket Pasa, considered changing their name to *Oguz Alaylari*, after the legendary *Oguz* tribe, the semi-mythical stem tribe of the first Turks.[38]

The *Hamidiye* policy is usually seen as a failure, and a costly one. Most of the *Hamidiye* were Sunni Muslims, and their protection by the state often provided the opportunity for them to oppress and kill their Shi'a brethren, the Zaza Kurds, as well as the Alevis. Recent research has pointed out, however, that the *Hamidiye* regiments were "an important stage in the emergence of Kurdish nationalism from 1891 to 1914, serving as a fulcrum of Kurdish power for over two decades."[39] It is clear that apart from the use of these regiments as irregular cavalry, the Ottoman center hoped to mobilize them as a population of Muslims trained as loyal Ottoman proto-citizens. Yet, paradoxically, just as Abdulhamid's Islamist policies served as the crucible of Turkish nationalism, the *Hamidiye* policies did the same for Kurdish nationalism.[40] As put by a recent historian of Kurdish nationalism, "The *Hamidiye* gave an opportunity for the Kurds to experience and attempt to fathom the wider world."[41]

THE HISTORICAL ROOTS OF THE IRAN-IRAQ CONFLICT

The early days of the Iran-Iraq war were seen by some of the Iranian press as the "twenty-fifth Ottoman-Iranian war." Saddam Hussein, for his part, maintained that he was fighting to reclaim land that had been part of Iraq during Ottoman times. Throughout the turbulent history of the region, the Ottomans have clashed with the Safavids. By the late nineteenth century another struggle was under way: the Hamidian campaign against Shi'ism. The Ottoman provinces of Mosul, Baghdad, and Basra had always been a crucible of Shi'ism. From the 1880s onward, the Ottoman center grew increasingly anxious about the spread of Shi'ism among the Sunni population. The tension was also overlaid with ripples from the Great Game as Britain, Russia, Iran, and the Ottoman empire vied for power in the region.[42] During the run-up to the disastrous 1877–78 Russo-Ottoman war, the Iranians mobilized and massed troops on the Ottoman border and made plans to take Kerbala and Baghdad if the opportunity arose, thus diverting important Ottoman forces from the Eastern front.[43]

In this context, the thousands of Iranian subjects that flocked every year to the Shi'a shrines in Najaf, Kerbala, and Baghdad became a security risk. Measures were taken to curtail their movements and restrict their number.[44] It was also felt that Qajar Iran was under the influence of British India, where there was a very large and wealthy Shi'ite population. Ottoman officials therefore feared that the British were using the Iranian pilgrims and holy men (mujtahid) as stalking horses to increase their influence in the area.[45] The tremendous power of the mujtahid in Iranian society was very clearly perceived by the Ottoman officials who served in the area in the 1890s: "They seek no official appointment (mansab) and have no fear of dismissal (azl). They are therefore very difficult to control. They have great influence among the people and the common folk see them as the vice-regents of the Imam. Their influence is a thousand times greater than that of the Shah . . . within twenty-four hours and at their merest gesture they can cause the people to rise against the Shah."[46]

The only preventative for the spread of Shi'ism was seen to be education. As 40 percent of Iraq was Shi'ite, it was out of the question to use military coercion. The Ottoman center therefore resolved to fight what it saw as a dangerously subversive ideology by education and counterpropaganda. It was decided that the state should send specially trained *ulama* to Iraq to instill the virtues of Sunni Islam in primary schools. Another emphasis was on the development of the Sunni *madrasas* in Iraq, which were in a state of disarray and dilapidation, while the Shi'ite *madrasas* flourished. It was determined that specially trained Sunni *ulamas* be sent out to Iraq to "explain the doctrinal fragility of Shi'ism to the people." They were not to let it be known that they were state officials but were to pose as simple travelers, and to report to the authorities any Shi'ite *ulama* whom they saw fomenting discord.

What seems to have been envisioned here was nothing less than a religious secret service.[47] The Ottomans actually instituted mobile primary schools and *madrasas*, which consisted of state *ulama* who traveled together with the nomadic tribes.[48] Local Iraqi *ulama*— including, interestingly, women—were also to be trained as Sunni propagandists. The documents refer to a certain Ayse Hanim who was to be paid three hundred kurus for her services in instilling Sunnism among Iraqi women.[49]

According to Suleyman Hüsnü Pasa, a distinguished Ottoman exile in Baghdad, the Shi'ite *mujtahids* were very dangerous: "As these men see all government as usurpers, the restriction of their influence is an inevitable necessity for the Ottoman State. They are a barrier to progress and very dangerous."[50] To counter their influence, he said, the state should train competent primary school teachers who would be fluent in Arabic and Kurdish and familiar with the customs of the local population.[51] A very clear example of the concept of education as propaganda is the Sultan's move to bring Shi'ite children to Istanbul to be trained in the imperial schools as loyal Ottomans. In some of these cases, as the children came from modest families, the Sultan paid for their travel expenses and education out of his privy purse. The Sultan's view of the matter was that, "since so much money [had] been spent on these children . . . the training of the Shi'ites among them should assure that they become Sunni in order to enable them to convert their brethren upon their return."[52]

One cannot escape a haunting feeling of familiarity when one reads the reports of Ottoman officials in the field—they seem to be conjuring up Imam Khomeini when they speak of the *mujtahids* who can mobilize the Iranian population "with their merest gesture." The same sentiment is experienced when today's Turkish press takes pains to point out how the recent religious revival in Turkey is not to be confused with the Khomeini revolution.

THE OTTOMAN IMAGE IN THE RECENT TURKISH PRESS

Hardly a day passes without a reference to the Ottoman past in the Turkish daily press. What is fascinating, however, is that very often the same past is being used to legitimate diametrically opposed views on Turkey's present and future. Staunch republican secularists as well as the Islamist Welfare Party (*Refah Partisi,* RP) take the Ottoman past as their point of reference. After the March local elections in which it won the mayoralty in Istanbul and Ankara, the RP declared that it would "institute the Ottoman tradition in municipal politics." No one is too clear just what this "Ottoman style municipal politics" means, least of all the RP.[53] In response, the old guard secularist newspaper *Cumhuriyet* published a long piece on the great Ottoman architect Sinan, who was depicted somewhat incongruously "as an Ottoman who would never have allowed the shantytowns that the RP is encouraging."[54]

As with every issue, the Ottoman past is called into the witness box. The grandson of the Kurdish leader Seyh Said, Abdülmelik Firat, said in an interview that "we [in Turkey] are the continuation of the Ottomans. There are many ethnic groups in Turkey." Thus, the Ottoman past is being put forward as a golden age in which Kurdish identity was allowed to flourish.[55] Most strikingly, President Süleyman Demirel made a historic statement on March 20, 1994: "If someone wants to call himself a Kurd, let him. Different races from different creeds have to live in Turkey under the flag of constitutional citizenship. This is what the Ottomans did."[56] Therefore the mainstay of Turkey's constitution as an "integral state" and its highest ranking official joins one of the foremost proponents of Kurdish nationalism in seeking legitimation from the Ottoman past.

Cengiz Çandar, one of Turkey's best investigative reporters and columnists, often waxes poetic about the Ottoman past. When the matter of Turkish troops being sent to Bosnia with UNPROFOR arose, he wrote in his column: "This means that the Turkish soldier is back in Bosnia, setting foot in the Balkans for the first time since the 1877–78 war, even if this is under UNPROFOR [command]."[57] On February 7, 1994, Russian nationalist leader Vladimir Zhirinovsky told CNN, "We support the Serbs because they have been done out of their heritage by the Turks." Thus both Cengiz Çandar and Zhirinovsky, from two opposite poles to be sure, base their Balkan projections on the Ottoman past.

Even more strikingly, in early April 1994, the Tansu Çiller government announced that it was establishing a "Political Psychology Centre" to do research into the reasons for Kurdish separatism and the rise of religious parties. The government spokesman, Yildirim Aktuna, once the director of Istanbul's major psychiatric hospital, told the press that religious politics was in the ascendant because "certain circles are nostalgic for the Ottoman Empire. They feel a sense of deprivation. This is because the Kemalist Republic was built immediately upon the demise of the Ottoman state. The speed with which the reforms took place did not allow anyone the time to mourn the passing of the Ottoman Empire."[58]

The meteoric rise of Istanbul in the last ten years, and its reemergence in some ways as the "Seat of Felicity" (Der Saadet) certainly has much to do with this process. The fact is, even the weakened and lumbering Ottoman Empire of the turn of the century had a far greater presence in the world than the present, much more healthy Turkish Republic. This leads to an atmosphere where even staunch Kemalists hark back to the "golden age" of an empire where "everything was ordered as it should be." On the other hand, Islamists yearn for some utopian "Ottoman Just Order," which defies definition.

It appears that, as the Turkish identity crisis deepens, the urge to identify with a romantic past increases. The republic cannot provide the romantic resonance that society craves, so the Ottoman "twilight zone," in its various constructs, is shoved into the breach.

CHAPTER THREE

TURKEY AND THE NEW MIDDLE EAST
A Geopolitical Exploration

Henri J. Barkey

The Middle East was immediately and dramatically affected by the end of the Cold War. The decline of Soviet influence in the area had a destabilizing effect that contributed to the outbreak of the Gulf War, which itself gave impetus to the Arab-Israeli peace negotiations and the signing of the September 13, 1993, Declaration of Principles between Palestinians and Israelis. Turkey's strategic posture was also dramatically affected by the end of the Cold War, as for the first time in three centuries, there was no longer a border with a Russian empire. The departure of Soviet forces from Turkish borders may, for the time being at least, mean that the conventional military threat from the north has disappeared. On the other hand, this also reduces Turkey's vital relevance to NATO, its primary alliance partnership. Turkey has also had to adjust to and contend with a series of new neighbors and their attendant problems. Azerbaijan, Armenia, Ukraine, and the new states in Central Asia all represent new economic and political opportunities as well as dangers.

In the past, Turkey's relations with the Middle East have taken a back seat to its larger alliance commitments. This is in the process of changing, as Ankara, willy-nilly, finds itself increasingly drawn into the affairs of the Middle East. There are four main reasons for this development, the first and most important being the Kurdish rebellion in Turkey. The severity of this rebellion and its connections to the Kurds of northern Iraq, and the future of Iraq itself, as well as of Iran and Syria, mean that attempting to resolve it will involve all the states of the region and may even define the next Middle East conflict. Second, the problem of water will assume greater political and strategic significance as Turkey's mammoth hydroelectric and irrigation schemes approach conclusion, affecting, as they have already done, the availability of water in Syria and Iraq. In addition, burgeoning populations and the resolution of the Arab-Israeli conflict, both of which will require a reconfiguration of water usage, will exert pressure on the region's total water table.

The third reason lies in worldwide changes in the strategic and geo-economic balance. As economic issues such as trade, investment flows, and employment assume greater importance, Turkey will need to bolster its position vis-à-vis its primary economic partner, the European Union, which, for the moment, is only prepared to allow it to participate in a customs union agreement. There are three immediate areas with which Turkey can seek to expand economic ties: the Middle East, the Black Sea region, and Central Asia.

Finally, continued uncertainty in the Gulf resulting from the challenge posed to status quo Arab powers by Iran and Iraq as well as by the Arab-Israeli peace process may provide Turkey with a regional role. The possibility of Turkey's playing the role of an active intermediary or even a balancer in the region, while remote at present, may nevertheless increase if in the future the United States is perceived as disengaging itself from the region in the wake of the Soviet collapse. Kuwait's experience with its local bully, which first offered it protection and then turned on it, has shattered illusions of Arab unity and exacerbated feelings of insecurity. This in turn could lead to changing alliance patterns in the Middle East with many possible configurations in which Turkey could be required to become an active player.

THE CHALLENGE OF THE POST–COLD WAR ERA

Turkey's future role in the Middle East is better understood in light of the developing international system. Some of the immediate and general repercussions of the Cold War's demise on the Middle East can be grouped under five general categories.

First, the significance of the Soviet Union's disappearance lies in the fact that it was a revisionist power that challenged the United

States both militarily and ideologically. Although the USSR was a direct threat to some Middle Eastern states, in its absence many find themselves exposed both economically and politically. For those that counted on the U.S. security umbrella, the end of the Cold War means that the United States will no longer be willing to extend its unconditional protection and political support and, as in some cases, contribute financially to their security. Except where vital U.S. interests are at stake such as in Kuwait, U.S. involvement will diminish considerably, as was evidenced in the Yemeni civil war. And for former allies and clients of the Soviet Union, the new Russian regime has neither the inclination nor capability to continue its predecessor's policies.

Of course, this does not mean that other revisionist powers will not emerge to challenge the status quo in the future. In fact, one can make the argument that Iran has already fashioned itself as one such. By categorizing Iran and other such powers as "backlash states,"[1] the United States has refused to engage it as a revisionist power deserving of the kind of attention and energy it devoted to combating the Soviet Union. This is because even an Iran determined to obtain nuclear weapons cannot possibly threaten the United States as did its former nemesis. Also, even if the U.S. government were to augment its pressure on Iran by sharpening trade sanctions, the size and industrial capacity of Iran means that "containing" it will be easier than past efforts at containing the Soviet Union. Therefore, it is unlikely that Middle Eastern powers will be able to use Iran in place of Russia to generate much strategic support in the West.

Without the overwhelming ideological division that shaped world politics—or, for that matter, pure superpower rivalry—relations between individual Middle Eastern countries will revert to being a function of their own differences over specific interests. Therefore, the superpower preferences will cease to be a determining factor in such relations. In the Middle East, much affected by the superpower rivalry, this has been felt already in the Israeli-Arab peace process and even in Turkey's relations with its neighboring states. One important consideration, however, is that though the superpower rivalry may no longer exist, the United States remains the single most influential state, one whose authority and preferences will have to be contended with.

Second, the bipolar era had ushered in a period of "rent-seeking" in many Third World countries. State elites unable to generate the resources needed to develop their societies or defend them from external threats often turned to the superpower competition. Especially since regime survival often depended on their ability to manipulate domestic groups either by buying them off or insulating the state and society from international economic changes they could not control, the bipolar competition provided the perfect arena in which Middle Eastern states could maximize their resources by making ideological and security-based appeals to greater powers. With the end of the Cold War, the strategic argument has lost its primary importance. Some states, such as Egypt because of its crucial positioning in the Arab-Israeli conflict, may continue to gather rents; others will see their share disappear. As Alvin Z. Rubinstein has remarked, in the new environment "there is a shift in influence from the weak to the strong . . . because their superpower patrons accorded [local actors] an importance far beyond their actual strategic-political value."[2]

Third, the demise of the Soviet Union also represents the victory of liberal capitalism and free markets over command economies. With states from Latin America, Eastern Europe, and even South Asia attempting to restructure their economies, an unprecedented worldwide consensus has emerged regarding the importance of trade and competition. There is no contending economic ideology—especially with China trying to emulate the market economies—that can provide the necessary justification to state elites for continuing the dirigiste economic policies that have accounted for so much waste and inefficiency. Unable to raise strategic rents by manipulating the superpower competition or trading on their geopolitical locations, these countries will have to adapt to the competitive market rules of the emerging order. While some, like Turkey and to a lesser extent Tunisia, have already started this process, others will have to compete for funds and foreign investment with former Eastern European bloc countries and Soviet-successor states.

The United States, for its part, has made it clear that it will favor those countries that are not protectionist and can participate fully in the international market. In the Middle East, where there is a divide between countries that export oil and those that do not, the United States will increasingly focus on those countries that are capable of participating in the world economy. Turkey, despite its current economic woes, is the only Middle Eastern country that has been earmarked by the U.S. Commerce Department as one of the ten "big emerging markets."

Fourth, the failure of the Soviet Union as a totalitarian state, the revelations regarding its past domestic practices, and the lack of enthusiasm in the West for authoritarian governments will increase the indigenous pressures in many Third World countries to democratize and liberalize. Just as with dirigiste economic policies, the failure of the Soviet Union eliminates the ideological underpinnings of one-party states and other forms of authoritarian rule.

As a result, human rights considerations will play a larger role in the formation of foreign policy and certainly in the dispensing of aid by both the United States and Western Europe. The application of human rights considerations to foreign policy may still remain selective—the case of China reveals that exceptions are made only when a country's economic importance is overwhelming. Yet there is no question that in the absence of the Soviet empire gross violators will find it difficult to get a sympathetic hearing in Washington. As a result, and because of the increased saliency of ethnicity in the post–Cold War era, multiethnic countries encountering intercommunal strife or ethnic rebellions will be the most affected by the change regarding human rights.

Finally, the intensity of the Cold War competition and the Arab-Israeli conflict served to disguise the fact that, as Ghassan Salamé suggests, many of the states in the Middle East were superficially constructed and were in fact regimes masquerading as states.[3] Hence the logic of their behavior was rooted in regime preservation rather than state interests. This is not surprising—as Levy and Barnett have argued, "state survival in the Third World is rarely at stake whereas governmental stability and survival frequently are."[4] Challenges to most states of the region have come primarily from domestic sources and, in the absence of the Cold War rivalry and a diminishing Arab-Israeli conflict, these will be further accentuated. The experience of Algeria and the civil war in Yemen are, perhaps, the most telling such examples of future instability.

Even states that were previously considered institutionally strong and unassailable, such as Turkey, are not immune to the winds of change. The rise of ethnic consciousness has affected Turkey most directly, as evidenced by the most serious rebellion mounted by its Kurdish minority since 1923. This Kurdish challenge to Turkey, if continued with the same intensity of violence, may threaten its territorial integrity. In the Middle East, preoccupation with regime preservation can be externalized and form the basis of some of the challenges to the region's state system. Saddam Hussein has twice demonstrated that his regime's survival was worth undertaking the risk of confrontation with its neighbors, and that it was also possible for an Arab power to question the region's boundaries. In doing so, he may have, in effect, called into question his own state's territorial integrity. For these reasons the Middle Eastern state system is unsettled and, in the short term, headed toward a period of insecurity, self-examination, and turbulence. The internal contradictions of these states will become more pronounced while state authorities simultaneously continue to seek alliances to bolster the ruling regimes' staying power.

TURKEY'S STRATEGIC DILEMMA

Turkey's immediate neighbors lie in four distinct geographical regions: the Balkans, the Middle East, the Black Sea, and the Caucasus. Ankara has the dubious, not necessarily earned, distinction of being viewed with great suspicion if not outright hostility by its immediate neighbors. While these regions are also inhabited by allies or future allies, an overwhelming majority of countries have come to fear Turkey's potential role in the post–Cold War era. Whether fueled by memories of Turkey's imperial past or, as in the case of Serbia, by domestic insecurities that are only marginally related to Turkey, the perception is that a Turkey unbound by Cold War constraints, which sees itself at the center of a Turkic-speaking world that stretches from the Adriatic to the Great Wall of China, will try to throw its weight around. This was reinforced by the initial zeal with which Turkey approached the Central Asian countries; in discovering a set of new countries to which it felt bound by bonds of kinship and language, Ankara may have taken on more than it could handle.

Despite its strategic location, Turkey's primary economic and political relationship has historically, by choice or Cold War–induced reasons, been with Western Europe and the United States. This was a comfortable—even if not always satisfactory—relationship that provided Turkey with security and access to markets in the West as well as to economic aid. But the chain of events unleashed by the end of the Cold War is forcing Turkey to become more engaged in its immediate environment. The end of the Cold War may have provided Turkey with opportunities it never imagined it could have: it appears, with the exception of Russia, to be the strongest regional military power, and few in the area can compete with the economic dynamism it exhibited from 1980 until recently. However, where Turkish interests diverge from those of the United States in an area or over an issue of vital U.S. interest, then Turkey will continue to find its ability to act on its own limited and even be liable to pay a price.

While the Caucasus, the Black Sea region, and the Balkans hold potential dangers and promises for Turkey, of the surrounding regions, it is the Middle East that contains the greatest promise and risks. In both the Balkans and Azerbaijan, the limits of Turkish influence were quickly realized. In fact, Turkish attempts at becoming a significant actor in the Caucasus have been checked by resurgent Russian power, as Russia has emerged the winner in the "three-tiered competition" over the Transcaucasus and Central Asia,[5] and the West remains, for political reasons, reluctant to intervene in the Russian sphere of influence. This has effectively curtailed serious support for Turkish positions in both Central Asia and the Caucasus, despite the initial encouragement offered to Turkey, partly in hope of checking Iranian expansionism.

In contrast, the strategic picture of the Middle East in the post–Cold War, post–Arab-Israeli rapprochement era is quite favorable to status quo powers such as Egypt, Israel, Saudi Arabia, and the Gulf monarchies, as well as to Turkey. With the active, even though distant, backing of the United States, these countries can constitute a natural if informal alliance. The demise of the Soviet Union has eliminated an important source of war materiel and political support for regimes such as Syria, Iraq, and Libya. Although it is willing to sell military equipment to all these and Iran, Russia's insistence on being paid in hard currency puts a significant limit on prospective buyers' capabilities to acquire large quantities of weaponry.

The signing of the September 13, 1993, Declaration of Principles moves the region one step closer to normalcy and to regular commercial and diplomatic relations. Thus Ankara, which for years had very carefully straddled the sharp divide between the Arab world and Israel, will have an easier time on both the economic and diplomatic fronts. Increased stability could translate into potential leverage over Syria and others, curbing their support of the Kurdish insurrection in Turkey. Ankara also expects that with declining military spending, opportunities for trade with the region will expand and Turkey, with its dynamic export and construction sectors, could emerge as a primary beneficiary. The prospects for peace open up the possibility of exporting water, which could also provide Turkey with substantial foreign exchange revenues.

TURKEY AND THE PERILS OF THE MIDDLE EAST

Among the major obstacles that lie ahead for Turkey are its Kurdish problem, the future of Iraq, the water question, its ability to fashion durable arrangements with other like-minded states, and, to restate Salamé's observation, the difficulty of dealing with the inherent instability that regime-dominated weak states give rise to.

The origins and intricacies of the Kurdish question in Turkey have been discussed elsewhere.[6] It has become the most dominant issue in both domestic and foreign policy. There are two important characteristics of the modern Kurdish problem in Turkey: first, it is a domestic problem long in the making that, in some parts of the country, has now assumed the mark of a full-scale rebellion. Despite the most ardent efforts of the Turkish state and military to eradicate the rebels, led by the Kurdistan Workers Party (PKK), the rebellion has, over the last ten years, continued to gain momentum, especially in the political arena. The military dimension aside, the danger of the Kurdish rebellion for Turkey lies in the politicization and radicalization of Turkey's Kurdish community estimated to be 12 million, or 20 percent of the population. Experience of ethnic conflicts shows that once past a threshold—although this is always difficult to pinpoint with accuracy—ethnic conflicts can rarely be resolved but only managed. Turkey may be quickly approaching this point.

The second concerning aspect of the Kurdish question is its potential regional repercussions and implications. It is not only Turkey's problem: more than 20 million Kurds live in Turkey, Iraq, Iran, and Syria, though Turkey has the distinction of having the largest single contingent and at present of being the only state actively engaged in military operations of some magnitude. As Hamit Bozarslan argues, the resurgence of the Kurdish question represents the failure of the countries involved to create their "state-nations." Cultural, military, economic, and political strategies designed to incorporate and assimilate the Kurds have failed despite considerable resources that had their origins either in the Cold War competition or oil rents.[7] By and large the Kurdish movement in each of these countries is guided by its own dynamics and does not owe its existence to support originating in any other state. The movements' mere existence, however, has enticed regimes in the area to use them against one another, while simultaneously putting into motion an effort at collaboration among themselves along a "parallel diplomatic" tract designed to contain the movement as a whole.[8] Not surprisingly, therefore, Turks, Syrians, and Iranians have periodically met to discuss the future of their Kurdish enclaves and to combat any secessionist aspirations (and even desires for autonomy) the Iraqi Kurds may harbor. Even Iraqi Kurdish leaders have been marshaled into an anti-PKK coalition by Turkey through co-optation and threats.

Whether or not Turkey manages to resolve its Kurdish problem peacefully, the very recognition of the existence of the Kurds in its midst makes it more difficult for it to reject the Middle Eastern identity. The fact that the PKK has managed to obtain support from Syria, Iran, and Saddam Hussein to mount multifaceted political and military operations demonstrates that resolving the internal conflict will require an internal strategy as well as an external one. The use of the PKK card against Turkey by its neighbors with varying degrees of intensity is a direct result of their need to balance Turkey's potential threat to them. Whether it is water problems, as in the cases of Syria and Iraq, or more complex calculations regarding the Caucasus, Central Asia, and mounting a challenge to a secularist regime, as in the case of Iran, their motivations are independent of immediate calculations regarding their own Kurdish populations. Syria and Iraq may also be motivated, respectively, by irredentist claims over Alexandretta or by desire for revenge for Turkey's role during the Gulf conflict.

Another instance of the regionalization of the Kurdish problem occurred with the creation of the autonomous Kurdish region in northern Iraq. This has significantly contributed to Turkey's woes. Even though it initially has made only a minimal military contribution to the PKK's operations, the Kurdish enclave is perceived by Turks (as well as by Iranians and Syrians) as a possible future model for their own Kurdish minorities. Such fears have resulted in promoting the Kurdish issue to the realm of foreign policy. At the same time,

Ankara has discovered that the Iraqi Kurdish issue has rebounded onto Turkish domestic politics and that it is unable to isolate the northern Iraqi question from its domestic one, as was made apparent when the Iraqi Kurdish leader, Jalal Talabani, brokered the PKK's March 1993 unilateral cease-fire announcement. In January 1994, the Turkish Air Force mounted the single largest raid of its history, when fifty planes attacked a PKK camp deep inside Iraqi Kurdish territory that also straddles Iranian territory. While the raid had more to do with domestic politics than with the fight against Kurdish rebels, it is another indication of how Turkey's relations with its neighbors are being driven by the exigencies of the rebellion.

Regardless of the neighboring states' attempts to keep it intact, there is serious doubt regarding Iraq's chances of rejoining the regional state system as it was constituted before the Gulf War. Saddam Hussein's resilience is the primary reason why both the sanctions regime and the Turkey-based Operation Provide Comfort, which supports and protects the Kurdish entity in northern Iraq, have been maintained. These together with the no-fly zone over southern Iraq's predominantly Shiite population only serve to further underscore Iraq's hybrid character and put a question mark over Iraq's future unity. As Graham Fuller suggests, it may be too late to halt the process of Iraq's disintegration,[9] and the future may contain only limited choices: a democratic but loose Iraqi federation or a Sunni-Shiite state coexisting with a Kurdish state to the north.

Because Ankara has repeatedly stated that any change in northern Iraq—from a possible breakup of Iraq to any arrangement that grants Iraqi Kurds territorial autonomy—would constitute a serious challenge to Turkey, it has indicated its preference for a strong centralized state in Baghdad capable of reining in disparate forces. This explains why the Turkish government has intensified contacts with Saddam Hussein's regime, indirectly offering it critical support at the United Nations and simultaneously trying to engineer a return of northern Iraqi territory to Baghdad by suggesting to Iraqi Kurds that their future would be best assured if they were to negotiate a deal with Baghdad.[10]

Turkish diplomacy in this regard is perilous and risks internationalizing its domestic Kurdish problem. Its efforts at lifting the embargo on Iraq could alienate the United States, its European allies, and its Gulf benefactors—Kuwait and Saudi Arabia. Similarly, the United

States, having made a commitment to the Kurds of northern Iraq, is unlikely to view kindly Turkish efforts to force them back under Saddam's yoke. And Ankara's search for a purely military solution to its domestic Kurdish problem has resulted in gross human rights violations including disappearances and village cleansings. The United States' fear of endangering Provide Comfort, which serves at the pleasure of Ankara, has been effectively used by Turkey to mute criticisms of its human rights policies. However, as human rights activists intensify their focus on Turkey, and governments, especially in Europe where large numbers of Kurds now reside, begin to pay attention to very visible cases, such as the imprisonment of Kurdish members of Parliament in 1994, Turkey will find that its domestic problems entail foreign policy considerations. By making 10 percent of the foreign aid it allocates to Turkey conditional on not using U.S.-supplied military equipment against civilians in the southeast, the Congress in 1994 served notice of the importance of human rights issues to its own post–Cold War policy. Turkey is experiencing similar problems in European bodies.

The Kurdish problem in Turkey has only recently attracted the attention of Arab elites. Some in the Arab world view the situation as a domestic concern and are alarmed at the potential instability in Turkey. Others have argued that the Israeli-Palestinian agreement may put additional pressure on Turkey to come to some kind of accommodation with its Kurdish minority,[11] and Saudi Arabia's leading daily, *Asharq al-Awsat*, has called on Turkey and the PKK to cease their hostilities and begin talks "about a deal upholding Kurdish cultural rights within a united Turkey."[12] Here, too, the Kurdish insurrection makes Turkey vulnerable to interference or to political jockeying by its regional neighbors. Ankara has already accused Greece, Syria, Iraq, Iran, and Armenia of directly intervening in its domestic affairs.

The internationalization of the Kurdish problem in Turkey may come about precisely because of Ankara's reliance on Saddam Hussein's ultimate ability to regain and maintain control over Iraq's northern territories. But how likely is Saddam, who has few options at present, to collaborate with Turkey in a post-sanctions environment—especially after Turkey cooperated with the Gulf War allies to provide protection to Iraqi Kurds? In the past, when he felt himself strong, or when other concerns predominated, Saddam Hussein quickly readjusted his attitude toward Turkey. Following the Iran-Iraq war he assumed an aggressive posture in negotiations over the allocation of Euphrates water and canceled agreements regarding Turkish "hot pursuit" operations in northern Iraq. In 1990, when the Turks asked Iraq for a renewal of their 1984 security protocol, the first deputy prime minister, Taha Yasin Ramadan, argued in refusing the request that without a resolution to the Euphrates problem it was difficult to see how the two countries could maintain cordial relations.[13]

The ramifications of the Kurdish problem extend to questions of democracy, human rights, and economic policy and endanger the balance between civil society, the state, and the military. Ankara's overtures to Baghdad, despite attendant risks and uncertainties, underscore the fear that the domestic Kurdish rebellion strikes at the contradictions that lie at the heart of Turkey's foreign policy objectives. The continued militarization of Turkey's Kurdish policy has meant that Turkish ground troops and air force are continuously involved in cross-border operations, and more and more the call for establishing a security zone in northern Iraq is heard in Ankara. In its desperation to resolve this issue, Turkey may strike out on its own. Whether this takes the form of a previously unused military or diplomatic track, it could result in further disrupting Turkey's relations with its neighbors. In fact, the late president Turgut Özal had, by diverging from standard Turkish foreign policy practices, first during the Gulf War and then in Ankara's dealings with Iraqi Kurds, put into motion a series of changes that could have culminated in precisely such an independent approach to the Kurdish problem.

WATER PROBLEMS AND RELATIONS WITH THE ARAB WORLD

As a result of the historic legacy of the Ottoman Empire, its links to Israel, and—most importantly—because of its NATO connections, Turkey has often been viewed with suspicion in the Arab world. And since the establishment of its republic, Ankara for its part has tried to distance itself from the Middle East. Its interest in the region has been aroused occasionally and then only from a narrow or nonregional perspective: it attempted to build an anticommunist alliance through the Baghdad Pact as a further extension of its own Western alliance obligations. Also, it tried to attract some of the petrodollars flowing into the Arab world following the 1973–74 oil price hikes by increasing its trade with the region, and it unsuccessfully sought support for its position in the Cyprus dispute.

With the end of the Cold War and the movement toward Arab-Israeli peace, two contradictory trends are emerging. While Turkey's ambitions in the region and beyond are the object of much suspicion in the Arab world, another view holds that Turkey is a vital component of a regionwide security arrangement that informally includes Egypt, the Gulf countries, and Israel—the countries that stand to benefit the most from the emergence of a stable region-wide market.

At the heart of Arab resentment is Turkey's dispute with Syria (and to a lesser extent with Iraq) over sharing the waters of the Euphrates and Tigris. At issue is the Southeastern Anatolia Project, known by its Turkish acronym GAP. When completed, this project is supposed to transform Turkey's southeast but, in the process, will also significantly affect the quantity and the quality of water available to Syria and Iraq.[14] A typical Arab view of the water question is articulated by well-known Arab journalist Riyad Najib al-Rayyes, who argues that "by rejecting a water-sharing agreement, Turkey is displaying a high-handed attitude that has created a legacy of Arab resentment, and engaging in a high-risk ploy to become the region's superpower by controlling its most vital resource and acquiring a strategic role to match."[15] This resentment is accentuated by the perception that the United States has pushed Gulf countries and Saudi Arabia to invest in the Turkish military and other industries as a hedge against resurgent Iraqi and Iranian power.

Turkey's stand on the water question and its attempts at linking it with Syrian backing for the PKK have elicited wide support for Syria in the Arab world.[16] Whether or not this issue will become a pan-Arab one in which Arab states make common cause with both Syria and Iraq, as some have suggested,[17] remains to be seen. In the coming decade, a Syria at peace with Israel might be able to devote more attention and energy to dealing with its northern neighbor. Militarily this implies that Syria and even Iraq will be freer to project their capabilities northward. At present, not a single one of Syria's eleven divisions is deployed north of Homs.[18] Water worries have even resulted in Iraqi-Syrian cooperation despite their long-standing mutual dislike and mistrust.

GEOSTRATEGIC AND ECONOMIC BALANCES

The unfolding Kurdish crisis, the future of Iraq, and the water-related discords with its neighbors portend future crises in Turkey's relations with the Middle East. These developments will occur at a time when Ankara's status with its allies and primary trading partners is on the decline and the Middle East, toward which it is being pulled, is on the threshold of a major transformation that carries with it the possibility of severe internal disruptions. Can Turkey's economic and strategic attributes and position provide compensation for all the difficulties it is likely to experience?

From a geostrategic perspective, Turkey faces a transformed Middle East where not only will Israel become an active participant but all the traditional alliance patterns have been altered. In the months following the signing of the Israeli-Palestinian agreement, Ankara suddenly discovered in Israel a potential ally. In the past, domestic hostility to Israel and Arab pressure had debased Turkish-Israeli relations, but even before the Israeli-PLO agreement Turkey's increasing difficulties with the Arab world and Iran had engendered the beginnings of a rapprochement. As one Turkish analyst has noted, Israel is the only country in the region that neither has irredentist claims on Turkey nor has attempted to alter its democratic makeup and replace it with a theocratic system.[19] Clearly relieved at no longer being limited in its contacts with Israel in deference to Arab wishes, Turkey has made tremendous efforts to engage Israel in its campaign against the PKK—a request the Israelis have steadfastly refused. What Israel offers Turkey is not only the possibility of exerting pressure on Syria but, in Turkish minds, a reliable and continuous conduit to Washington, with which Ankara needs to bolster its links. In effect, the old courtship game has been reversed: it used to be that Israel vied for Turkish support. While Turkey will retain its important psychological role as a non-Arab Muslim state that balances Iran and the Arab countries, the advent of peace will undoubtedly alter Israel's perception of Turkey. In the future, individual Arab countries will assume a far different significance for Israel, which will be more responsive to the intricacies of inter-Arab developments and efforts at coalition building than to the needs of its "periphery" allies, including Turkey. Post-Özal Turkey's pursuits, specifically in Iraq, have put Ankara at odds with a number of Middle Eastern countries. On the

Iraqi issue, for instance, Israel is closer to the Kuwaiti and Saudi positions than is Turkey.

An unexpected source of opposition to Turkey may originate in Egypt. In the aftermath of the dramatic developments in the region, Egypt, which has traditionally vied for the mantle of Arab-world leadership, is presently in search of a regional role. Although Egyptian officials and opinion makers have never considered Turkey a model, but rather an "experience,"[20] the possibility that Egypt may emerge as a loser in the coming economic competition with Turkey and Israel is of some considerable worry.[21] Although Egypt, as Abdelmon'em Said of al-Ahram's Center for Political and Strategic Studies argues, may not have any choice but to rejuvenate its economy if it wants to maintain its traditional civilizational role in the Arab world and international influence,[22] in view of the monumental economic problems it faces, the regime in Cairo may seek to bolster its regional role by staking out a role in important issues, ranging from nuclear disarmament to water problems. Egypt which, like Iraq and Syria, is a downstream riparian state, has two incentives to engage itself in the Turkish-Syrian and Iraqi water dispute: Not only can it enhance its regional stature, more importantly it could work to discourage the creation of precedents that could bind it in the future vis-à-vis the use of the Nile. It is already worried that the Gulf states, having spurned Egypt's offer of a security partnership against Iraq and Iran (the Damascus Declaration), might seek Turkish protection instead.[23]

Egyptian unease notwithstanding, Iran is the one country that can provide Turkey with an unequivocal entry into the future good graces of both the Arab world and Israel. As the primary revisionist power in the region, Iran has not hidden its dislike of existing security arrangements and alliance patterns. These are likely to assume a larger anti-Iranian character in the future because of Iran's fierce opposition to the Arab-Israeli peace process and its desire to project its power over the Persian Gulf region. Iran reacted angrily to suggestions by then-Prime Minister Demirel during a visit to Gulf countries that Turkey wants to participate in regional security arrangements.[24] Especially with a weak Iraq unable to balance Iran, or one still ruled by Saddam Hussein still intent on playing a disruptive role, Turkey's role as a possible ally and staging post for U.S. forces will provide Ankara with the requisite strategic anti-Iranian clout.

Turkey's dynamic and growing economy may also shore up Ankara's diminished strategic importance. However, the economy has been ailing of late under the combined weight of the mismanagement of structural reform programs and the ever more costly war with the PKK. Turkey's economic success dates to its 1980 stabilization program and its attempted transformation of an inward-oriented economy into an export-driven one. As a result, it expanded its exports to the Middle East, in particular taking advantage of the Iran-Iraq War by selling to both warring nations. Turkish construction companies followed suit. The export drive to the Middle East eventually stalled due, in part, to declining oil prices, the end of the Iran-Iraq War, and associated political problems. In fact, most of Turkey's long-term post-1980 export gains have come in the more competitive Organization for Economic Cooperation and Development (OECD) markets. Similarly, imports from Turkey represent a small percentage of total Arab world imports. Turkish businessmen, government officials, and political parties (except for the Islamist Welfare Party) have never considered the Middle East market an alternative to Western ones.[25] The average share of Turkish exports to *all* Islamic countries was 18 percent for 1992–93, with Persian Gulf countries accounting for almost 50 percent; by contrast, the share of OECD countries was 61.5 percent, demonstrating the unlikelihood that there will be a major change in economic orientation toward either Iran or Arab countries. The political problems experienced by Turkish industrialists in some of the Arab markets—large unpaid debts, workers who were either not paid or kept against their wills—soured bilateral commercial exchanges. Nonetheless, the Turkish economy has developed sound practices and, in this respect, it is far ahead of any other Middle East state except Israel in implementing economic reforms. Although Turkish reform attempts have presently stalled, the progress achieved hitherto creates a considerable distance between it and other states in the region. If Turkey succeeds in recuperating from the stalemate it is presently experiencing and proceeds with privatization and other reforms, its potential as a major economic power in the region is unrivaled.

Anxious to participate in the new competitive international economy, many states in Eastern Europe, Latin America, South Asia, and East Asia are actively pursuing economic reform programs to open their economies to foreign investment. Increasing competition for capital and export markets makes it imperative that Turkey develop alternative markets to its traditional OECD-based ones. The European Union, with which it has signed a customs union agreement, has made clear that for both economic and political reasons it prefers not to admit Turkey anytime soon. Of the three possible regions—the Middle East, the Black Sea, and Central Asia—where Turkey can seek to rapidly expand its economic ties, the Middle East remains the most promising. With its burgeoning domestic market resulting from expanding population and income levels, Turkey represents an attractive market for foreign investment that can take advantage of its proximity to build plants to serve Turkey as well as the whole region.

Although the Middle Eastern market has been a mixed success for Turkey in the past, several factors might benefit it in the post-peace settlement period. The reduction in tension will ultimately lead to a decline in arms expenditures, freeing up resources for more productive uses. Political stability and the depoliticization of trade links will, in the long run, enable Turkey to compete on a level playing field. Israeli-Turkish economic cooperation and the decision to proceed with negotiations on a free trade agreement following Prime Minister Tansu Çiller's visit to Israel can be mutually beneficial, especially in solidifying markets in the developed world. While bilateral economic links between these two states will in all likelihood blossom, especially in tourism—Israelis have flocked to Turkey in increasing numbers—Turkey will find in Israel a long-term rival for access to Arab countries.

CONCLUSION

Charting a course through the Middle East will prove a challenge for Turkey primarily because its future economic or political role in the region is ambiguous and not easily definable. As during the heyday of the U.S.-Soviet rivalry and the Arab-Israeli conflict, Turkey can no longer isolate itself from developments in the Middle East. Ankara has found that its own Kurdish problem is intrinsically linked to those of its neighbors. All states with a Kurdish minority have to contend with the fact that their domestic policies will increasingly be influenced by those of their neighbors. The Allied-run Operation Provide Comfort is an apt example of the regionalization and internationalization of the Kurdish problem. The Kurdish rebellion and the GAP project have brought Turkey back into the Middle East. Given the unprecedented interaction between domestic and external security concerns, presently these two issues of vital importance to Turkey defy simple solutions.

This, in turn, complicates Ankara's task of constructive engagement with other regional powers to shore up Turkey's declining strategic importance to the Western alliance. Similarly, attempts to bolster Turkey's sagging fortunes with the European Union through a revival of commercial relations with the Middle East will also be compromised by the complexity of regional political differences.

Turkey's ability to balance its regional security interests without sacrificing potential economic gains will very much depend on Ankara's willingness to redefine its environment. The transformation of the international system necessitates a redefinition of its interests and the means of achieving them. The growing importance of economic factors; the rediscovery of human rights concerns; the reemergence of ethnic nationalism; and the demand on scarce resources and a fragile environment mean that previous alliance commitments and relations with other states will be subject to new criteria for evaluation. In the past, Turkish foreign policy has been risk-averse and status quo oriented. Only once in recent memory did a Turkish leadership break with the domestic and international mold that Ankara had fabricated, during the Gulf War when Özal decided to cast his lot with the coalition despite protests at home.[26] Disappointed with the results, Turkey returned to its reactive mode following the 1991 elections and Özal's death. In fact, it is often overlooked that a Turkish refusal to side with the coalition in 1991 would have led to its complete isolation after the war. Similarly today, what Ankara requires is a new approach to its domestic and external ills, especially its Kurdish dilemma. Until such time that Turkey can regain the initiative— by resolving the Kurdish problem politically and putting its economic house in order—it will remain vulnerable to the manipulations of its neighbors and unable to take advantage of the Middle East to improve its international stature.

POSTSCRIPT

In March 1995, the Turkish military moved into Iraq with a force of 35,000, ostensibly to deal the PKK a devastating blow. Well-advertised in advance, it is unlikely that the operation succeeded in achieving more than such minimal objectives as the destruction of food and ammunition stocks. Politically it served to highlight the uneasiness with which Ankara perceives the absence of authority in northern Iraq and it may have been a warning shot across the bows not only of its allies, principally the United States, but also of the warring Iraqi Kurdish factions whose internecine duels have contributed in Turkish opinion to the expansion of the PKK infrastructure. On the other hand, the timing of the intervention, soon after the European Union voted to admit Turkey into a customs union arrangement, led to a backlash in European capitals. In effect, it may have had unanticipated impact by internationalizing what had been an internal situation. Although this would not ultimately affect Turkey's entry into the customs union, the furor caused by the Turkish intervention in northern Iraq further emphasizes the degree to which Ankara has mortgaged its relations with its neighbors, not to mention its allies, on the Kurdish problem.

CHAPTER FOUR

TURKEY AND IRAQ

Phebe Marr

There are few countries where the Gulf War and its aftermath have left greater policy dilemmas than in Turkey. Before the war, relations between Turkey and Iraq, while not warm, were pragmatic and cooperative on most issues of concern to both countries, despite their very different regimes and foreign policy orientations. Economic ties were strong, based on transshipment of oil through a pipeline from northern Iraq to the Mediterranean port of Dörtyol, expanded to carry more oil in the 1980s. Oil provided Turkey with rental revenue worth up to $1.2 billion a year.[1] For Iraq it provided an outlet to the Mediterranean that allowed it to bypass Syria, whose frequent disruptions of the Iraqi pipeline through its territory had finally caused Iraq to seek a replacement. Water problems, based on Turkey's progressive construction of the Southeastern Anatolia Project (GAP), have been serious but not sufficient to disrupt relations. Besides, most of the blame for the diminution of the water flow into the Euphrates in these periodic crises has been accorded to Syria, with whom Iraq had extremely acrimonious relations. On the key issue of importance to both countries—the Kurds—there has been positive cooperation, particularly during the Iran-Iraq war, when the Turkish government was allowed to help police the frontier by pursuing its own dissident Kurds across the Iraqi border. And while Turkey maintained diplomatic relations with both Iran and Iraq during the war, even providing Iran with a commercial outlet to the West, Turkey saw Iraq's final —if Pyrrhic—victory as in its interest, that is, in containing the spread of Iran's revolutionary impulse.

Although early signs of tension between the two countries appeared during the first months of 1990, the relationship was dramatically changed by Saddam Hussein's invasion of Kuwait in August 1990 and subsequently by Turkey's support of the Gulf War coalition. The Kurdish rebellion and subsequent deluge of Kurdish refugees on the Turkish border, the successful coalition resettlement effort, and Operation Provide Comfort, the groundbreaking experiment in protection of the nascent local Kurdish regime in northern Iraq, all served to heighten the tension. Economic cooperation between Turkey and Iraq was temporarily ruptured by UN sanctions and the shutdown of the oil pipeline, while political cooperation at the border was severed by Turkish participation in the northern protection regime. Diplomatic relations with Baghdad were broken, although they have been partially revived by the return of a Turkish chargé who holds ambassadorial rank.

How permanent are these changes likely to be? What, if any, lasting effects are likely? And, in an increasingly uncertain situation, what are the most important factors likely to determine the future of Turkish-Iraqi relations? Both the links and divisions between Ankara and Baghdad hold important clues to the answer. Some issues cut both ways, depending on how they are viewed and handled in the two capitals. In addition, outside influences, especially U.S. policy, will play a role in shaping the direction these relations take. Seven key issues are likely to shape the future relationship. They are water resources, the oil pipeline and other economic interactions, the Kurdish question, issues of boundary determination and maintenance, the new regional security environment, the relationship of Turkey and Iraq to the U.S. and Europe, and finally, the impact of domestic politics in both countries on their foreign policies. The two most immediately important geostrategic issues for Iraq and Turkey are water and oil.

THE ISSUE OF WATER RESOURCES

The water issue illustrates the primacy of geography in the relationship and one reason why relations are uneasy. Iraq's dependence on Turkey for water resources tends to create frictions between the two countries and could cause serious problems in the future. However, no matter how severe these frictions become, Iraq will have to deal with Turkey on the water issue.

The facts of the case are well known. The sources of Iraq's irrigation lifeline—the Tigris and Euphrates—lie in the highlands of eastern Turkey. Some 96 percent of the Euphrates headwaters and 60 percent of the Tigris headwaters are in Turkey.[2] A substantial portion of the Euphrates also passes through Syria, giving it control over some of Iraq's water supply, while the main tributaries of the Tigris also lie outside Iraq's borders in Turkey and Iran, making Iraq almost totally dependent on its neighbors for its irrigated agriculture. Some areas in northern Iraq support rain-fed agriculture, but 48 percent of its arable land is dependent on irrigation from its river systems.[3] The Tigris irrigates about 2.2 million hectares; the Euphrates, about 1 million.[4]

This agriculture has already been affected by Turkey's ambitious GAP, an impact that will increase in the future as the project nears completion. GAP will tap the sources of both rivers for a massive agricultural development program in eastern Turkey. GAP is to be composed of some twenty-two dams and power plants on the Tigris and Euphrates to irrigate 1.7 million hectares (over half Turkey's current irrigated area) and double its hydroelectric power.[5] Because of costs and other difficulties it is unlikely to meet its scheduled completion date of 2002; its finish is more likely a decade or even two decades away. Nevertheless, the dams already completed have caused problems and strained relations with Syria and Iraq. The completion of the Keban Dam in Turkey and the Thawrah Dam in Syria in 1973, both on the Euphrates, caused serious water reduction and displacement of villages in Iraq in 1975 when both dams were being filled. There were further problems after the construction of the Atatürk Dam in 1990 caused cutbacks in downstream flow. These were temporary, however, and subsided when the dams were filled. Nonetheless, by the time the GAP scheme is completed, Turkey will require 17 to 34 percent of the Euphrates water, reducing its flow in Syria by about 40 percent; and in Iraq by 50 to 60 percent.[6] Thus, over time, Iraq can expect reduced utility from the Euphrates despite its own planned irrigation works on the river.

It is ironic that GAP is being instituted by Turkey in part to improve the economic conditions of its Kurdish population in the east, as well as to make up for its shortage of electric power. Given these dynamics, one might conclude that the Turks are attempting to solve both their energy and their Kurdish problems at the expense of Iraq and Syria. It is also worth noting that the greatest impact of GAP in

Iraq is likely to be felt in Arab areas watered by the Euphrates. Kurdish agriculture in Iraq is more closely tied to Tigris tributaries, such as the Zab rivers, one of which is dependent on Iran.

A riparian agreement over water-sharing is needed but, despite international pressure in its favor, is not in place, leaving Iraq vulnerable to Turkey and causing periodic flare-ups of tension between them. At the end of 1993, for example, an official in Iraq's Ministry of Irrigation publicly criticized Turkey's water policy in connection with the new Birecik power-generating project, claiming it would deprive Iraq (and Syria) of power and violate a 1964 protocol on water-sharing.[7] Water is likely to be hostage to other political problems as well. In the past this problem has been managed by both countries in a way that has prevented serious ruptures. If relations are normalized in the future, they may be able to continue this pattern.

In dealing with the water issue, Iraq has several advantages. First, the Tigris has not yet been tapped and can be used to supplement the Euphrates, partially mitigating the problem in the near to mid-term. Iraq has already dug a channel between the two at Tharthar and plans more in the future. And even after Turkey taps into the Tigris source, Tigris water in Iraq is protected by a number of tributaries— the Greater and Lesser Zab and the Diyala—two of which arise in Iran, not in Turkey. Unfortunately, Iraq is also vulnerable to Iranian water projects on the Zab. Iraq is also vulnerable to action on the Euphrates by its Ba'thist rival, Syria, with whom it has worse relations than it does with Turkey. That was clear during the water crisis of 1975, after both countries built dams on the Euphrates. Iraq's animus was entirely reserved for Syria, and the two engaged in military posturing, indicating that more was at stake than water resources.[8]

A second offset for Iraq lies in its oil revenue, which can be used to purchase foodstuffs from abroad once sanctions are lifted. Indeed, the trend has long been in that direction. In the past three decades, Iraq's agriculture, particularly in the south, has declined, mainly through neglect, especially after the Iran-Iraq war. In 1960, agriculture contributed 17 percent of Iraqi GDP; in 1989, it contributed 5 percent.[9] The decline of production was offset by rising agricultural imports. In 1958, Iraq imported little food and exported some grains; by the end of the 1970s, it was importing a third of its food supply.[10] Food imports have again declined since the imposition of sanctions in 1990, which have paradoxically given a boost to attempts at self-sufficiency. Urban migration from rural areas of the south tended to reduce the farm population, though it was later supplemented by imported Egyptian labor. Notwithstanding Baghdad's huge new scheme to drain the river marshes, largely to control the rebellious population in the south, reviving agriculture in Iraq will be expensive due to overuse of the land and progressive salinization. Once oil starts to flow again, the trend to exports will resume. These social and economic factors point to less Iraqi dependence on domestic agriculture and irrigation and more on oil revenues for the import of needed food. Oil resources also put Iraq in a better position to resist Turkish leverage on its water resources, should Turkey attempt to use it.

On the Turkish side it seems clear that Ankara intends to forge ahead with GAP, relying on economic development to raise living standards in the southeast and damp down ethnic tensions, whether or not these schemes strain relations with its neighbors. The pace and timing of this project will depend more on Turkey's financial resources and the course of its military actions against insurgents in this region than on any protests from Syria or Iraq. All indications are that progress will be slower than planned, giving Iraq more time to adjust to its effects.

While Turkey's GAP can be expected to cause stresses in future relations with Iraq, on balance, the water resource problem is more likely to compel the negotiation of water-sharing provisions than to rupture relations. However, geography cannot be altered—Iraq is in the weaker position. At the same time, however, it has a third powerful offset to Turkey's actions on water—its oil pipeline through Turkey and the revenues this can bring to the Turkish economy.

THE TURKISH PIPELINE

Unlike the common water sources, which tend to divide the neighbors, the double oil pipeline that runs from Iraq's Kirkuk field through Turkey to the Mediterranean at Dörtyol ties them together. The pipeline has many benefits for both, and few disadvantages. The first pipeline was opened in 1977, mainly to replace the Mediterranean pipeline through Syria, which was constantly held hostage to poor bilateral relations between the two countries. Initially the Turkish pipeline carried 700,000 barrels per day (b/d), expanded to 900,000 b/d in 1984 by the addition of slip chemicals. In 1987 a parallel loop was completed, which almost doubled the capacity to 1.5 million b/d.[11] The line not only provided Iraq with a much-needed outlet for its oil during the Iran-Iraq war when its Gulf ports were shut down, but gave it alternative outlets for oil—the Gulf and the Mediterranean—depending on market demand. Estimates have placed Turkey's foregone revenue from the pipeline at $1.2 billion a year, and it is no secret that Turkey would like the pipeline reopened to help alleviate its current economic problems.[12]

Notwithstanding the benefits for both countries, there are some disadvantages as well. For both, the pipeline creates political vulnerabilities. As the recent war illustrates, Iraq must rely on the goodwill of its neighbors for access to markets. And Turkey could find itself suddenly deprived of an important source of revenue in case of a crisis. For both, the pipeline runs through Kurdish-inhabited territory, making the line vulnerable to sabotage. This is less serious for Iraq, where the pipeline stays well away from Kurdish areas until it leaves the country near the border with Zakhu, exposing a relatively small portion of the line to sabotage. In Turkey, however, much of the pipeline traverses Kurdish-occupied territory north of the Syrian border. However, the pipeline has been relatively free of sabotage.

Over the long run it is more significant that both countries have alternatives to this pipeline. Turkey has been involved in negotiations with Azerbaijan to build a pipeline from lucrative oilfields in Baku to run through southeast Anatolia to the Mediterranean. It is hoped that this line can connect with those in Kazakstan. However, these new pipeline projects will see fruition only after a number of years, and they are, if anything, fraught with more uncertainties and difficulties than the Iraqi pipeline. A pipeline through Turkey from Azerbaijan, although strongly supported by the United States, has met with opposition from Russia (which wants the line run through its territory) and from Iran, which claims to provide the shortest route to the sea.[13] Until these disputes, essentially political in nature, are resolved, the lines cannot be built. Even if the Azeri pipeline is constructed through Turkey, it faces the problem of a sixty-seven–kilometer gap between Azerbaijan and the Azeri enclave of Nakhichevan. To cover the gap the line would have to traverse Armenian territory—a problem for the Turks, or Iran—a problem for the oil companies.[14] These difficulties indicate why both Turkey and Iraq are anxious to activate the already existing pipeline from the Iraqi fields. Indeed, of all Iraq's neighbors, Turkey has shown itself the least volatile and the most pragmatic business partner. Although that reputation has been damaged in Iraqi eyes as a result of Turkey's participation in the Gulf War, it is still a more likely export venue for Iraqi oil than other neighbors through which pipelines already pass—Syria, Lebanon, and Saudi Arabia.

Moreover, the Turkish pipeline is connected to Iraq's strategic pipeline, built in 1975 to connect its northern and southern oil fields. This pipeline gives Iraq flexibility, since it can carry Kirkuk oil south to the Gulf and oil from the southern Rumailah fields north to the Mediterranean, depending on need. Although the northern Kirkuk fields are declining, there is no reason why Turkey could not continue to benefit from oil flows from southern Iraq. And Iraq's oil potential is clear. It has over 100 billion barrels of proven reserves, 10 percent of the world's total, and is second only to Saudi Arabia, with the possibility of more to be discovered.[15] Within a few years of the lifting of sanctions, and some investment in infrastructure, Iraq could bring its oil-exporting capacity up to 6 million b/d.[16] The far more certain prospect of participating in the export of this oil in the near future must outweigh the uncertainty of yet-to-be-built pipelines through Central Asia and the fractious Caucasus.

Iraq will put emphasis on rebuilding its offshore Gulf oil terminals, Mina-l-Bakr and Khor al-Amayya, destroyed in the Iran-Iraq war, since they give it maximum independence. But these ports are not without their own problems. Iraq's troubled relations and unresolved border problems with Kuwait and Iran and its more limited access to the Gulf, as a result of its wars, raise uncertainties here as well. Both offshore facilities are vulnerable to sabotage and military action from neighbors, especially Iran. Moreover, for markets in Europe, the Mediterranean is a cheaper, faster outlet than the Gulf. Thus there is little evidence that the Turkish pipeline is likely to have declining relevance for either Turkey or Iraq; indeed, given Iraq's oil potential, it may come to have increased attractiveness for both, if relations between the two countries can be put on a pragmatic basis.

In addition to the oil connection, trade is important to both countries. As the following table indicates, the embargo has slowed this to a trickle.

Table 4.1 Turkish Trade*

Main Trading Partners % of Total	1987	1988	1989	1990	1991
Exports to:					
Germany	21.4	18.4	18.7	23.7	25.1
Italy	8.3	8.2	8.4	8.5	7.1
USA	7.0	6.5	8.3	7.5	6.7
UK	5.3	4.9	5.3	5.7	5.0
Iran	4.3	5.7	4.8	3.8	3.6
France	4.9	4.3	5.1	5.7	5.1
USSR	1.6	2.3	6.1	4.1	4.5
Iraq	9.3	8.5	3.8	1.7	0.9
Saudi Arabia	4.0	3.1	3.1	2.6	3.6
Switzerland	3.5	2.3	1.5	2.3	1.8
Imports from:					
Germany	14.8	14.3	14.0	15.8	15.4
USA	9.7	10.6	13.3	10.2	10.7
Iraq	8.2	10.0	10.4	4.7	—
Italy	7.6	7.0	6.8	7.7	8.8
France	4.3	5.8	4.7	6.0	5.8
UK	4.9	5.1	4.6	4.5	5.5
USSR	2.2	3.1	3.8	5.6	5.2
Japan	6.1	3.9	3.3	5.0	5.2
Libya	2.2	0.6	1.8	2.2	1.3
Iran	6.7	4.6	1.5	2.6	0.4

* Excluding transit trade.
Source: The Economist Intelligence Unit, Country Profile, *Turkey*, 1993–94, p. 44.

In 1987 Iraq was Turkey's second largest customer after Germany, and Turkey third after Germany and the United States as a recipient of Iraqi goods. By 1991, Iraq was at the bottom of the list on imports and exports. (Some of the decline, of course, was due to the end of the Iran-Iraq war.)

Some of that trade was cross-border exchange, affected by the double embargo on northern Iraq (imposed by the UN on Iraq and by Saddam on the Kurds); this trade has also been reduced by the Turkish war against the PKK in the east. Much of the trade was carried on by and benefited Kurds on both sides of the border. With some justification, the Turkish government claims that a revival of Turco-Iraqi trade would boost the economy of the southeast and dampen the intensity of Kurdish alienation from the central government, although it would not eliminate it. Saddam Hussein, for his part, does not have an interest in removing his own embargo on the north before he has a negotiated settlement with the Kurds, since it would help alleviate the poverty of the Kurdish area and support the faltering government set up in the north. For these reasons, the restoration of the pipeline and oil flows and the revival of trade are clearly in the interest of both countries.[17]

THE KURDISH ISSUE

There are few issues more likely to have a permanent impact on Turkish-Iraqi relations than the Kurdish question. Will the status of the Kurds serve to divide Ankara and Baghdad or induce them to cooperate? Are the current arrangements in the north likely to endure or become transformed into something more permanent? If so, how might that affect these relations? Are there any potential changes in the situation that could permanently alter relations between the two governments? It must be borne in mind that while the Kurdish issue is the most important factor affecting relations between Turkey and Iraq, it is not the only one. In the calculus of both countries, the Kurdish issue is offset by economic and strategic considerations. Nonetheless, the Kurds loom very large in the equation, particularly since they constitute not only a strategic issue but one bound up with such potent, but intangible, factors as national identity and sovereignty.

Analysis of the Kurdish issue must start from the present position of both governments on northern Iraq. This position is clear; it is to contain Kurdish separatism and to keep both Turkey and Iraq intact as states. Within both countries there is a range of views on formulas to achieve these ends, and differing levels of tolerance for a devolution of local authority to the Kurds. In Iraq, these range from acceptance of minimal or superficial decentralization in an autonomous zone, the position of the Ba'th leadership, to broad tolerance for a "federal" state in the north, the position of the opposition Iraq National Congress. In Turkey, the government would presumably settle for any solution agreed on by all Iraqis, but they would be unhappy with anything approaching real autonomy lest it set a precedent for their own Kurds. The Turkish establishment—the military, the Foreign

Office, and most mainstream politicians—would like a return of the central government of Iraq, preferably under new leadership. Other Turks, including many intellectuals, take a more liberal view. They would accept genuine autonomy for the Iraqi Kurds, although they would be far less likely to countenance the same arrangement in their own country.[18] In both countries, however, virtually no one espouses a change of boundaries or a dismantling of the state system, except for the more extreme elements among the Kurds themselves. Among liberal Turks and Arabs, the federal solution is advanced as a formula to keep the state intact.

Both states have made different, unsuccessful attempts to resolve the Kurdish problem. Since 1974, Iraq has granted its Kurds considerable autonomy, at least on paper. Kurds in Iraq have been allowed the use of Kurdish language, they had a Kurdish press, and Kurdish was taught in schools at all levels. Within an area comprising the three governorates of Irbil, Dohuk, and Sulaimaniyyah, Kurds had their own legislature and an executive, with authority to deal with local affairs. Of course, as elsewhere in Ba'thist Iraq, the local authority was a facade; real power reposed in the hands of Saddam Hussein and the top Ba'th leadership whose representatives in the Kurdish area carried out his orders. In the central government there was a Kurdish vice president and Kurdish cabinet ministers—there ostensibly as Kurdish representatives—but they were without any real power. Nor did the Kurdish legislature in the north represent the free choice of the inhabitants. That choice reposed, for the most part, in the two major parties who won the 1992 election—the Kurdistan Democratic Party (KDP) and the Patriotic Union of Kurdistan (PUK). Both had been in opposition, in exile, or fighting a sustained guerrilla war for much of the last three decades.

Nevertheless, since March 1970, the Iraqi government formula for dealing with the Kurdish question recognizes Kurds as a distinct group, with a specific linguistic and cultural identity, acknowledged in constitutional arrangements that provide (at least on paper) for a devolution of authority. This has now become part of Iraq's constitutional legacy and is accepted by the bulk of the population. Under different leadership in Baghdad, with a different outlook and agenda, it could form a workable basis for a new institutional framework. Still, the flaws in the arrangement are glaring. Without a real voice in the power structure in Baghdad, the Kurds could not prevent the devastation visited on them during and after the Iran-Iraq war: the razing of 4,000 villages, the resettlement of Kurds in their tens of thousands, the Anfal campaigns that resulted in many thousands of deaths and disappearances, and finally the use of chemical weapons on civilians. This suggests that local autonomy, no matter how strong, cannot protect Kurds against a determined central government. There is no substitute for a system that provides for real Kurdish participation at the center.

The Turks, on the other hand, have handled the problem in the opposite fashion. They can claim, with justification, to have a democratic system, with Kurdish representation in parliament and at the cabinet level. But the price of Kurdish entry to the political structure has been Turkification, the renunciation of Kurdish linguistic and cultural identity. Although these restrictions have been loosened in recent years, especially under former President Turgut Özal, concessions on the use of the Kurdish language in print have been too slow and limited to satisfy Kurdish aspirations. The use of Kurdish in broadcast and TV media and in the school system has been denied, as has representation by parties with programs deemed to endanger the integrity of the state—that is, Kurdish political parties. On these grounds, parliament voted to revoke the immunity of seven deputies belonging to the pro-Kurdish Democratic Party (DEP), and six were charged under article 125 of the penal code, which prohibits threats to state integrity, and jailed pending trial. These acts, and the constitutional provision on which they are based, brought international opprobrium to the Turkish government. The Turkish dilemma is this: How far must the government move down the path of greater "cultural" autonomy to satisfy moderate Kurds, and how far is too much to preserve the cohesion of their state?

It is widely conceded that Turkey must move from the Kemalist formula of an identity based on Turkish language and culture to a new, more comprehensive definition of citizenship, one that will sustain a sense of community and strengthen a functioning democracy. Such a compromise will require that Kurds accept reduced demands for separatism and a more ecumenical view of their identity, and requires of the Turks a flexibility that they have not demonstrated. With all its faults, the Turkish experiment appears to have more promise than Baghdad's, although some combination of the two may be essential. The formula to be used, however, is more a domestic issue for Turkey and Iraq than an international issue, although how each deals with this problem is bound to influence their relationship. The longer Turkey fails to solve its Kurdish dilemma, the more it will affect Turkish views on the Kurds of northern Iraq and government policy toward Baghdad. The same is true of Baghdad, although it is difficult to see a satisfactory resolution of this problem as long as Saddam Hussein is in power.

At present, the governments in both Turkey and Iraq share a common goal with respect to the Kurds in northern Iraq, so the Kurdish issue is more likely to bring them together than to drive them apart. Both want to contain Kurdish aspirations for self-determination within the bounds of their current state systems and within the state boundaries as currently drawn. Both urgently need to address formulas by which this can be achieved. Achievement of this goal is highly unlikely under Saddam Hussein, but might be more attainable under a successor. As long as Saddam remains in power, this situation will confront the Turkish government with a political dilemma— whether to accommodate Baghdad, hoping that Turkey will not face a renewed refugee problem on its borders, or to assume more responsibility for the northern Iraqi region, an equally onerous and unsatisfactory undertaking. The Turkish government appears to have better prospects for a resolution of its Kurdish problem, but a settlement may be some time in coming. In the meantime, the issue is profoundly destabilizing domestically.

Failure to successfully address these domestic issues is likely to produce more Kurdish separatism in both countries. An erosion of central government authority in Baghdad—unlikely at present writing—could produce an insurgency that destabilizes the border with Turkey and Iran and helps further PKK efforts in Turkey. Sentiment in Baghdad and the rest of Iraq could turn against retention of the Kurdish area, excluding Kirkuk. But this eventuality seems highly unlikely and would surely be a long-term proposition. It would also be a costly process for the Kurds in terms of lives lost and economic prosperity forgone. It is not clear that time is on the side of Kurdish separatism. Central governments in post-Saddam Baghdad and in Ankara may come to offer enough benefits—economic, cultural, and political—to keep most Kurds satisfied within their present boundaries. Meanwhile, both governments will continue to repress extremists who resort to violence.

It is far more likely, barring dramatic changes in Ankara, that Turkey will work to reduce and contain any development of Kurdish self-determination in northern Iraq and its subsequent spillover into Turkey, and that it will try to do so in cooperation with Baghdad and other regional governments. Fighting between the PUK and the KDP throughout 1994 has increased the possibility of instability in the region, and reduced confidence that the nascent Kurdish administration can govern effectively. Should the situation in the north deteriorate further, Turkey will probably attempt to exercise as much direct control over the territory as it can, without actually absorbing the area. If Turkish influence in the north acquired a degree of permanence over time, this would worsen relations with Baghdad, which needs the weight of the Kurds as a Sunni balance to the majority Shiite population, as a secular balance to Islamic influence emanating from Iran, and as a mountainous barrier guarding Iraq against invasion from the north. Any attempt by the Turks to change this strategic reality would surely create permanent fissures in its relations with Baghdad. Needless to say, it would also be strongly opposed by Iran, Syria, Armenia, and Russia.

What of a third alternative—the gradual emergence of a de facto Kurdish buffer state in the north, one protected by and oriented toward Turkey, rather than Iraq? Much has been written about the long-term potential for this option, and even its desirability.[19] This eventuality looks increasingly less likely, at least in the near term. Until 1994, when partisan fighting broke out in the north, the Kurds had done a credible job of working together to create a functioning administration under very trying conditions and much uncertainty. But by any "capacity" test, the Kurds do not have the wherewithal to establish a de facto state. Their strongest suit has been the quasi-democratic regime that had been governing much of the north, even beyond the thirty-sixth parallel. But this government, as events have shown, was a fragile coalition at best, kept together by the agreement of the two main contenders for power, who had much to lose in the event of its collapse. The election of 1992, won by the KDP by a razor-thin margin of two votes, was not accepted by the PUK. In a long behind-the-scenes bargaining session, KDP leader Massoud Barzani was persuaded to give up his margin of victory in favor of a coalition government on the basis of equality. As long as the coalition held up, so did the government, but in April 1994, the coalition broke down, with serious consequences for the future of the Kurds in the north. Local fighting over a land dispute between individuals belonging to the two parties broke out in Rania and quickly spread throughout the Kurdish region, and several hundred Kurds were killed. Although the two leaders gradually reconciled, their differences run deep. Although the coalition had been patched up, its fragility is clear as are the real disagreements between the two leaders and their parties. Fighting resumed in December and continued despite mediation attempts by the United States and others.

In addition to problems of governance, the Kurds do not have some of the other requisites for independence. Their economy is limping along just above the survival level. The continued double boycott has prevented the development of any self-sustaining industries. Even farming, a mainstay of the economy, is only slowly coming back to life. Aside from outside aid, smuggling, and some transit traffic, little exists on which to build a viable economy at present. Unemployment is rife and a large refugee population and a substantial civil service need to be paid from "state subsidies." Suggestions by various policy analysts that Kurds be allowed to develop local industries to make their economy more self-sustaining have fallen on deaf ears; these ideas have been opposed by regional powers, especially Turkey, as the first step on the road to an independent state, or they have fallen into the "too difficult" category. Kurds themselves have apparently not done enough to take the initiative in generating financial support from Kurds outside.

Finally, the Kurds do not have the military potential to defend and protect an independent state from well-armed, hostile neighbors. The 30,000 to 50,000 peshmergas designated for the Kurdish army cannot defend the north against Iraq or any neighbor, even if they were unified, which they are not. Militarily, any developing buffer state in the north would have to be a protectorate—of the United States, the international community, or the Turks. Aspirations for self-determination are high, especially among the educated population, and even among the poor and less well educated.[20] But the political foundations of a state cannot be built solely on aspirations; indeed, unrealistic aspirations may seriously impede progress in establishing a government on the ground. In any event, creating the sinews of an independent state, even a federated province, is a project that seems further off than ever.

There is little doubt of Baghdad's preferred policy; it wants to regain control over the north. Under Saddam, it would probably prefer to remove the current Kurdish leadership in the north. Failing that, it would prefer to make arrangements through negotiations that it could later undo. Any such process would put the Kurds in substantial danger without ironclad protection guarantees from the West. A successor regime in Iraq might be more willing to make limited accommodations with the current leaders under appropriate international encouragement. But under most conceivable circumstances, Baghdad would want a return to the status quo ante—with Iraqi troops at the border, and good relations with Turkey.

Turkish policy in the short term will be critical in this regard. Will Turkey be better off with Baghdad, even under Saddam Hussein, in control of the north and the border? Or would a friendly, pliant, but weak local Kurdish government, unable to resist Turkish encroachment on its territory, be preferable? The first alternative has its dangers. An armed, aggressive Saddam is likely to make a threatening neighbor, particularly if he acquires new weapons of mass destruction. The Turks will constantly have to look over their shoulders and wonder whether vengeance is harbored in Baghdad for Turkey's role in the Gulf War and afterward. Indeed, a rebuilt Iraq with Saddam at its head could become a major threat to Turkey, particularly if Turkey's ties to NATO and the United States weaken and Saddam retains his distrust of Ankara. Despite these dangers, however, all indications point to a reluctant preference for dealing with Baghdad —even under Saddam—as the lesser risk. Recognized in this risk, however, is the calculation that if Saddam remains in power, his continued presence will guarantee Western cooperation in a policy to contain his military buildup and deter any future aggression.

The alternative—recognition of a temporary buffer zone or quasi-state in the north—even under considerable Turkish influence or protection, would create real problems for Turkey. It would generate serious friction with Iran. It would overextend Turkey's military commitments and create one more headache for Turkey in a post-Soviet world. It would force Turkey to absorb and administer more Kurds. And it is a formula for continuing tensions with Baghdad, jeopardizing other positive interests, especially economic ones. There is little evidence that Turkey's ruling establishment is likely to espouse this option if it can avoid it.[21] A Kurdish buffer state that cuts Turkey off from Baghdad, and from contacts with the oil states to the south, would be counterproductive in the extreme.

Actions of the Turkish government indicate a desire to normalize relations with Baghdad. These include the presence in Baghdad of a chargé of ambassadorial rank; opening the frontier at Zakhu to truck traffic; insistence that Turkey's aid program in Iraq benefit all communities, not just the Kurds;[22] and Turkey's announced preference for lifting the oil export embargo and reopening the pipeline, as Iraq fulfills its nonproliferation obligations. A persistence of the current standoff between the West and Baghdad over a long period of time, without any change of government in Baghdad, will be increasingly uncomfortable for Ankara and could eventually jeopardize Turkey's long-term strategic interests in Iraq.

There is a third possible scenario, one that could face Turkey and the West with a very undesirable outcome. This would be a collapse of order in northern Iraq, which would make the region increasingly unmanageable. The Kurdish zone could become a haven for the PKK and Islamic elements from Iran, as well as saboteurs from Baghdad. Under these circumstances, Turkey might be drawn into the north to a greater extent than it wished to shore up its position in eastern Turkey, and it could end up playing a role analogous to Syria's in Lebanon. The implications of this situation for relations with Baghdad are serious and would not bode well for Turkey's future.

BOUNDARY ISSUES

Unlike boundary issues between Iraq and Iran, and Iraq and Kuwait, those between Turkey and Iraq have, for the most part, been laid to rest. However, some suspicions still lurk in Baghdad over lingering Turkish irredentist claims to the Mosul province and its oil. The Turks only relinquished the Mosul province in 1926, when Iraq's northern boundary was set by an international commission sponsored by the League of Nations. Although the loss of this territory with its oil resources was resented in Turkey, relinquishment of empire was part of the Atatürk legacy and one that has remained relatively unquestioned. Some right-wing Turkish groups continue to hanker after Mosul, but successive Turkish governments have not renewed these claims, preferring cooperation with governments in Baghdad.

Recently, however, actions by Turkey have renewed Iraqi suspicions of Turkish aspirations in the northern provinces. These include Turkish acquiescence in the establishment of a Kurdish Conservative Party, a small, marginal group in northern Iraq that advocates the establishment of an independent state of Mosul, to include Kurds and Arabs, that would cooperate with Turkey and act as a buffer against a truncated Iraq. The fact that this group, which openly espouses the partition of Iraq, has an office in Ankara has raised eyebrows in Baghdad. More significant have been close, continuing ties with Iraqi Turkmen and the Iraqi National Turkmen Party headquartered in Ankara. Turkmen form a substantial population in northern Iraq, at least 500,000 and possibly more, and they look to Turkey for support. Turkey's ties to both groups, established during Özal's presidency, may be seen as a hedge against Kurdish separatist aspirations in the north. Should Turkey move to extend its influence further into Iraqi territory, these suspicions will be exacerbated. Thus far, however, the Turkish government has been at great pains to support Iraq's territorial integrity.

More problematic is the issue of boundary maintenance. During the Iran-Iraq war, Turkey and Iraq concluded an agreement giving Turkey the right of hot pursuit of the PKK for up to three miles across the Iraqi border.[23] This lapsed with the end of the war in 1988. With the collapse of Iraqi control in the north, Turkey has resumed the practice and recently bombed presumed PKK camps as far south as Sulaimaniyyah. Agreements with the KDP and PUK to exercise control over PKK units in Iraq have often broken down. (Indeed, differences on this issue between the PUK, more favorably disposed toward the PKK, and the KDP, more willing to take action against them, has been a major cause of the friction between the two parties.) In the current political vacuum, the Turks can be expected to be more, not less, intrusive.

Even if the Baghdad government should reassert control over the north in the future, maintenance of border security would be difficult and require cooperation with local Kurds. For the Turks, it is a question of who is more reliable—the central government in Baghdad, even under Saddam, or the Kurds of northern Iraq? Ankara's answer is not yet clear, but the issue is one with the potential to cause friction with Baghdad. Turkey cannot be entirely comfortable with Iraqi forces under a leader like Saddam Hussein up against their own on the frontier, or with Saddam's having greater access to the PKK. The longer the north of Iraq remains a problem, the greater the danger that Turks will take police functions in the area into their own hands. This action would create increased animosity toward Turkey among local Kurds as well.

In sum, the Mosul province issue has been largely laid to rest, although greater extension of Turkish authority into northern Iraq is reviving Iraqi fears of Turkish irredentism. Far more serious is border control, given PKK activity inside Iraq and across the frontier. Cooperation with Baghdad on this issue is more likely than the reverse, but lack of any control over the frontier and the increased use of Iraqi territory by the PKK are likely to cause serious friction with Baghdad if they persist for any length of time. On the other hand, support for the PKK is a weapon Saddam can use against the Turks as well.

THE NEW REGIONAL ENVIRONMENT

At a broader level, future relations between Baghdad and Ankara will depend on the regional interests of both countries as perceived in each capital. Here, the collapse of the USSR and the end of the Cold War have created substantial new realities for both countries.

For Turkey, the overarching threat of a monolithic Soviet Union's impinging on its territory has disappeared. In place of the old menace has come a new situation with both opportunities and challenges. The opportunities lie in the potential for renewed economic, political, and cultural ties with the Turkish-speaking states in the Caucasus and Central Asia. Already Turkey has reached out to these states, only to discover, on closer examination, that their expectations may have been exaggerated. At the same time, the collapse of the former Soviet Union (FSU) has unleashed a whirlwind of ethnic struggles within and between the states of the FSU, leading not only to instability on its borders but spilling over into domestic Turkish politics. Ethnic wars in Georgia, Azerbaijan, and Armenia, as well as in Bosnia, are cases in point. The creation of an independent—indeed expanding— Armenian state impedes Turkey's links to Azerbaijan as well as to Central Asian states further east. Moreover, while Russia is no longer a next-door neighbor, it is a powerful nearby state harboring some deep suspicions of Turkey, a NATO power anxious to expand its influence into the Russian "near abroad." This new environment, while more promising than the old, will continue to create challenges for Turkey and complicate its regional relations.

In addition, the change in the regional landscape has now made Iran an increasingly important factor for Turkey, culturally and strategically. No longer held in check by the USSR, Iran is freer to support Islamic movements across its borders in Iraq and Turkey. Turkey may have cause to fear Iranian support, not only for the PKK, but for their Alawite minority, as well as Turkish Sunni fundamentalists. The victory of the Islamist Refah (Welfare) Party in the 1994 municipal elections, not only in Istanbul and Ankara, but in Kurdish areas in the east, could be unsettling. How this will affect conservative Kurds, not yet won over by the PKK but alienated by the Turkish government, remains to be seen, but it could allow Iran to fish in troubled waters, as it is already doing in the eastern regions of northern Iraq. On the strategic level, the growing connection between Iran and Russia, designed to keep Turkey out of the Caucasus and Central Asia, must also be of concern to Ankara.

Thus far, Turkey has avoided full-scale involvement in neighboring strife. It has tried to establish a web of relations with regional states, the better to neutralize the impact of hostilities on Turkey and to hedge its bets. The best examples of these are the Black Sea Economic Cooperation Initiative, which includes the states that rim that body of water, and the Economic Cooperation Organization, including Iran, Pakistan, and Central Asian states. But this strategy has not worked well in northern Iraq, where Turkey finds itself drawn into a conflict it cannot avoid. Turkey has followed a hedging strategy here, as well, by participating in the Provide Comfort regime with the coalition, while resuming relations with Baghdad; at the same time it presumably coordinates Kurdish strategy with Tehran and Damascus as well.

For Turkey, maintenance of Iraq as presently constituted is an important counterweight to disruptive regional conflicts on two counts. First, Iraq's government, and much of its society, is secular and can be counted on to balance, and oppose, the spread of Islamic influences across the border. Second, Iraq can act as a powerful balance against Iran, but only if its sovereignty and territorial integrity remain intact. Iraq can also act as a balance against Syria with whom Turkey has always had antagonistic relations. A truncated Iraq, one from which the Sunni Kurdish areas have been removed, would be far more Shi'a in composition and therefore subject to Iranian influence. Alternatively, a stable Kurdish regime in northern Iraq, friendly to Turkey, is likely to stir countervailing intervention from Armenia, Iran, Syria, and even Russia. These countries have ample instruments for intrusion through support for the PKK and nascent Islamic parties in Turkey proper and in northern Iraq. Maintaining Iraq intact, as a geostrategic balance against Iran, is certainly in Turkey's interests for the foreseeable future.

Iraq's strategic situation has changed even more radically than that of Turkey. The loss of the Soviet Union as a patron and a "balancer" against the United States and the role of the United States as the sole superpower in the region have left Saddam with few options. He has made numerous attempts to restore the axis with Russia, but thus far with little effect. However, right-wing Russian groups, including a parliamentary contingent led by Zhirinovsky, have been welcomed in Baghdad. Russia increasingly sees Baghdad as a market for arms and a much-needed source of hard currency. In part, this accounts for the visit of the Russian foreign minister to Baghdad in October 1994 in an effort to resolve the crisis arising from Iraq's mobilization of its troops on the Kuwaiti border. Some would like a return to the era of Russian advisors. Should the situation in Russia change, this link could be quickly established to the detriment of the West, and Russia could end up in a position similar to the one occupied by the USSR during the Iran-Iraq war as the one country able to deal with both Iran and Iraq. Such a possibility would certainly strain Iraqi-Turkish relations and would also concern the United States, already worried about Russian intrusion into its "near abroad."

Commercially, Iraq would prefer ties to the West and to Turkey, and it will work to improve them. But a weakened and continually isolated Iraq will most likely incline the country in the direction of Russia, if not further afield to North Korea and China.

TURKEY'S RELATIONS WITH THE UNITED STATES AND THE WEST

One of the most important factors affecting future Turkish-Iraqi relations will be Turkey's ties to the United States and Europe. And this, in turn, will depend on Turkey's evolving vision of itself and its future direction. The Turkish-U.S. partnership will be critical in helping to shape this vision.

It is already clear that some in Turkey, swayed by economic and strategic arguments, feel that partial removal of the embargo on Iraq and opening the pipeline would improve both their general economic situation and their ability to deal with the Kurdish situation. In the short term, the Turks are deterred from moving in this direction by UN Security Council resolutions and the consensus, still operative in the Security Council, that Iraq has not met conditions for removal of the embargo, as well as by strong U.S. persuasion. Cooperation is also in Turkey's interest. The Turks' worst nightmare is a collapse of coalition policy in the north and a renewed exodus of Kurds to the Turkish frontier. But the most important constraint on improved relations with Baghdad is Turkey's reluctance to seriously jeopardize its relations with the United States, its most important international ally. Turkey will calculate long and hard before creating a permanent fissure in the relationship or initiating a long cool period, such as ensued from the 1964 crisis over Cyprus, when President Johnson indicated he would not support Turkey as a NATO power if it decided to intervene militarily in Cyprus. Much will depend on how the United States handles this relationship, and the degree of firmness it shows along with sufficient compensation to Turkey for the real economic and political costs it is paying. An indication of such compensation is the transfer of $1.2 billion to a special defense fund for Turkey, to be spent on a joint U.S.-Turkish aerospace venture.[24] Notwithstanding these factors, as well as Turkey's own interests in keeping peace in northern Iraq, Turkey's threshold for tolerance of these arrangements could reach their limits if Turkey fails to settle its own Kurdish problem or feels its national cohesion threatened by events in northern Iraq. The longer the present policy obtains, the higher the costs to the United States, not only financially, but in other policy trade-offs; this cost is already apparent in Turkey.

Turkey faces a second consideration inhibiting normalization with Baghdad while Saddam is in power—its self-image and its image in the eyes of Europe. Turkey's sensitivity over Europe's failure to include it in the European Union, despite its good NATO record, is a continuing psychological sore. The wound has been exacerbated by the domestic repercussions of Europe's failure to come to the aid of Muslims in Bosnia, and outbreaks of violence against Turks in Germany. Nevertheless, Turkey is sensitive to Europe's criticisms of its human rights record, especially with respect to the Kurdish issue.

Openly flouting the sanctions regime and restoring relations with Saddam can only widen the perception in Europe of a gap between "Muslim" Turkey and "democratic" Europe. Turkey's policy toward Iraq, at least while Saddam Hussein is in power, will therefore be tied up with the far more significant but intangible question of Turkey's identity. Will it continue to aspire to become a member of the European community, remaining a secular state with democratic institutions? Or will it gradually turn elsewhere for inspiration and support—to eastern Europe, to the Caucasus and Central Asia, or the Middle East? The onus of dealing with Saddam Hussein may be considerably lightened if other European powers—Western and Eastern—decide to do business with him themselves.

On the Iraqi side, Saddam can be expected to apply maximum pressure to dislodge Turkey from the Western coalition and move it back to the pre-war status quo. This process is well under way. In addition to the "carrot" of renewed income from the pipeline, Saddam can also use the "stick" of support for the PKK. The Turks must also fear a revived and possibly vengeful Saddam on their borders. In sum, the single most important factor in preventing a renewal of more normal Turkish-Iraqi relations while Saddam is in power is the determination and consistency of U.S. policy in preventing it, and U.S. and allied willingness to absorb the costs.

THE IMPACT OF DOMESTIC POLITICS

Last, Turkish-Iraqi relations will be affected by changes in domestic politics in both countries, which cannot be predicted with any certainty. The removal of Saddam Hussein and his replacement by a new government provides the best hope for a negotiated settlement of the Kurdish problem in Iraq. Such an eventuality would almost certainly provide the Turks with the justification for a return to previous relations with Baghdad. On the other hand, if Saddam's removal were followed by severe instability in Baghdad and in the north, the Turks might reluctantly move to control—or close—Iraq's northern border, creating a repetition of the crisis that confronted the West in 1991. Some wonder whether, under these circumstances, the north could become a haven for refugees fleeing a chaotic Baghdad. While not currently in prospect, the political situation in Baghdad needs to be carefully watched. A new regime in Baghdad, once it stabilized itself, would certainly seek to regain control over the north and to reopening the pipeline. Prospects for better relations would be largely dependent on whether a new government could secure an amicable settlement with the Kurds and a relatively quiet frontier—or whether guerrilla activity and instability would continue. In the latter case, the Turks could be drawn into frontier actions that would once again cause friction with Baghdad.

Domestic political changes in Turkey also have to be considered. A weak and unstable central government, increased military influence in the councils of government, greater Islamic pressures, and possibly more collaboration between the Refah Party and the PKK in the east could all prevent the central government from taking the measures required to settle the Kurdish problem. Conversely, the emergence of a stronger government, able to seek a political rather than a military solution to the Kurdish problem, and an improvement in the economic situation would allow Turkey to take a more relaxed position on Iraq and the situation in the north, more sustained cooperation with the coalition in protecting the Kurds, and a continuation of the current de facto separation of the Kurdish zone from Iraq proper.

CONCLUSION

Turkey's geostrategic and economic interests point to a gradual, if reluctant, normalization of relations with Iraq, even while Saddam is in power. Were he to be replaced, this process would be speeded up. These strategic interests are strong. To shore up its fraying economy, Turkey would like its pipeline opened and the resumption of cross-border trade with Iraq. To contain the PKK rebellion and the rise of Kurdish aspirations inside Turkey, it would like to contain the development of separatism in northern Iraq and secure the border. In Turkey's view, this is still best accomplished by supporting Iraqi sovereignty over the north. In addition, Turkey would like a independent, reasonably stable, secular Iraq as a balance against Iran and the spread of its influence—nationalist and ideological—northward.

However, these factors are offset by others that are likely to keep the Turkish-Iraqi relationship uneasy. The most important is the continued presence in Baghdad of Saddam Hussein and the implications of his rule for regional and international politics. Turkey has much to fear from a rearmed and potentially vengeful and mercurial Saddam

Hussein, and it will surely keep him at arm's length. Moreover, the onus under which the Baghdad regime labors under his leadership will continue to bring constraints on Turkey's dealings with him, certainly from the United States and the West. His presence will also make the solution of the Kurdish problem far more difficult. It could perpetuate continued protection of the northern enclave in Iraq, complicating Turkey's ability to deal with its own Kurdish problem. For as long as the protection regime exists, frictions between Ankara and Baghdad will persist.

While much Western analysis has focused on the emergence of a separate Kurdish entity in northern Iraq and on the role Turkey might play there, this seems less likely today than it did in 1993. The ability of the Kurds to sustain the cohesion of their government, to move toward economic development, and create a reasonable security force —all factors necessary for real self-determination—do not seem promising in the face of determined opposition from Baghdad and regional neighbors. Rather, another scenario must be considered— one in which the situation in the north becomes more unstable. This could gradually draw Turkey further into northern Iraq to protect its frontier and to control the situation. This would certainly revive Baghdad's fears of "Mosul revisited," and further strain relations, particularly if the United States continues to be successful in keeping Saddam isolated.

From Iraq's perspective, virtually all its national interests point in the direction of a desire for improved relations with Turkey—with or without Saddam. The need to break out of its isolation, to secure its northern frontier, to contain Kurdish aspirations, to regain its sovereignty—all indicate an imperative to establish better relations. Iraq has some cards to play as well, threatening to use the Gulf as an outlet for the oil when sanctions are removed, rather than using the pipeline; supporting the PKK; and keeping the Kurdish north destabilized to bring pressure from Turkey—and other neighbors—on the Kurds. If Saddam remains in power, however, tensions are likely to persist.

Any attempt, either to permanently detach the north from Iraq or to extend Turkish control over the northern region, is a formula for creating lasting hostility between the two countries. Turkey is unlikely to be drawn into this scenario willingly, but unless there is a change of regime in Baghdad or of the situation in the north of Iraq, this could become a possibility. Since it is not one desired by either Iraq or Turkey, it is more likely that both will work for a gradual return to something approaching the status quo before the Gulf War, however reluctant Turkey may be and however uneasy a neighbor it finds in Iraq; indeed, the process is already well under way.

The views expressed in this paper are those of the author and should not be construed as reflecting the policy or positions of the National Defense University, the Department of Defense, or the United States government.

CHAPTER FIVE

TURKISH-IRANIAN RELATIONS
An Iranian View

Tschanguiz H. Pahlavan

The history of the relationship between Turkey and Iran is old and complex. The foundation of modern Turkish-Iranian relations was laid by the founder of the Pahlavi dynasty, Reza Shah, when he visited Turkey in 1934, at a time when both countries were struggling to overcome constraining historical traditions and establish modern institutions to gain access to Western civilization.[1] Overcoming a legacy of conflict and warfare, the 20th century ushered in a new era of cooperation between the two countries.

At the time of Reza Shah's visit, Turkey and Iran had several common goals. They were both working to separate the state from tradition and religion. Both countries also perceived a common threat from the spread of communist influence from abroad as well as internally. In their view, communism, like tradition, could interrupt the modernization process and damage their burgeoning relations with the West. Similar predicaments facilitated the signing of several agreements, and between 1926 and 1937, a set of tariff, border, trade, and security agreements were signed between the two countries.[2]

Though this period was not devoid of its share of tensions, the goodwill engendered by the new relations generally prevailed and culminated in the 1937 signing in Tehran[3] of the Sadabad Treaty[4] between Iran, Turkey, Iraq, and Afghanistan. The West welcomed the treaty as a step toward maintaining and improving regional peace and stability. The events of World War II, however, and the occupation of Iran by Allied troops demonstrated that the agreement was not effective in a crisis, as the entry of Allied troops into Iran in 1941 had severe consequences for its political stability. Yet that development also showed that Iran had special strategic significance for the world powers, even though it was not, even then, comparable to Turkey's. Still, in the Western strategy against Soviet communism during the post-war period, Iran and Turkey each had particular importance. This importance was reflected in the Baghdad Pact (1955), the Central Treaty Organization (1959), and the Regional Cooperation for Development (1964), all designed to counter the expansion of the Soviet Union.[5]

The history of Turkish-Iranian relations during the twentieth century, however, also shows that the relationship sometimes experienced some difficulties. For example, in 1927 the Turkish army entered Iranian territory to chase and capture Kurdish rebels. Instead, a column of Turkish soldiers was seized by the Kurds, and the Turkish government, assuming they had been transferred to Tehran and detained by the government, recalled its ambassador from Tehran. Tensions mounted and relations deteriorated until explanations from the Iranian government defused the crisis and negotiations were renewed, culminating in a tariff treaty in June 1930 and a border agreement in January 1932.

During the reign of Mohammed Reza Shah from 1941 to 1979, there were also underlying strains in relations. For example, there were disagreements about Turkish regulations for Iranian trucks using Turkish roads. In another instance, the Iranian ambassador was temporarily recalled in response to comments made by the Turkish ambassador, who, after returning to Tehran from his vacation in Turkey, said in a lecture that while driving from the Turkish border to Tehran he had felt as if he were in his own country. The shah was angered by this obvious reference to the prevalence of Azeris in Iranian Azerbaijan, who speak a language related to Turkish.[6]

More generally, Tehran viewed Ankara's promotion of Turkish nationalism as a method of withstanding the Soviet threat. The Pahlavi dynasty's use of Iranian nationalism was defensive; it aimed to keep the country unified, whereas Turkish nationalist ideology was perceived as expansionist.[7] Although Tehran was sometimes anxious, believing it could not depend on Turkey in a crisis (especially since the Sadabad Treaty had proved ineffective during World War II), the two governments continuously worked to ease tensions through negotiation.

Oil-poor Turkey struggled economically after the hike in oil prices in 1973–74 and its economy was continuously affected by shortages of foreign currency. At the same time, Turkey was undergoing momentous changes, including internal disturbances and military takeovers. Iran too, between 1941 and 1953, had experienced similar upheavals. Still, despite their domestic instability, the two countries' common stance against the Soviet Union and communism made them valued Western allies and encouraged their peaceful coexistence.

ISLAMIC IDENTITY AFTER THE 1979 REVOLUTION

Turkish-Iranian relations entered a new phase after the 1979 Islamic revolution in Iran.[8] The goal of this revolution was to influence and sway the Islamic world, though the exact definition of the "Islamic world" was not made clear. Turkey, secular in orientation, wished to remain faithful to Atatürk's secularist and Turkish nationalist legacy. This contrast in worldviews created some difficulties in their relations; for example, because Iranian revolutionaries viewed Kemal Atatürk as a friend and intellectual peer of Reza Shah, they disapproved of laying wreaths on his grave even during official visits. Turkey, enduring this slight against its founder with difficulty, steadfastly emphasized its secular culture.

The Islamic Republic of Iran does hold some natural attraction for Turkey's religious elements. It should be noted, however, that domestic Turkish religious movements are not products of the Iranian revolution, and it would be a mistake to consider Iran the sole source of religious movements in the region. Such conclusions are misleading, not least because they exaggerate Iran's ability to influence domestic religious movements. In Turkey, as in other Middle Eastern countries, the transition from old political structures to modern governments has yet to be completed. Sections of society that still feel alienated from the present political structure are seeking the realization of their ideals through different channels—religious, political, or something else.

Still, Turkish newspapers claim that the country's internal religious movement is a product of the movement in Iran.[9] In recent years, various reports have indicated that Turks are increasingly turning to Islam.[10] Turkish religious tendencies, though, particularly during times of high inflation and economic insecurity, are the product of

Turkey's *internal* situation, not outside interference. The Turkish government itself has engaged in religious activities in order to hinder, or at least control, radical religious tendencies.[11] The religious establishment in Turkey functions as a bureaucracy, and the people who work for it are civil servants. Ironically, this government-sponsored religious agency has been instrumental in spreading and deepening religious tendencies in Turkey. Thus, Turkey continues to come up against an old question: Can one be a Turk without being a Muslim? This question, never an issue in Iran, has always been an integral question for Turkish identity.

MAJOR ISSUES IN TURKISH-IRANIAN RELATIONS

Aside from the differences in approach to religion, there have been other causes for tension between the two countries since the Islamic revolution in Iran, including the problem of the Kurds, the situation of the post-Soviet Republic of Azerbaijan, and the activities of Iranian emigrants in Turkey. Yet in spite of these differences, they have found ways to cooperate, as in the case of the establishment of the Economic Cooperation Organization.

Turkey's nationalist ideology since the disintegration of the Ottoman Empire after World War I has long exerted pressure on its non-Turkish minorities. Originally, the idea behind Turkish nationalism was to create a force that would extend beyond Turkish borders and create a "Turkish nation," to unify all Turks within a new, although undefined, structure.[12] This ideology was to appeal to Turks as far away as Central Asia and as close as Iran and the Caucasus. Maps and encyclopedias printed in Turkey and articles by Turkish intellectuals aimed at influencing Turkish foreign policy toward this goal. Such expansionist views always disturbed Iran because of the perception that nationalists had set their eyes on Iranian territory, sometimes from the frontier to Tehran.[13]

In contrast, after 1979, Iranian nationalist ideology, always aimed at bolstering national unity, was met with a great deal of consternation among regional powers made anxious by the propaganda associated with apprehension about the possible export of Islamic revolution. Ideas regarding the export of revolution after the onset of the revolution itself had a great deal to do with attempts to unify the whole Islamic world. In practice, however, the Islamic revolution of

Iran not only was not capable of exporting Islamic revolution, but even failed to generate a model of Islamic government acceptable to other parts of the Muslim world. In fact, the Islamic Republic of Iran, with its unique government, was even the target of strong domestic criticism.

Nevertheless, the Islamic revolution in Iran has inspired and animated Islamic movements in other countries. At the same time, it should be mentioned that Islamic movements have occurred, especially in the Middle East, since at least the beginning of the twentieth century; the Ottoman Empire was itself an instigator of some of these movements.[14] The majority of the thinkers of these movements were from Middle Eastern countries other than Iran, but there is no doubt that they influenced Iran too. This applies as well to movements other than Islamic ones—for example, the Palestinian movement has had more influence on Iranian revolutionary youths than the other way around; many noncommunist, revolutionary Iranian youths sympathized with the Palestinian movement during the shah's regime.[15]

Thus, to ascribe to Iran the causation of all regional Islamic movements is to simplify a complex phenomenon that needs a separate and comprehensive analysis. While the Islamic revolution of Iran has had an inordinate degree of influence on Shi'a groups in the region, by no means has this extended to all Islamic or even all Shi'a groups. The revolution is primarily based on Twelve-Imami Shi'ism and has not succeeded in attracting all Shi'a sects or mystic groups. Smaller groups, and those adhering to the Alawite sect, have never considered themselves part of the Islamic revolution. Many religious Iranians frustrated with the Islamic revolution turn to one of these sects to seek guidance from their spiritual leaders, often considered undesirable by the regime.

Despite Ankara's efforts at preventing a repetition of Iran's Islamic revolution, there has been a rise in Islamic movements there. However, this rise has come from purely domestic sources in Turkey. In view of the negative image most Turks hold of Iran, it is quite unlikely that Iran or Iranians can exert a great deal of influence in Turkey. Still, the Turkish government, which enjoys the protection and support of NATO,[16] does not miss an opportunity to warn against the danger of Islamic expansion. This policy has an ulterior motive: it seeks not only to coalesce the country's secular forces but to demonstrate to the West that Turkey plays an active role in blocking

Iranian influence. This claim, though untrue, has provided Turkey with a variety of economic benefits.

Generally speaking, Turkey and Iran have differing worldviews and ideologies that are probably impossible to reconcile fully. These kinds of differences, however, should not necessarily affect their respective strategic positions and international affiliations.

TURKEY: ALLY OR AGENT OF THE WEST?

Just as the Iranian image in Turkey has been less than positive, Iran has held a negative view of Turkey since the revolution. Leaders of the Islamic revolution have always perceived Atatürk, the founder of modern Turkey, as an ally of Reza Shah, an enemy to Islamists, and believe Turkey has deviated from the path of Islam. More importantly, though, they are convinced that as an ally of the West, Turkey simply acts in the interests of the United States.

Constrained by short-term interest and calculations, Turkey was unable to play an intermediary role during the Iran-Iraq war. Nevertheless, the war benefited Turkey. Both Iran and Iraq, as a result of their international isolation, were forced to rely on Turkey as a major source of needed commodities imported from Turkey itself or from the West. Turkey's expectations of its relations with Iraq were higher than its expectations of Iran. Throughout the 1980s, the war with Iran gave Iraq an incentive to cooperate fully with Turkey, including in the establishment of commercial exchanges between the two countries. Turkey quickly became one of Baghdad's main customers. Sixty percent of the oil consumed in Turkey was imported from Iraq. When Turkey saw that "Iraq was threatened with collapse under the battering of the Iranian advance," the Turkish nationalist minister of state, Kamran Inan, publicly warned that 40 percent of Turkey's oil supplies came from the Iraq's Kirkuk region. Also, he suggested that "no less than one and a half million Turks and Turkomans [live] in the northern regions of Iraq." Inan, in effect, wanted to assert Turkey's preemptive right in the event that an Iranian advance led to the breakup of Iraq.[17]

Although an Islamic country, Turkey's constant attempts to project a Western image have obscured its regional role. This is partly the result of its geopolitical position on the border of both Europe and Asia, and partly the outcome of having adopted Western norms which, in turn, favor political and cultural links with the West at the expense of the Islamic world. Turkey is the only Islamic country that continues to participate actively in Western cultural and military organizations.[18] Iran rejects this involvement with the West and firmly believes that these attachments hinder Turkey's successful integration in regional organizations.

The Turkish government perceives its country as a frontline member of NATO. The former chief of staff of the Turkish military, Dogan Güres, has argued that the Straits of Bosporus and the Dardanelles along with the Black and Mediterranean seas are an axis connecting the Straits of Gibraltar to the Middle East and Central Asia.[19] This explains why Turkey inhabits a dangerous part of the world and why its importance will continue to increase. Güres also cites Syria, Israel, Palestine, and Lebanon as strategically important to Turkey. In an obvious reference to Iran, he expresses concern over the existence of chemical weapons and ballistic missiles in the region, and over the efforts of some countries to build atomic weapons.[20] The Turkish army's emphasis on a military role for Turkey heightens the level of anxiety in neighboring countries. This vision is accompanied by the constant overestimation by some in Turkey of the danger of fundamentalist Islam.

After the long war with Iraq, Iran has every reason to avoid conflict with Turkey, and Iranian officials have persistently tried, in spite of their differences, to reach an accord with Turkey. Some of Turkey's actions, however, have resulted in crises and provoked emotional responses in Iran. In February 1994, for example, the Turkish army bombed Iranian border villages in its pursuit of Kurdish activists from the Kurdistan Workers Party (PKK).[21] Nine were killed and nineteen were injured in the incident. The Iranian government's response to the bombing was cautious, enabling a group of Turkish investigators to go to Iran, after which the Turkish government apologized to Tehran.[22] Another example of poor Turkish judgment in Iran's view was the year-long detention of the freighter *Cap Maleas* on suspicion of arms smuggling for the PKK, and its release after an admission by the Turkish interior minister that the incident was the result of a mistake.[23]

A March 10, 1994, editorial in the Iranian government newspaper *Kayhan* depicts Turkey as being in a crisis situation, with its economy in shambles, the Kurdish problem unsolved, internal democratic forces repressed, and Islamic activism on the rise.[24] The same editorial suggests that, correspondingly, militarism in Turkey is on the rise and armament industries are anxious to expand. Consequently, Turkey has the potential of becoming one of the greatest military powers of NATO. This kind of editorial, published in an official Iranian newspaper, indicates the intense anxiety that prevails in Iran. It is Tehran's belief that due to domestic problems, including the conflict with the Kurds, Turkey may resort to war in the region. For example, General Güres's argument about Turkey's regional importance, published in an Iranian military journal, indicates just how much the Turkish situation might concern Iran. Since Turkey tries very hard to be perceived as a defender of Western policies and a friend of the United States in the region, it is natural for Iran to feel that Turkey actually acts as a Western agent.

Kayhan published a series of articles about "Turkey, the West and Islamism" in January and February 1994. The series outlined the growth of revolutionary Islam and quoted the Iranian ambassador in Turkey as saying "Turkey has simple people who are faithful Moslems and interested in religious topics. But the image of Turkey which has been shown is non-religious and anti-religious. . . . The government of the country, which is a separate entity, is secular, but Turkish people like the Koran and Islam. . . . People are interested in religious topics and in participating at religious gatherings."[25]

The same newspaper published the results of an academic study, which concluded that 80 percent of Turkish university students were in favor of establishing an Islamic government in Turkey. The article elaborated that although 31 percent of these students believe that true Islam could become a reality through democratic processes, 33 percent viewed this idea with skepticism.[26] Thus the report concluded that not only is official Turkey obsessed with the West, but that the United States had a hand in preventing the rise of Islamism in Turkey. Turkish officials, according to the newspaper, have created a "Turkish-Islamic synthesis" in their attempt to win over Islamic groups and prevent an Iranian-style revolution in Turkey.[27]

Government-run newspapers in Iran constantly write about the rise of Islamism in Turkey, its subservience to the West in general and the United States in particular, and express concern over Turkey's military buildup. The Iranian government's foreign policy, however, promotes neighborly relations with Turkey. The deputy secretary of the

Iranian Foreign Ministry explained that the Iranian arsenal is smaller than those of neighboring countries. Without specifically mentioning Turkey and, in an attempt to allay the concerns of the West and its neighbors, he pointed out that Iran's total weapons imports in 1989–91 were on the order of $2.8 billion, while Iraq and Saudi Arabia had imported weapons worth $10.3 and $10.6 billion, respectively. Iranian weapons imports in 1992 amounted to $850 million.[28]

KURDISTAN

Turkey is one of the countries in the Middle East most concerned about its territorial integrity. The primary reason for this insecurity lies in the Kurdish question, but another is the existence of past treaties, such as the 1920 Sèvres Treaty, that called its territorial integrity into question.[29] As early as 1880 the Ottoman Empire was faced with the problem of Kurdish demands for autonomy, or for the right to secession and full independence. From the outset, the Kurdish problem in Turkey has necessitated the cooperation of its neighbors, including Iran. The events following the Persian Gulf War show that Turkey has still not been able to muster the force needed to extinguish Kurdish demands.

There are two facets to Turkey's Kurdish dilemma, one domestic and one involving Turkey's neighbors to the south and east. History has shown that with regard to the Kurds, Turkey has generally acted in a way that has created problems with the countries on its border. Part of the problem stems from the operations of the Kurdish armed groups; beginning in the 1980s, for example, the PKK acquired more fighting power and operational capability. In 1984, Turkey succeeded in obtaining some cooperation from Iraq on the matter, cooperation that, along with disputes between the PKK and the Kurdistan Democratic Party of Iraq (KDP), so weakened the PKK that it could not easily continue its attacks against Turkish forces. Thus, the PKK was forced to concentrate its operational forces in Syria. In 1987, the Turkish prime minister signed an agreement with Syrian officials to strengthen cooperation on security matters between the two countries and compel Syria to curtail the guerrilla activities of the PKK.[30] For its part, Syria tends to use the "Kurdish card" in exchange for concessions on its dispute with Turkey over use of water from the Euphrates.[31]

The effective curtailment of the PKK's activities, first in Iraq and then in Syria, led the organization to establish a cooperative relationship with the KDP of Iran (KDP-I), resulting in the PKK's gravitation toward Iran in order to strike at Turkey under the umbrella of the KDP-I. Turkish newspapers in 1988 continuously reminded Iran of its obligations under the 1937 Sadabad Treaty,[32] which called on the cosignatories (Iraq, Iran, Turkey, and Afghanistan) to avoid interference in each other's internal affairs, cooperate on security matters, and maintain the security of their common borders. During various Kurdish crises, Turkey has pressured Iran to restrain the Kurds' movements along its borders. Iran's policy toward its own Kurdish population contrasts with that of Turkey, as Iran, because of its culture and history, has had a different approach. Iran cannot risk being perceived as a collaborator of Turkey on the Kurdish problem.

In 1988, when Turkey and the PKK were engaged in serious fighting, Iran made some overtures toward the KDP-I. Tehran had been cracking down on KDP-I's rival, the Kurdish Komala Party, and wished to differentiate between these two political factions of Iranian Kurds. Abdul Rahman Ghasemlu, the KDP-I leader, began negotiations with the Iranian government and insisted that a compromise be reached. However, in July 1989, Ghasemlu was assassinated during a secret meeting in Vienna with Iranian government representatives.[33] The assassination caused a great deal of consternation and frustration for the Kurdish movement in Iran, and as a result, the conflict between Tehran and the Kurds deepened. Nevertheless, this hardening of their respective positions should not override the fact that, from a historical perspective, there has always existed a greater desire in Iran for developing an atmosphere of cooperation with the Kurds.

Even before the Islamic revolution, the shah's regime had complex relations with the Kurds, and not all Kurds were pleased by the demise of the Pahlavi dynasty. Although some Kurdish groups benefited from the fall of the shah,[34] a powerful and influential group of Kurdish tribal chieftains, such as the Jaf chiefs, the Ardelan family, and the Palizban tribe and their followers, lost their economic and political influence and continued to make trouble for Tehran after the revolution.

Iran is the only country in the region with a province that is legally called "Kurdistan." In addition, many cultural restrictions that existed during the pre-revolutionary period are disappearing. As one author states, "permission to publish and sell materials in Kurdish—

even if these are censored—marks a substantial departure from the regime under the shahs. Some materials in Kurdish on Iranian or Kurdish political history have been marketed in Iran without difficulty."[35] Additionally, there is more freedom for Kurds to be culturally active in Iran. Even governmental organizations are publishing materials in Kurdish and on Kurdish language and culture.[36] This is because there is generally no restriction on the publication of Kurdish newspapers and magazines, or materials regarding Kurds or Kurdish history. There is general censorship in Iran, but it is not limited to the Kurds, as all citizens, regardless of ethnicity, race, or regional origin, are subject to governmental supervision. The only real cultural discrimination that exists is on religious grounds, and it should be stressed that while Kurds may not receive preferential treatment because they are predominantly Sunni, it is a religious rather than an ethnic situation that they share with other Iranian Sunnis. In Iran, "Shi'as are preferred for government appointments, just as Sunnis tend to be preferred in Turkey and Iraq."[37]

Kurds are an inseparable and important part of Iranian civilization. Their ethnicity and language prove this as well as their traditions, such as the new year (Nevruz) festivities and the cultural patterns of their daily life, which closely resemble those of the rest of the population of Iran. The conflicts and clashes between the government and Kurdish organizations have been predominantly of a political nature and not the result of ethnic discrimination. Therefore, in the twentieth century, the Kurdish question in Iran never attracted any international attention, nor were there any ethnic massacres or genocide in Iranian Kurdistan committed by government forces. In fact, since the 1930s, many Turkish and Kurdish Iraqi Shi'a leaders who had to give up their struggles have sought asylum in Iran.[38]

Certainly, in recent history, the Iranian government has combated secessionist demands by the Kurds and has not tolerated claims to "self-determination." Such demands have not been consistent, varying over time with changing political conditions. In principle, there has never been any objection to the Kurdish desire for self-governance, only to the threat of separatism and territorial dismemberment. An additional concern for Tehran has been the traditional ties Kurdish political organizations have had with other opposition forces. All these facts illustrate the limits of any Iranian-Turkish cooperation on the Kurdish question.

Turkey's troubles with its neighbors on the Kurdish issue extend beyond Iran. For instance, in 1989, Turkish newspapers published the confession of a PKK activist who said that "the Soviet Union was the mastermind of the guerrilla operations in southeastern Turkey in a triangular alliance that involved Syria and the PKK."[39] Bulgaria, another neighbor, was also attacked by some Turkish circles for allegedly helping the PKK, as was Greece. A training camp for PKK members was reported to exist on the Greek island of Lavrion.[40] These examples serve to illustrate how Turkey's domestic problem with the Kurds involves neighboring countries and weaves complex and entangled relationships. The only solution is for Turkey to reach an agreement with the Kurds and other domestic opposition forces and to avoid involving regional countries in its internal problems.

IRAN AND TURKEY IN CENTRAL ASIA AND THE CAUCASUS

The disintegration of the Soviet Union gave rise to the expectation that the Great Game in Central Asia might be replayed, this time by Iran and Turkey. The "Great Game," as it has been called for almost 160 years,[41] was the bloody nineteenth century contest between Russia and England for supremacy over Central Asia and India, from Elbrus to Everest, the Black Sea to the Bay of Bengal, and the Ural Mountains to the Khyber Pass. Those who thought that they would witness a repeat of the game were mistaken, however. Iran and Turkey are simply devoid of the capabilities necessary for such a contest—they are regional, not world, powers, after all.

After the fall of the Soviet empire, Turkey moved quickly to extend its influence to Central Asia and the Caucasus. Turkey was motivated by historical and emotional bonds as well as a desire to dominate the new markets in these regions. Despite its closer ties to the Caucasus, Turkey wanted also to be present in Central Asia. Ever since the demise of the Ottoman Empire, some Turkish intellectuals have harbored a sentimental view of Central Asia and developed feelings of "belonging" in relation to it. Author Tekin Alp has written that the four volumes of Turkish and world history used to teach school-children in Turkey since the 1930s contain "the new estimate of the role of the Turkish nation in the cultural development of humanity

from prehistoric times until our own days." The following are some
of the points made in this work:

> The motherland of the Turkish people is Central Asia, which extends
> from the . . . Baikal Basin through the Altai mountains to the Basin of
> the Itel, the Caspian Sea, the Hindu Kush, and the Karakorum and
> its neighborhood. While the rest of humanity was living in caves, lead-
> ing a most primitive life, the Turks . . . began to emigrate to China,
> India, the Asian hinterlands, North Africa, and Europe to which they
> brought the cultural gains acquired from their motherland. Other
> roads which the emigrants chose took them through the Ural moun-
> tains, the Caspian Sea and via the northern side of the Black Sea.[42]

The West, fearing the spread of Iranian-style "fundamentalist
Islam" in Central Asia, supported Turkey's presence there. When the
Soviet Union began to disintegrate, the Islamic Republic of Iran did
not initially have a clear policy. At first Iran sought to negotiate with
Moscow alone and not directly with the newly independent states
(NIS); gradually, however, Iran accepted the new situation. Still, the
first phase of Iranian-NIS relations was characterized by confusion.
The Iranian government, which since the revolution had proclaimed
its desire to have an independent policy between East and West,
was suddenly confronted with the disappearance of the "East" and
caught unprepared for the consequences of the splintering of the
Soviet Union and the emergence of the new republics.

In the second phase, pressure from some domestic groups forced
the Iranian government to express solidarity with its Muslim
brethren in the new republics. Inexperienced, the Iranian government
was confronted with a situation it did not fully understand; as nation-
alistic tendencies were rising, it stressed Islamic unity. At this junc-
ture, two countries—Turkey and Saudi Arabia—strongly opposed
the Islamic unity advocated by Iran. Turkey, which tried to counter
Iran with its own brand of secular culture, was somewhat successful
in this endeavor, but needed the support of its powerful economy. In
contrast to Iran, Turkey focused on the unity of the Turks and sought
to strengthen a particularly Turkish presence in Central Asia.[43]
Turkey, in this venture, encountered Uzbek aspirations to become
the leader of the region, leader of "greater Turkestan," an idea, however, unwelcomed by other Central Asian leaders. Kazakstan and
Kyrgyzstan, in particular, showed no inclination toward pan-Turkic
and pan-Turanist thinking. Turkey's only (and temporary) success

materialized with the election of Abulfez Elchibey, a strong supporter of Turkey, as the first president of Azerbaijan.

Ankara followed a two-pronged policy: it introduced the NIS both to its secular culture and to its particular kind of Islamic movement. When the Soviet republics became independent, Western countries, especially the United States, expected that "Turkey should expand its role from bulwark of the Western alliance to patron of emerging nations stretching east to the Chinese border. The idea had instant allure for many Turks, reviving forgotten dreams of pan-Turkism among distant Muslim kin awaiting a march toward Western prosperity. For the United States . . . as Soviet power crumbled, Turkey seemed a reliable proxy to fill the Central Asian vacuum."[44] Turkey's efforts in challenging Tehran in Central Asia, however, fell short of the mark. "These days that dream appears to be fading. Facing its own economic troubles recently, this nation of 60 million has been unable to provide the aid to cement its influence over the region. Only now are its policymakers acknowledging how difficult the region's ethnic and political cross-currents can be."[45]

At the same time, Turkey and the West were exaggerating the threat of Iranian religious fundamentalism in Central Asia. "The fear of fundamentalist Iran spreading throughout the region has been much exaggerated. Certainly thousands of mosques have been built and reopened, some with Iranian help. But over 90 percent of Central Asians who consider themselves Muslims are Sunni rather than Shi'a as in Iran; and after decades of a forced denial of religious values, a revival of interest in Islam is scarcely unexpected. Although most interest is home-grown, both Turkey and Saudi Arabia are promoting Islam as well. The Turkish newspaper *Zaman* is funding religious schools, while the Saudis have distributed over two million Korans and are bankrolling the building of new mosques."[46]

Iran's other opponent in Central Asia has been Saudi Arabia. Relying on its great monetary resources and the fact that Sunni Islam is the religion of the majority of the people in Central Asia, Saudi Arabia rose to the occasion. However, Saudi Arabia had to be cautious in Azerbaijan, not only because the Shi'a sect is strong there, but also because other countries of the Caucasus, such as Armenia and Georgia, had good relations with Iran.

The third phase of development in Iran's relations with the Central Asian republics saw a more realistic approach that understood the complexity of the region. The Islamic Republic of Iran realized that there was no "Islamic response" to the problems existing and arising in Central Asia. Even in Tajikistan, for example, where the people and many political groups share a common cultural heritage with Iran, they do not relate well to the present Islamic government of Iran. As a result, Iran decided to pay attention to the different tendencies prevailing in Central Asia. Despite the many areas held in common with Iran, including the same faith, these regions were indeed significantly different, something that Tehran had to respect.

At present, the primary aim of the Islamic Republic of Iran is to establish and consolidate economic ties with Central Asia. The goal of the 1993 visit of Iran's president to the region was to strengthen general relationships, not to propagate an Islamic model or to allow for Iranian Islam to play a dominating role in decision making. Economic relations can enhance Iran's position in relation to Turkey, especially because of common borders with a number of these countries. The main difficulty being encountered by Tehran, though, is the worsening economic situation in Iran, which, as in Turkey, is making it difficult to satisfy the increasing needs of the Central Asian republics.

With the implementation of the treaty with Turkmenistan on the transport of natural gas, to be moved through Iran to Turkey and then to Europe, Iran and Turkey have the potential for developing a common ground for future cooperation. For Iran, Turkmenistan has a special importance among the Central Asian countries, as it borders with Iran and its internal stability and economic prospects have created opportunities for both countries to strengthen their relationship. The projected completion date of the pipeline project is 1995. One-third of the gas to be exported will go to Iran, and half will be delivered to Europe through Turkey, which will keep the rest for its internal consumption. Presumably, Turkmenistan will be able to deliver its surplus to other Central Asian countries and even to the Caucasus.[47]

At the same time, it is important to note that Iran, without having to depend on Turkey, has the potential to connect Central Asia to world markets. Ports on the Persian Gulf and Indian Ocean could act as possible connecting points for Central Asian countries. In addition to being economically feasible, using these ports may contribute to the peaceful resolution of differences in the Persian Gulf. Many countries in the region stand to benefit from such a development, provided the West agrees with these additional routes. Not only would the implementation of such projects help countries like China or Afghanistan, but all the Persian Gulf states might enjoy new economic possibilities beyond their oil production. The well-developed banking system of the Gulf states is one source of capital needed to finance these and other economic activities in the region.

Azerbaijan is the only place where Turkey and Iran have actually entered into a conflict. Although they do not have a common border, the geographic proximity of Turkey and Azerbaijan and their linguistic similarities, coupled with the historical hostility between Turkey and Armenia on the one hand, and the current animosity between Azerbaijan and Armenia on the other, created a false situation of sympathy and solidarity between the Turks and the Azeris. This situation did not last long, however. The downfall of the pro-Turkish Azerbaijani president Elchibey, who became the symbol of Turkey's ill-conceived policy in Azerbaijan, made possible Russia's comeback to dominate internal political games there. Turkey's failure showed that it cannot rely on pan-Turkist ideology to secure a permanent presence for itself in Azerbaijan.

Both Russia and the West are skeptical about Turkey's role and abilities in Azerbaijan. When General Güres, the commander-in-chief of the Turkish army, declared that Ankara intended to participate with the CSCE's peacemaking forces in Nagorno-Karabakh, the spokesperson of the Russian Foreign Ministry immediately responded that the Turkish conditions for participation were "complicated" ones. Accordingly, Armenia and the separatist forces of Nagorno-Karabakh would also have to approve the military presence of Turkey.[48] Long before this incident, Western countries also showed their dissatisfaction with Turkish achievements in the Caucasus. One Western diplomat said: "A couple of years ago, it was possible to talk of Turkey being the patron of Central Asia, but the results have been different. If they can't do it in Azerbaijan, who thinks Turkey is going to be a major player in other places?"[49]

In order to gain influence in Azerbaijan and prevent Iran from developing relations with Baku, Turkey invested a good deal in former Azeri president Elchibey. Elchibey was propagating pan-Turkism, unity with Turkey, and finally unification of the two Azerbaijans—that is, the republic and the province of Azerbaijan in Iran. Such policies during World War II had led to conflicts between Iran and Russia. At that time, indigenous communists were pursuing the secession of Iranian Azerbaijan with the help of the Soviet army. In addition to the Western powers and Iran, the people of Azerbaijan themselves strongly resisted Soviet efforts, condemning the communist takeover and the separation of this province from Iran. Since then, Iranian Azerbaijan has become even more integrated into the national structure of Iran; the increasing involvement of Iranian Azeris in the national economy and state administration makes a separation difficult to conceive.[50] Therefore, separatist slogans have little to appeal for Iranian Azeris. Even on the eve of the collapse of the Soviet Union, they perceived that they would be better off as part of a greater country than as part of a poor and troubled republic.

Turkey's efforts to keep Elchibey in power not only failed, but also earned the enmity of Russia, which has been worried about, among other things, Azerbaijani oil. According to the Western press, "government officials and diplomats also speculate that disputes are likely to surface between Turkey and Russia over the single issue that may end up at the center of the regional struggle: oil."[51] Turkey's protégé in Baku was overthrown and this resulted in "devaluing Turkey's influence in the eyes of countries farther east."[52]

The change in leadership and the return of the old communists gave Iran a better opportunity to make advances in Azerbaijan. Heidar Aliev, the communist veteran who became president of Azerbaijan after Elchibey, kept his distance from the anti-Russian and anti-Iranian slogans followed by the former leadership. Tehran, even before Aliev became president, endorsed his ambitions and declared its readiness to support him. Afterward the leaders from both countries visited each other and declared their willingness to strengthen the relationship. When Aliev visited Tehran in the summer of 1994, negotiations were carried out on the abolition of visas, construction of a gas pipeline from Iran to Nakhichevan, and cooperation in the fields of transportation, agriculture, shipping, and oil.[53] This is an extensive framework for further cooperation and a significant platform for Iran's comeback in Azerbaijan. The collaboration also covers the Caspian Sea, where Iran has proposed a new organization to be established on its shores. The foreign minister of Azerbaijan, Hassan Hassanov, declared that he considers Iran a bridge connecting his country to the Persian Gulf.[54] This is a clear sign of changing attitudes in Azerbaijan since Elchibey's fall.

At the same time, the Islamic Republic of Iran is worried about the increasing improvements in the relationship between Azerbaijan and the West. In July 1994 an American military mission visited Azerbaijan to supervise the implementation of the Conventional Forces Europe treaty on the dismantling of non-nuclear weapons. President Aliev used this opportunity to state that his country would like to have better relations with the United States in numerous areas, including military cooperation.[55] In June of the same year, *Alghods*, a Moscow-based magazine, reported that Iran was seeking cooperation with Russia to forestall an American presence in the region.[56] In view of Turkey's past efforts, it is not surprising that not only Iran, but also Russia and Armenia observe Turkey's presence in the region with skepticism. It is likely, as a result, that Western countries will increasingly seek to establish contact with the Caucasus states independent of Turkey.

The geographical location of both Armenia and Iran presents physical obstacles to Turkey's entry into the Caucasus and Central Asia. Therefore, Turkey is in need of good neighborly relations with Iran more than any other country in the region. At the same time, all these events show that there are numerous other conflicting interests. Each country has to seek out various alliances with other players and parties to be able to assume a role in the region. In other words, the present situation shows that overly ambitious policies have no chance of succeeding. In general, taking conflicting interests into consideration, one can argue that from a historical perspective Iran is in a better position in the region than Turkey. Armenia would not easily accept a dominant Turkish role, but it would have no objections, provided the West gave its support, to Iran's efforts at being an intermediary.[57] Although Iran has made significant efforts to be accepted as an intermediary in the Azerbaijan-Armenia conflict over Nagorno-Karabakh, Turkey and other Western states are reluctant to accept an Iranian role in this matter. Russia is pursuing the same policy.[58]

CONCLUSION

According to A. Sheykh Attar, an Iranian diplomat, the official Iranian analysis of Turkey's role and position in Central Asia and the Caucasus may be summarized as follows:

- The Turkish governmental model, with its policy of secularism, seeks the separation of church and state.
- The Turkish model is contradictory to Islamic ideology and serves only those rulers in the region who are afraid of religion.
- NATO countries, particularly the United States, have generally supported Turkey's attempts to penetrate Central Asia and the Caucasus.
- The ideology of pan-Turanism will be supported by the West, Russia, and the rulers of the new republics as long as Turkey is acting to prevent the intellectual and political influence of Iran in the region.
- Turkey's endeavors to be more successful in the region have included the publication and dissemination of religious propaganda and the training of religious students. This will ultimately result in the strengthening of Islamic tendencies and movements, which is contrary to the real intentions of the Turkish government.
- Turkey's anti-Armenian strategy will finally lead to a confrontation between Turkey and the West.
- The absence of contiguous borders with the Central Asian countries, together with economic difficulties, will prevent Turkey from making significant investments in the region without the financial support of Western countries.
- Due to a lack of success in economic fields, Turkey has increased its cultural activities (like expansion of television networks, publication of books, distribution of press) and promotion of pan-Turanism.[59]

AREAS OF COOPERATION

Despite the tensions between Iran and Turkey, cooperation between them continues—and is even improving in some areas. The mere fact that Iran and Turkey are neighbors and face some common problems forces them to cooperate rather than enter into conflict. In both countries there are forces looking for collaboration who are resisting those favoring confrontation. One can classify the fields of cooperation into two areas: regional cooperation and bilateral agreements.

In regard to institutional forms of cooperation at the regional level, the most important organization is the Economic Cooperation Organization (ECO). This organization, founded in 1985 by Iran, Pakistan, and Turkey, is actually a continuation of the Regional Cooperation for Development which these countries established in 1964.[60] Since the collapse of the Soviet Union, the ECO has been able to expand its scope and encourage a number of other countries to become members, including Afghanistan, Azerbaijan, Kazakstan, Kyrgyzstan, Tajikistan, Turkmenistan, and Uzbekistan.

The role of the ECO is to facilitate cooperation among member states and coordinate their regional activities in order to prevent unnecessary competition. It will take time, however, for this organization to have a comprehensive structure. Not only is the existence of such other organizational forms of cooperation as the Commonwealth of Independent States (CIS), the Black Sea Economic Cooperation zone,[61] and the Organization for Cooperation of Caspian Sea Countries causing some confusion, but the different levels of development and experience of the member states themselves will likely prevent the realization of the objectives declared by the ECO. In fact, the ECO may prove only to be a framework for a minimum of cooperation at the regional level. In the absence of historical regional cooperation among the majority of the member states of the ECO, it will be very difficult to form strong and effective collective regional organizations. Most of the member states are at least associated with other neighboring structures. Yet, despite these realities, the ECO might be able to present a framework for certain kinds of collective action, though in order for this to occur, the founding members—Iran, Pakistan, and Turkey—will need to coordinate their efforts and interests and set aside their independent plans.

There are also regular consultations between Iran, Turkey, and Syria to discuss common interests. The sixth of these meetings, held in Damascus, was devoted to the situation in northern Iraq, including the Kurdish movement and the safeguarding of Iraq's territorial integrity.[62]

There is a history of bilateral cooperation between Turkey and Iran since the 1930s. Currently, there are even more plans and projects to strengthen the relationship. The project for transmitting Iranian gas through Turkey to Europe is quite attractive to Ankara.[63] In addition, Turkey's secured share in the project for transmitting Turkmenistan's gas to Europe could facilitate their cooperation in Central Asia.[64] Turkish companies have shown a keen interest in participating in the realization of such projects. In this vein, one can project into the future and point to the creation of a free trade zone in the Iranian city of Maku near the borders of Turkey, Armenia, and Nakhichevan (the Azeri enclave between Turkey and Iranian Azerbaijan) as one possible collective project that could benefit all the countries concerned.[65]

Iran and Turkey have also signed a protocol for cooperation in security matters to exercise control over their common borders. In this June 1994 protocol, both countries agreed not to let their territories be used by the other's opponents.[66] In other words, Turkey will not allow Iranian exiles within its borders to be politically active against the Islamic Republic of Iran, and Iran should prevent the PKK from making use of Iranian territory in its fight against Turkey.

In July 1994, when Turkish President Demirel visited Iran, the following subjects were negotiated as part of a comprehensive plan: the transport of goods from Iran to Europe via Turkey and from Turkey to Asian countries and the Persian Gulf; connecting the railways of the two countries; the construction of roads; strengthening ECO; the transmission of Turkmen gas from Iran to Turkey; and collaboration on security matters.[67] Interestingly, no agreement of note regarding cultural issues was discussed, let alone signed. Emphasizing the differences on approaches to culture, Demirel pointed out that because 98 percent of Turks are Muslims, it would be incorrect to interpret the results of the most recent elections as a victory for Muslims because the secular state in Turkey is not against religion, but is simply opposed to its use as a political tool.[68]

Iran and Turkey are two important countries which, despite all their differences, have been able to demonstrate the will to coexist peacefully in the twentieth century. Whether they will be able to continue their amicable neighborly relationship depends on two factors: how they interpret events in their region and the rest of the world and who is in power in each country. There is enough room for both countries to live together peacefully, provided they do not follow policies that are too ambitious.

CHAPTER SIX

FACING THE CHALLENGE
Post-Revolutionary Relations with Iran

Atila Eralp[1]

Since the nineteenth century, questions of modernization in Turkey have been closely related to issues of identity, and therefore of internal order and foreign policy. For Ottoman reformers and their successors in the Turkish Republic, modernization has meant the fashioning of the polity along European lines, or "Westernization."[2] Over a period of a hundred years, the polity has transformed itself from an Eastern empire to a modern nation-state seeking inclusion within the institutional and cultural fold of the West. This transformation of the land of the infidel from enemy to societal blueprint has brought in its wake serious, not yet fully resolved, problems regarding identity.

This makes Turkey an interesting case from several standpoints. It is unique not only in that it is unlike many other non-Western countries whose identity is strongly influenced by notions of opposition to the "West," but also that, because of the transformation process, its consolidation of a distinctly Turkish and Muslim, yet secular and Western, identity remains incomplete. In searching for a deeper understanding of the status of the Turkish endeavor, the ramifications and dilemmas posed in adopting an "imagined" identity, Turkish foreign policy in general, and Turco-Iranian relations in particular, represent useful indicators. Examination of this issue sheds light on how Turkey perceives itself and hopes to resolve the contradictions implicit in consolidating its Western identity, because Iran poses a special challenge beyond that of other neighboring countries.

The very character and orientation of post-revolutionary Islamic Iran—and the strongly anti-Western flavor that marks its rhetoric and foreign policy forays—represent both direct and implicit challenges to Turkey's much desired Westernization project. While the seriousness of this challenge is open to debate, it should be apparent that not only are traditional shared and conflicting geopolitical interests between Iran and Turkey of importance, but a host of deeper, often intangible, ideological-cum-identity problems are posed when Iran and Turkey, and their respective foreign policies, are juxtaposed.

A SKETCH OF TURCO-IRANIAN RELATIONS, 1923–78

Despite a legacy of conflict, relations between Iran and Turkey were mostly unproblematic until Iran's Islamic revolution in 1979. Their good relations stemmed from striking similarities in the views of both countries' leaderships with respect to nation building and development generally and, later, from shared perceptions of threat.

For Turkey under Atatürk and Iran under Reza Shah, development meant modernization, inextricably tied to Westernization. An elite-led civilizing mission inspired both men. Lifting their respective peoples necessitated increased association with the West and the ready adoption of Western ways. On the Turkish side, the rejection of earlier views that had resulted in military conflict (such as pan-Turkism), the emphasis on national as opposed to Islamic identity (thereby reducing the importance of the Shi'a-Sunni schism in relations between the two), and the focus on internal development generally are likely to have contributed to this cordiality.

A common hostility to communism reinforced this bond, especially in the wake of World War II. Turkey and Iran were important frontline states and partners in the West's policy of containment of the Soviet Union, constituting the reliable core of the "northern tier." In search of security, development assistance, and increased respect, the two were willing participants in Western-led (or -backed) regional security arrangements during the Cold War years. For Turkey particularly, the post-war international system offered a fertile ground for establishing institutional links with the West and boosting a Westernization project increasingly defined by the country's belonging to the Western Alliance. One's friends defined who one was; progress in Turkey's Westernization and democratization efforts was equated with its connections, not internal developments.

Two events shattered the stability and cordiality that marked Turco-Iranian relations: the 1979 Islamic revolution in Iran and the later dissolution of the Soviet Union. Suddenly, the potential for a much more difficult and complex relationship became apparent. Iran posed a challenge to Turkey in the aftermath of its revolution because of Iran's adoption of a new, revolutionary anti-Western and Islamic vocabulary and orientation. This would pit Iran as a banner-carrier of Islam against secular, pro-Western Turkey.

After the Islamic revolution, Turkish efforts have been directed to restrain such a polarization along these lines, primarily because such an escalation of tensions would not only create regional problems but could negatively affect Turkey's attempts at Westernization. In addition, the unconsolidated nature of the project leaves Turkey potentially vulnerable to Iranian-led efforts to radicalize non-Westernizers within the Turkish polity and thereby polarize the country internally. In short, identity-related problems in Turkey need to be internally and gradually solved; any justification for outsiders to artificially stimulate this process is viewed as undesirable.

This perception has only been reinforced by the new regional environment that has arisen in the wake of the Soviet Union's collapse. With the dissolution of the Soviet Union, Turkey and Iran were suddenly confronted with an entirely new environment, unprecedentedly conducive to their efforts to enhance their influence and prestige. This set of circumstances prompted a stepping-up of competition between Turkey and Iran to influence Middle Eastern as well as Central Asian and Caucasian developments. To the extent that the issue was seen within the framework of "Islam versus the West," this would lead to serious upheavals within Turkey as well, not least because the Islamic Republic of Iran is perceived within Turkey as being just that, an Islamic Republic, rather than in terms of an alien, Shi'ite force.

This new reality was not immediately obvious to Turkish policymakers and other observers. The high speed at which events in the former USSR unfolded, the tendency to be overly optimistic, as well as the inherent weakness in Turkish thinking on Eastern matters as a legacy of its preoccupation with the West, all played roles. This process is of considerable interest and a fuller understanding of it requires retrospective examination of Turkish reaction to both events.

The relationship between Iran and Turkey is best viewed in a regional rather than a bilateral context, primarily because the governing elites of both have tended to view each other within such larger frameworks. Since the dissolution of the Soviet Union, the meaningful regional context for both countries has expanded from the Middle East to include Transcaucasian and Central Asian developments.

THE NEW REGIONAL CONTEXT

The Islamic revolution in Iran coincided with several other major regional and international developments, including the conflict in Lebanon and the Soviet invasion of Afghanistan. These developments again emphasized Turkey's importance to the West, which had been somewhat undermined when superpower tensions eased in the early 1970s. They also helped the country overcome part of the Western opposition to Turkey's 1974 military intervention in Cyprus. With hindsight, one could say that these events helped to reaffirm the outlook among the Turkish governing elites of Turkey's value and connections to the West, shattered after the Cyprus crisis.

The perception of the West as a bloc—with no distinction drawn between the United States and Europe—was undergoing a major transformation at the end of the 1970s. While friction between Turkey and the European countries increased, events in Afghanistan and Iran enhanced Turkey's geopolitical significance for American Middle East policy. These developments led to a quick resolution of several issues that had soured American-Turkish relations, the most important of which were the conclusion of the American-Turkish Defense and Economic Cooperation Agreement and Turkey's acceptance of the Rogers Plan, which enabled the return of Greece to NATO's military structure. In this climate, the United States undertook the modernization of airfields in eastern Turkey, and American assistance to Turkey quadrupled between 1978 and 1981, reaching an all-time peak in 1985.

Initially, links between Turkey and the Middle East were security-oriented, in response particularly to the Soviet invasion of Afghanistan, the Iranian revolution, and the Iran-Iraq war. As Albert Wohlstetter has pointed out, the Gulf region—and with it Turkey—gained a strategic significance in the aftermath of these events.[3] Turkish policymakers adopted an engaged but cautious posture regarding the

Gulf region, showing their readiness to cooperate with the United States, but within the framework of NATO rather than under any bilateral agreement. For example, Turkey refused to take part in the rapid deployment force set up by the United States to ensure the security of the Gulf region. Even with its pro-Western attitudes, Turkey had to take Iran into account, as evidenced by its neutrality during the Iran-Iraq war.

In addition to security concerns in the Gulf, Turkish elites turned toward cultivating their economic ties with the Middle Eastern countries. Although this policy had its roots in Turkey's financial and political problems after the 1973 oil crisis and the Cyprus crisis, the downturn in relations with the European Community gave an additional urgency to its search for new markets in the Middle East. One of the means by which Turkey attempted to secure a steady supply of oil was to build pipelines to transport Iranian and Iraqi oil and gas to Mediterranean ports. While pipeline projects in Iran were still being discussed, Turkey and Iraq constructed a pipeline. In this way, Turkish elites hoped to reduce the national oil bill as well as to ensure mutual dependence.

Turkey's exports to the Middle East rose significantly—but fleetingly—in the 1980s, reaching a peak of 44 percent of total Turkish exports in 1982.[4] Trade with Iran and Iraq constituted the great portion of this new export activity. This increase in exports to the region was accompanied by a stepping up of the activities of Turkish contractors in the region.[5] Further signs of Turkey's commercial drive into the Middle East can be seen in its involvement in the 1981 establishment of a standing committee for economic and financial cooperation under the auspices of the Islamic Conference Organization, of which Turkey had hitherto been an inactive member.[6]

Greater involvement in the Middle East at both private and state levels coincided with important changes in the ranks of the Turkish governing elites. The "traditional" Republican elite—staunchly secular and Western-oriented—found itself confronting a new, pragmatic-technical elite in the 1980s. Active in the bureaucracy as well as in the private sector, they were more concerned with integrating Islamic values with a pragmatic, policy-oriented approach than with the transmission of Western values and "civilizing" the people through education. Also, rather than upholding anti-Western Third-Worldist views, as did the more Islamist followers of the National Salvation

Party of the 1970s, this new elite tried to reconcile Muslim cultural orientations with the requisites of economic growth.[7] Integration in Western financial and trade markets and importing Western technology and know-how became one of the most important goals of this new elite, rather than the civilizing mission of the secular traditional elites. As fragmentation took place among the governing elites of Turkey in the 1980s, a type of "entrepreneurial politician" emerged, at ease with numbers rather than words, ready to find an immediate solution to immediate problems and more inclined to act according to contingency than principle.

It was from among the ranks of this new elite that Turgut Özal's party, the Motherland Party, was able to draw its leadership. These elites tried to enhance Turkey's economic links with the Middle East in a manner unprecedented in its history. Turkey's response to the Iranian challenge was shaped in pragmatic terms by this emerging elite, and the creation of trade and economic relationships constituted the backbone of Özal's policy with regard to Iran. He was a strong believer in the functionalist proposition that building economic links and networks would eventually promote the resolution of political problems. In addition, the backing provided by the United States to more moderate Islamic regimes in the Middle East strengthened Özal's attempts to promote a form of modernization in Turkey to balance the inclinations of the Western-oriented traditional elites and a newly emerging, more Islamist one. On the basis of his success in integrating Islamic identity with Western modernity, Özal hoped to act as a role model and broker for Western interests in the region—which in turn would help Turkey obtain more financial and political support from the West.

The promotion of trade as a way of minimizing political tensions was an important part of Özal's approach with regard to the Middle East in general and Iran in particular. Trade agreements made with Iran in April 1981 and March 1982 called for barter deals and a trade volume of $1.8 billion. Turkey agreed to buy up to six million tons of crude oil, and in return to deliver manufactured industrial and agricultural items. As the trade figures show, there was a dramatic increase in trade relations between the two countries: Turkish exports to Iran, rather insignificant in 1978 ($44 million) and 1979 ($12 million), reached $1.1 billion in 1985. An additional source of income came from transit fees ($200 million in 1984 and $162 million in

1985).[8] Turkish companies benefited from Turkey's geography as well as its neutrality in the Iran-Iraq war, during which Turkey reexported Western goods at a profit. Turkish private firms were able to act as partners of European firms in circumventing Iran's foreign exchange and import restrictions. Tehran's and Ankara's interest in increased trade also showed itself in the revival of the dormant Regional Cooperation for Development grouping among Turkey, Iran, and Pakistan, which was renamed the Economic Cooperation Organization in 1985.

During the period after the revolution, this pragmatism was welcomed by Iran, which faced an embargo from the United States after the hostage crisis. Announcing the Turkish refusal to impose sanctions in April 1980, the Turkish Foreign Ministry pointed out that Turkey had explained to the United States the "special nature" of Turco-Iranian relations. As Süha Bölükbasi stated: "Having endured an American arms embargo between 1974–1978 and thus not an ardent believer in the effectiveness of sanctions, Turkey opted to follow an independent course vis-à-vis Iran. The Turks chose to do so, because they thought that isolating Iran was not in their national interest."[9] The ensuing war with Iraq also made Iran more pragmatic toward Turkey, as Turkey remained one of its main trade routes to Europe.

During the Iran-Iraq war, Turkey adopted what its policymakers called an attitude of "active neutrality," which effectively meant that, contrary to overall "Western"—particularly U.S.—policies, the Turkish government did not pursue a policy that Iran could consider hostile. This posture not only demonstrated the unwillingness of the Turkish authorities to antagonize Iran, but showed that Ankara considered constructive engagement with Iran not only desirable, but the best means of moderating the challenges posed by its revolution. Ankara maintained its neutral position during the Iran-Iraq war despite the increasing dissatisfaction with the support given by Iran to Iraqi Kurds. Iran on its part continued its pragmatic orientation vis-à-vis Turkey despite its displeasure with Turkey's hot pursuit treaty with Iraq.[10]

On November 28, 1984, Tehran signed a security agreement with Turkey that required each party to prohibit any activity on its territory aimed against the other's security, that is, designed to allay Turkish anxieties on the use of Kurdish Democratic Party (KDP) camps in

Iran by the Kurdish Workers Party (PKK). As one analyst has pointed out, "the Iranians lived up to their words. Since November 1984 there have been only a few PKK attacks originating from Iran."[11] Tehran has generally been careful to restrict the PKK's activities in Iran. Apparently, the importance of economic relations between Turkey and Iran acted to dampen the likelihood of politico-military problems between them. While both Ankara and Tehran were suspicious about each other's intentions over northern Iraq, they did not let these concerns lead to an escalation of tensions.

In this climate, pragmatism prevailed and Iranian efforts to export Islamic revolution to Turkey remained limited—at least in comparison to activities observed in other parts of the Middle East. Iran has largely refrained from involvement in covert activities in Turkey, though there have been propaganda broadcasts. Inevitably, there have been some incidents on both sides, but it appears that both parties have concluded that open channels and avoiding an escalation of tension are more desirable than fostering tension.

Iranian caution may be a function not only of Iran's understanding of pragmatism in its foreign relations, but of objective problems in attempting to influence the larger Turkish public. Groups that theoretically might be receptive to Iranian blandishments—such as Turkey's Shiite community—have long been among the most pro-secular elements of Turkish society. Also, Sunni religious orders (*tarikats*), which became more important with the rise of Islamist elites in Turkey in the 1980s, are known to have strong anti-Iranian sentiments. Finally, the ruling party of the 1980s, the Motherland Party, was quite sensitive in trying to reconcile Muslim cultural orientations with the requisites of economic growth and Western democracy. Özal's balancing act helped prevent the widening of the divide between Westernizers and non-Westernizers in Turkey, and acted as a restraint on Iranian influence.

THE END OF THE COLD WAR AND TURKISH-IRANIAN RELATIONS

At the close of the 1980s, there were again dramatic regional and international events affecting Turkey's relations with its neighbors. The war between Iran and Iraq, which had been quite important in determining the course of Turco-Iranian relations, ended in July 1988.

Trade relations, which had decreased with a dramatic decline in Iranian oil revenues, fell even further in the aftermath of the war as Iran began to diversify its trade relations and became increasingly focused on Western European countries, particularly Germany. It seemed that Iran's interest in trade with Ankara had been mainly due to the exigencies of the war. Initially, there were expectations that Turkish construction companies would be involved in post-war reconstruction projects, but as it turned out, these expectations remained largely unfulfilled. Thus, as the decade ended, economic links between Turkey and Iran, in particular trade relations, were not as vigorous as at its beginning. Iran was trying to lessen its dependence on Turkey while Turkish entrepreneurs were turning to European markets realizing the instability of the Middle Eastern market.

In June 1989, Iranian spiritual leader Ayatollah Khomeini died. He was succeeded by Ayatollah Khamanei, and Ali Akbar Hashemi Rafsanjani was chosen president in an apparent victory of moderates and pragmatists over radicals, especially with regard to foreign policy matters.[12] This change, however, did not cause any major shift in Turco-Iranian relations, already characterized by pragmatism for a decade, though for ideological reasons Tehran and Ankara might have been expected to have a more confrontational relationship.

The decade closed with dramatic changes in Eastern Europe and the demise of the bipolar world. Turkey's geopolitical position as a frontline state in the containment of the Soviet Union lost its significance, and it seemed for a while that Turkey would no longer have a bargaining position vis-à-vis the United States and the West more generally. With the end of the Cold War Turkey's priorities in foreign policy entered a period of uncertainty. Despite attempts to forge closer relations with the Middle East, particularly at the economic level during the course of the 1980s, these relations remained rather limited.

Members of the Turkish elite had always believed that Turkey held sufficient strategic value that continued Western economic support was assured.[13] There was increasing anxiety and uncertainty among the elites at this stage as it was perceived that Turkey had lost its trump card with the end of the Cold War. This perception increased internal discussion about a new role and style in foreign policy that would stress regional orientation of a more "active" manner.

The Gulf crisis helped to resolve this debate by striking a new balance between Turkey's attachment to the West and its links with the

Middle East. By taking on the broker's role, remaining all the while a close ally of the West, Turkish policymakers attempted a decisive step to prevent Turkey from being isolated after the end of the Cold War. In the process, its strategic role was redefined and expanded. Involvement in the Middle East, however, meant taking sides in intra-Arab conflicts, a drastic change in post-Cyprus foreign policy orientation.[14]

The Gulf crisis also prompted an intense debate about the style of Turkish policy and whether it should continue its cautious approach or adopt an active style. While Turkey's traditionally Kemalist institutions, such as the Foreign Ministry and the army, continued their cautious approach, Özal championed an active approach to the Gulf crisis. He hoped to act as a role model and become a viable broker for Western interests in the region, for which Turkey might obtain the financial and political support of the United States. The removal of the Soviet threat created a propitious climate for closer bilateral relations with the United States rather than the multilateral frameworks to which the Turkish elites were very sensitive in the Cold War years.

The change in the strategic environment and a greater Turkish role in the region were expected by some Turkish policymakers to increase inflows of external funds, as had occurred in the beginning of the 1980s and during the early Cold War, and to help develop the country and modernize its antiquated military machine. While there was wild speculation with regard to the amount of external funds likely to become available in the aftermath of the Gulf crisis, the public became increasingly frustrated as the balance began to show more economic losses than gains. Furthermore, in the aftermath of the Gulf War, Arab nations proved unwilling to offer Turkey a greater say in regional issues.

The impasse regarding Turkey's efforts to obtain regional prominence in the Middle East led to an enlarged definition of Turkey's regional policy efforts.[15] They began to seek stronger relations with Turkey's northwestern neighbors in the form of the Black Sea Economic Cooperation Initiative, as well as to establish relations with such Balkan countries as Albania and Bulgaria. The end of the Cold War thus served to re-involve Turkey in the Balkan countries after a period of almost a century. This dramatic shift presented new economic opportunities for Turkish businessmen who had already gained useful experience from their relations with the Middle Eastern countries in the 1980s and now wanted to channel their energies to a wider region.

The disintegration of the Soviet Union in the wake of the failed putsch of August 1991 also enhanced the momentum of change. Both the birth of the newly independent states and the changed world climate converged with Turkey's designs. Turkey, again working independently but with special ties to the West and particularly the United States, sought to insert itself as a key actor, especially in the Caucasus and Central Asia. However, it was this very new configuration of forces—and fluid ones at that—which would prompt an increase in competition between Turkey and Iran in their effort to influence developments in the Middle East as well as Central Asia.[16] In other words, the winds of change and domestic perceptions of the benefits to be gained from them had great potential to pit Turkey and Iran against each other.

COMPETITION FOR REGIONAL INFLUENCE

Turkey's policy during the Gulf War demonstrated its pursuit of regional influence. It was also the Gulf crisis that conclusively induced the Turkish leadership to recognize divisions within the West and opt for the United States rather than Europe—and to emphasize the concept of "strategic cooperation" between the United States and Turkey. In addition, the Gulf War and its aftermath increased tensions in Turco-Iranian relations, as Iranians believed that Turkey was extending its control over northern Iraq and increasing its sway over the Iraqi Kurds there. Iran also believed that Turkey was cooperating with the Western powers, particularly the United States, in undermining its influence throughout the region, and Turkey, for its part, appeared concerned about the growth of Iranian regional influence that would come with the weakening of Iraq.

The dissolution of the Soviet Union and the emergence of independent states in Central Asia reinforced the sense that a competition for influence was under way between Turkey and Iran. As analysts have pointed out, the demise of the Soviet Union raised fundamental questions about the geographical extent of the Middle East and how the term is to be interpreted.[17] Questions were raised about whether Arab domination of Middle Eastern issues was coming to an end, as Turkey and Iran were increasingly seen as integral parts of the

Middle East. It seemed that both Iran and Turkey were interested in an expanded definition of the Middle East, a definition that would include the Central Asian republics of the former Soviet Union. This would buttress Turkey's influence in the enlarged region and in Islamic forums generally.

Perceptions of competition between Turkey and Iran centered on whether one or the other would be adopted as the model for the Central Asian republics. However, while they and other outsiders were focused on this matter, it appears that the Central Asians themselves took sides only rhetorically and for diplomatic and commercial gain.

The emergence of the Central Asian states generated considerable excitement in Turkey. Turks felt as if they had found their lost brothers. Increasingly it was believed that Turkey could export its political model, entrepreneurial know-how, and consumer goods to the Central Asian republics all the more easily because of a common linguistic, religious, and ancestral heritage. This attitude was encouraged by the United States and the West generally, as Turkey was viewed as a suitable role model and useful conduit in integrating these newly independent countries into the international system, as well as an ideal candidate for containing Iranian influence in both Central Asia and the Caucasus. This is clearly evident in U.S. President George Bush's statement of February 1992 when he said that "Turkey is a beacon of stability in a region of changing tides. . . . Turkey is a friend, a partner of the West and . . . a model to others."[18] The statements, made in support of the secular and democratic "Turkish model," bolstered the impression that there was indeed a competition for influence between Turkey and Iran in Central Asia, and that Central Asians were faced with a choice between secular, ethnically based democracy on the one hand or Iranian-style theocracy on the other.

The prospect of Turkey's thus becoming a regional superpower grew in the Turkish popular imagination from the close of 1991 through summer 1993.[19] Although Foreign Ministry officials were rather cautious about the "model" issue, individuals and organizations long associated with the pan-Turkist movement suddenly found a new legitimacy and cropped up in and out of government circles involved with Turkey's Eastern ventures. These groups found an environment in which they could promote their long-standing thesis that Turks are encircled by enemies and that only other Turks are the friends of the Anatolian. Then-president Özal encouraged this activist stance implicitly being adopted, capturing well the spirit of the moment when he noted that the twenty-first century would be the "century of the Turk." Turkey's long-time right-wing nationalist leader Alparslan Türkes put it even more succinctly—"Everyone is a pan-Turkist now."

The trend to a more active foreign policy, which had begun during the Gulf War, was reinforced in this period, as were discussions about its very style and character. Still, those institutions long committed to traditional Kemalist, secularist principles continued to push for a cautious approach. On the other hand, most of the political parties, particularly such nationalists as the Nationalist Action Party and Great Unity Party, as well as those on the religious right, notably the Welfare Party, advocated a more activist stance, having long felt that Turkey should do everything possible to assert itself as leader of the wider Turkic and/or Islamic world. Özal also advocated an activist position, believing that Turkey should take advantage of opportunities emerging in the new international order. However, he differed from the nationalists and religious right in his belief that Turkey could proceed only in cooperation with the West, particularly with the United States, while the others saw the new Eastward turn as an alternative to Turkey's long-standing Western orientation.

Interestingly, those groups which were least committed to secular Atatürkist principles or the Westernization project were given a lift domestically and catapulted onto the Central Asian scene when Turkey was touted as a model for Central Asia. As they found a new basis of legitimacy in the emerging climate, they had a disproportionate role in shaping popular Turkish perceptions and expectations concerning Turkey's role in Central Asia and Caucasus. They were also critical in shaping the image of Turkey held by Central Asians and Azerbaijanis, in the process setting off alarm bells among Turkey's neighbors, particularly Iran.

The climax in this competitive phase between Turkey and Iran was the coming to power of the Popular Front government and the election of Abulfez Elchibey as president in Azerbaijan in June 1992. Azeris are closely related to Turks historically and ethnolinguistically, and to Iranians historically and religiously.[20] Azerbaijan, due to geographic proximity and linguistic affinities, occupied a special place in popular conceptions of Turkey's immediate and future role in the ex-Soviet Muslim East and consequently had been the focus of particular attention on the part of activist groups in and out of government.

This attention to Azerbaijan—though not fully supported by the cautious secularists in the foreign and defense establishments and in center-left circles like the Social Democratic People's Party—surely alarmed Iran, with its own large Azeri population. Iran predictably would be discomfited by any significant growth in Turkish influence in Azerbaijan. Turkey has never had any particular influence over Iranian Azeris—indeed a sign of the stability and cordiality long marking Turco-Iranian relations can be seen from the fact that Turkish pan-Turkists rarely, if ever, dwelt on the plight of their Azeri "kin," undoubtedly thanks to government concern for unduly upsetting Tehran. But the rapid growth in pro-Turkish sentiment in Azerbaijan—a divided nation—meant that Turkey could appear to be involving itself in a long-term venture involving the unification of Azeris in Iran with Azerbaijan. Azeri rhetoric, notably that of President Elchibey, his interior minister, and others, had a definite pan-Turkist character; many Azeri political parties adopted platform statements in support of uniting "northern" and "southern" Azerbaijan. Iran became increasingly alarmed, believing that Turkish designs in the Caucasus as well as the Middle East, backed by the West, were behind Elchibey's activities. It is unsurprising that as a counterbalance Tehran subsequently adopted a friendly posture toward Azerbaijan's enemy Armenia and cultivated relations with Moscow at this stage.

During this competitive phase, one of the most important incidents was the murder of Ugur Mumcu, a prominent Turkish journalist and writer, in a car bomb explosion in Ankara on January 24, 1993. Turkey's minister of interior affairs, Ismet Sezgin, linked the murder of Mumcu to the activities of organizations located in Iran and stated that these organizations were also involved in the murders of Çetin Emeç and Turan Dursun, also prominent journalists and writers. Prime Minister Süleyman Demirel also spoke of "certain powers" trying to create division in Turkey. At the Iranian consulate in Istanbul and elsewhere protesting crowds shouted, "We are not Iran!" An Iranian connection was also implied in the attempted assassination of Jak Kamhi, a prominent Jewish businessman, a few days later on January 28, 1993. There were also frequent reports in the press during this period of Iranian support for Hizbullah, which was reportedly

involved in many murders in southeastern Turkey. Within this climate, Iranian Prime Minister Hasan Habibi canceled his planned visit
to Turkey scheduled for February 8, 1993.[21]

In this context, the fall of Azeri President Elchibey in July 1993 was
heralded in Tehran as much as Moscow, signaling as it did a decline
in Turkish fortunes in Azerbaijan. This development was significant
from another standpoint—it appears to mark the end of the active
promotion of a blurry "Turkish model" in Turkey's relations with the
Caucasus and Central Asia. Needless to say, "the loss of Azerbaijan,"
as some termed it, stimulated something of a general reassessment,
caution and sobriety replacing the unprepared activist approach earlier apparent. Such a turn of events may have alleviated Iranian anxieties generally and helped bring to a close, on the Turkish side, a
phase of escalating tension between Turkey and Iran.

Turkish officials have realized that expectations both in Turkey
and abroad were too high and that Turkey's resources are simply
inadequate to play out the activist role in the region. There has also
been growing frustration with the level of support and commitment
Turkey has received from the West. There were expectations in
Turkey that Western (read American) enthusiasm for the "Turkish
model" would turn into significant inflows of external aid and investment, and that in return, Turkey would act as the principal broker
between the West and the Central Asian states. This, however, has
not been the case. Turkish government officials believe the West
should do more for Turkey, arguing that it is critical to stability not
only in the Gulf but also in the wider regional context stretching from
the Balkans to Central Asia. Increasingly these officials stress that
domestically and externally stimulated competition with Iran created
tensions in an already volatile region. Instead an active policy of
cooperation with such key regional actors as Iran would have been
more desirable.

AREAS OF COOPERATION

After the competitive relationship between Iran and Turkey reached
its climax in mid-1993, there was a period of increased cooperation.
Now, both sides emphasize that there is competition between them in
neither Central Asia nor the Caucasus. After the fall of the Popular
Front government in Azerbaijan, Iran became less pro-Armenian;

Turkey and Iran now seem to share common views in opposing the occupation of Azeri land by Armenian forces. Discussions aimed at increased economic cooperation and on bilateral as well as regional security issues continue.

The signs of this cooperation were seen even during the competitive phase. Turkey and Iran both supported the revival of the inactive Economic Cooperation Organization (ECO) formed by Iran, Pakistan, and Turkey in 1985. In reviving the ECO, Turkey and Iran thought of incorporating the newly independent states of Central Asia and Azerbaijan; memberships were granted to each of the new states with the exception of Kazakstan (which became an observer), and along with Afghanistan, they became formal signatories of the ECO founding charter on November 28, 1992. This organization attempts to promote transregional trade, banking, transportation, and telecommunications. In this context, it is notable that Iran and Turkey are focusing on two transregional transportation projects to revive the ancient "Silk Road" connecting East and West, involving the construction of a transregional highway and a railway network. Particular emphasis has been placed on the railway network, since the Central Asians possess a viable network already, and Iran and Turkey need to link into it. Iran has already started the construction of its segment and Turkey plans to begin work on its in 1995.

Turkey and Iran also signed a transportation protocol to solve problems related to transit through Iran. For Turkish entrepreneurs doing business with the Central Asian republics, the transit route through Iran is the only available one as long as the war between Armenia and Azerbaijan persists. Turkey has realized that Iran has a crucial geographical advantage with regard to Central Asia, just as Iran has understood Turkey's geographical advantage vis-à-vis Europe. Mutual interest has encouraged both to come to agreement on the principle of free transit.

In addition, the two countries are discussing several pipeline projects to carry natural gas and petroleum from Central Asia to Europe. One aims to build a pipeline to carry natural gas from Turkmenistan to Europe; another involves the transport of Iranian petroleum and natural gas to Europe. The viability of these projects is connected to the availability of Western credits, which have not been, and are unlikely to be, forthcoming so long as Iran and the West, particularly the United States, view each other with so much suspicion. The United States does not want to provide credits to Iran, and Iran is not yet ready to accept having such crucial pipelines pass through Turkey.

Both Iran and Turkey have expressed the desire to regain the $2 billion trade volume that existed in the beginning of the 1980s, twice the current figure. Turkey is primarily buying petroleum from Iran and selling machinery, agricultural products, and chemicals on a barter basis. For Turkey, access to Iranian oil is particularly important, as petroleum imports from Iraq have been cut off in the aftermath of the Gulf War.

In addition to these areas of existing and hoped-for economic cooperation, there has been increasing collaboration in the security field. Shared security concerns and willingness to undertake confidence-building measures have both played a part. Turkey's most pressing security concern comes from the PKK, which Ankara does not want Iran to support. Second, Turkey does not want northern Iraq and the Kurds there to be dominated either by Iran or any other force that would support the PKK or play the Kurdish card against Turkey. Both countries are suspicious of the ramifications of Western policy toward Iraq, and both oppose anything that undermines its territorial integrity. In this regard Iran is unhappy with the support Turkey has given to the enforcement of the no-fly zone in northern Iraq; Tehran has been attempting to convince Turkey to bring an end to the flights out of Turkey and find a regional formula to replace the multinational force. The complex situation involving not only bilateral relations but the situation of northern Iraq and the Kurds has resulted in increased dialogue between the two sides.

Recently, there has been a rise in the number of working visits between Turkish and Iranian high-level officials. Emerging from this dialogue has been consensus on one key question: both sides oppose the establishment of an independent Kurdistan in Iraq. While neither side is happy with the regime of Saddam Hussein, they attach great importance to the maintenance of the territorial integrity of Iraq and are searching for approaches to ensure it. To that end, Tehran and Ankara have been involved in a diplomatic initiative to coordinate regional policy toward northern Iraq; five meetings among Iran, Turkey, and Syria were held between November 1992 and February 1994.

In addition, Turkey and Iran have established a working security committee and a higher security commission, composed respectively of lower- and higher-ranking security officials from both countries. The basic aim in establishing these mechanisms is to facilitate exchange of information as well as to establish joint inspection and observation teams on issues related to border security. Turkey is hoping to increase its border security with the more specific goal of lessening the possibility that the PKK will establish bases in Iran. Iranians have expressed concern over the activities of the People's Mojahedin Organization (Mojahedin-e Khalq) in Turkey and have tried to link this with the Turkish concern over the PKK in recent negotiations. While the Turks do not want to see a direct link between these two issues, they have been increasingly willing to take Iranian concerns into consideration.

The foregoing analysis shows that both countries have been showing increasing concern about the principle of territorial integrity and have been willing to create mechanisms (bilateral as well as trilateral with Syria) to reduce anxieties about each other's intentions and prevent outside powers from undertaking policies perceived to be detrimental to local ones. The existence of sizable minority ethnic groups in both countries that are, or may be in the future, involved in separatist activities has reinforced this, as has the situation in northern Iraq. Restraint and cooperation have been the outcome. Neither the Kurdish nor Azeri cards are likely to be played, nor will either Tehran or Ankara tolerate the dismemberment of Iraq—for different, if self-interested, reasons. Iranians believe, too, that an independent Kurdistan would be under the influence of Western powers and Turkey, while Turks fear such an entity would cause major problems for Turkey internally, ultimately leading to a major challenge to the existing unity of the Turkish state.

CONCLUSIONS

Turco-Iranian relations since the establishment of the Turkish republic have overall been quite good, determined in large part by the overwhelming and shared security threat from the USSR. The Islamic revolution in Iran did not alter this significantly, though the tenets of Iran's new state ideology could have put Turkey and Iran on a collision course. This did not occur because of the exigencies of the Iran-Iraq war, Turkey's pragmatic approach to it, and the country's general search for new regional commercial ties and political influence.

The appearance of rivalry between Turkey and Iran grew out of perceived opportunities inherent after the collapse of the USSR. Turkish involvement, in Azerbaijan as well as in Central Asia, with the stated backing of the West is likely to have fueled considerable short-term anxiety in Tehran. A phase of competition, which came to a halt with the downfall of Azerbaijani President Elchibey, has since been replaced by an emphasis on cooperation and restraint.

Although the future may witness more confrontation between Iran and Turkey, it is not desirable for either country nor for the larger region. Being key regional actors in a volatile neighborhood going through a massive transition, both countries must make efforts to develop mutually beneficial projects that serve the larger purpose of integrating former Soviet states into the international community as independent entities. This should be done by providing support for infrastructure projects linking Central Asia and the Caucasus with the outside world, via both Iran and Turkey, and encouraging trade generally.

Juxtaposing secular, Westernized, democratic Turkey and fundamentalist Iran with an emphasis on competition is a dangerous course on two levels. On the one hand, traditional animosities and unsolved ethnoterritorial problems at work in the now conceptually enlarged Middle East mean any nation that feels anxious and isolated can exploit a wide array of vehicles to destabilize its neighbors. On the other, adjusting a self-image, as Turkey must, to achieve new goals in an unprecedented regional context is a more complicated, troubling endeavor than it might first appear. The danger for Turkey is that its long-pursued Westernization project may be challenged in the process—either by Iran directly or, more gradually, by internal forces long opposed to that project and in search of an alternative to the West. Thus a black-and-white juxtaposition of secular Turkey with fundamentalist Iran should be undertaken with great caution. As emphasized by several analysts,[22] a Central Asia policy that has the containment of Islam and Iran at its heart could well be counterproductive to the United States and regional inhabitants as well as Iran. Any cooperation from Turkey in this effort might help polarize Turkey along a secular-Muslim divide.

Turkish policymakers have been rather careful not to escalate tensions with Iran along lines that pit "Islam against the West." They argue that Iran should not be isolated but constructively engaged;

that Iran is not a uniform society but one with representatives of pragmatism as well as more radical, religious orientations and that efforts should be made to cultivate good relations.

If one thinks of Turkey's relations with Iran within the broader context of its drive into the larger Middle East, there are some crucial lessons. Turkish policymakers found themselves facing major problems relating to the country's orientation and national interest with the end of the Cold War. Unprepared for the challenges implicit in this because of Turkey's long-held Western focus and the relative simplicity of operating in a bipolar world, Turkey embarked, without adequate preparation or essential background information, on a venture to capture influence in the former Soviet Union, prematurely exposing itself to unnecessary risks and raising false hopes.

For Turkey to play the kind of role it initially aspired to, important hurdles must be overcome, not the least of which relates to the overall strength of the Turkish economy, and the persistence of profound political problems as manifest in separatist terrorism in the southeast and the growing strength of the religious right. The first lesson would seem to be "heal thyself"; countries—like individuals—are exemplary first and models second.

The other lesson, which is easier to act upon, relates to Turkey's overall information and expertise on the ex–Soviet Union and the Middle East. Experience has shown that extravagant rhetoric and hope played a greater role in fueling Turkey's initiatives than well-informed, prudent calculations. Clearly, Turkey has a great deal to learn about its neighbors. It seems that if Turkey focuses on healing itself and understanding its neighbors, the country will easily face down the Iranian challenge or any others that emerge in the region.

CHAPTER SEVEN

SYRIA AND TURKEY
Uneasy Relations

Muhammad Muslih

Although the Euphrates dispute and the controversial issue of Syria's support for the Kurdistan Workers Party (PKK) have created serious tensions between Ankara and Damascus, Syria's conception of Turkey's role in the region is the chief factor that underlies its policies toward its northern neighbor. From the standpoint of the Syrian ruling elite, Turkey's identification of itself as a Western ally and an "island of stability in a turbulent geographic area"[1] serves as confirmation of the Syrian belief that Turkey is a gendarme through which Western influence—benign or otherwise—is exercised over the region.

The tense relations between Syria and certain Western powers, particularly between Damascus and Washington up to the Gulf War, reinforced Syria's suspicions regarding Turkey's intentions. Of course, these suspicions were also shaped by such factors as the long history of Arab-Turkish antagonism, the loss of Alexandretta (Hatay), suspected Turkish designs on Mosul, Turkey's recognition of Israel, and its water policies.

Even though the Euphrates dispute is the most immediate problem so far as Syria's relations with Turkey are concerned, Syrian political elites view this dispute as a symptom of a larger problem. It is the problem of Turkey's role, and of her conscious efforts to pressure Syria not simply to serve her own policy ends, but also the policy ends of foreign powers, in this case Israel and the United States.

It is therefore important to recognize that Syria's relations with Turkey have evolved in the context of a mutual decay of confidence on both sides, a process fed by conflicting Syrian and Turkish positions toward a host of issues, as well as by Washington's hesitation to normalize its relations with Damascus. Understanding this context will shed light on Syria's strategic perspective. This is a matter that has relevance not only to interested observers, but also to policymakers.

SYRIA'S GEOSTRATEGIC PERSPECTIVE

President Hafiz al-Asad's image of the world and his country's role in it is the underpinning for Syria's geostrategic outlook. The Asad view claims for Syria the responsibility of taking up the Israeli challenge and leading the way toward genuine Arab independence—the vision of the Ba'th party as articulated by its founders Michel 'Aflaq and Zaki al-Arsuzi in the 1940s. The core of the theory underlying this vision was that the Arabs had a glorious past, and in order for the Arab nation to shake off backwardness and foreign control, the Arabs must believe in and have boundless love for it.

To capture this belief in the oneness of Arab history and destiny, 'Aflaq coined the phrase: "One Arab nation with an eternal message" (*ummah arabiyyah wahidah thatu risalah khalidah*). 'Aflaq also suggested a guide to action based on three principles: "Unity, Freedom, Socialism." The underlying assumption is that Arabs belong together not by virtue of race or narrow chauvinism but because of bonds of history, language, religion, tradition, and common aspirations.

Four centuries of Turkish rule and the imposition of Western control in the form of the mandates system after World War I provided the historical background for the ideas of the Ba'th. But the more immediate and compelling reasons for its founding and its growing popularity among the young were the events that took place in the years 1939-48. These years witnessed France's relinquishment of the Sanjak of Alexandretta to Turkey, the defeat by British troops of Vichy forces in Syria and Lebanon, the collapse of the Mandates system, and Syrian independence, as well as the Arab defeat in the Palestinian war of 1948 and the emergence of Israel.

The two events that left a lasting imprint on Asad and his Ba'thist comrades were the loss of Alexandretta to Turkey and the loss of Palestine to the Zionists, though the former was distinctly secondary in importance. From Syria's perspective, everything related to other foreign policy should be secondary to the task of taking up the Israeli challenge.

Still, Syrian political elites have never reconciled themselves to the loss of Alexandretta, which they always considered an integral part of the Syrian homeland. For many years, Syria raised the issue of Alexandretta in its negotiations with Turkey. However, Syria put this issue on the shelf after the October war of 1973. Since then, Syria's attention has been focused on resolving the various aspects of its conflict with Israel.

Though it is not to be supposed that Syria will confront Turkey over the Alexandretta issue in the near future, three factors keep this issue alive. The first has to do with Syrian patriotism. The Syrians view Alexandretta's cession not simply as an affront to their national pride, but also a clear indication that Syria's territorial integrity was fair game to the European powers. It must be noted here that in the 1930s, France was particularly worried about Italian designs in the eastern Mediterranean. By French calculations, a neutral or friendly Turkey could serve as an important bulwark against such designs, and to win over Turkey, the Sanjak of Alexandretta happened to be an attractive inducement.

The second factor is demographic and happens to have a profound emotional and symbolic significance as far as dominant political elites in Syria are concerned. According to the statistics of the French High Commissioner, the Sanjak of Alexandretta had a total population of approximately 220,000 in 1936. Although the Turks constituted the single largest ethnic community at 39 percent, Arabic speakers outnumbered Turkish speakers. Nearly 80 percent of the Arab population were Muslim and 20 percent were Christian. About 50 percent of the local Muslim population were Sunni Muslims, with the Alawites making up the difference.[2] Some Syrians claim that there are in Turkey today about 4 million Syrians, with members of the Alawite community constituting a significant number. This is a factor in itself with special emotional influence on the Alawite-dominated government in Syria.

The third factor has to do with the Syrian intellectual Zaki al-Arsuzi, an Alawite from the Alexandretta region. Arsuzi took command of the Arab movement that protested Turkey's acquisition of Alexandretta in 1938 and 1939. As a result, Arsuzi landed in jail, and in the end took refuge in Damascus with thousands of Arabs who had left their homes in the Sanjak of Alexandretta.

Once in Damascus, Arsuzi set up his headquarters in the Havana, a political cafe, and from there preached to his followers that the *Ba'th* (renaissance) of the Arabs was within reach and that independence from foreign rule would revive the ancient glories of the Arab nation. The ideas of Arsuzi made a profound impression on a number of young people who were furious at the Franco-British betrayal of Arab interests.

When Michel 'Aflaq and Salah al-Din al-Bitar adopted the word Ba'th as the name of their political movement in 1941, Arsuzi claimed that they had stolen the name from him. Some Syrians, including members of the Alawite community, agree, and even consider Arsuzi to be the more significant contributor to the theory of the ruling Ba'th party in Syria. Thus from the standpoint of some Alawites, the fact that Arsuzi hailed from Alexandretta sets the province within a special frame of emotional and symbolic significance.[3]

SYRIA, TURKEY, AND THE MIDDLE EAST

Syria and Turkey adopted positions towards regional and international conflicts that reflected the differences in their worldviews, as well as preexisting misunderstandings and divergent state interests with respect to specific issues. On the Arab-Israeli conflict, Syria's position has been shaped by the belief that Israel was a state of alien settlers created at the expense of the Palestine Arabs and that the purpose behind its creation was to compel the Arabs to live in the shadow of its overwhelming military power. Syria believes that Western support and funding made the creation of Israel possible.

Turkey, on the other hand, adopted a different position toward Israel. Although it remained neutral during the Palestinian war of 1948 and prevented Turkish volunteers from joining the Arab forces, Turkey dispatched to Syria a small training cadre and some supplies to Palestinian refugees.[4] When a number of other countries extended recognition to Israel, Turkey did the same, in March 1949, and soon started to develop its economic relations with Israel.[5]

Syria was critical of the Turkish decision, but willing to live with it. After all, more than thirty countries had already recognized Israel, and Syrian and other Arab representatives were holding talks to reach armistice agreements with their Israeli counterparts in Rhodes under the auspices of the United Nations. During the 1950s, however, Turkey followed policies that Syria considered favorable to Israel. What made Syria particularly suspicious of Turkey's intentions were provocative Turkish "maneuvers" on Syria's northern frontier, and hints in the Turkish press that Turkey might move into Syria if a Soviet-controlled government took over in Damascus. The fact that the hints were dropped at the time of the 1956 Suez crisis created in Syrian official circles the impression that Syria was the target of a Western-sponsored conspiracy.

Syria's suspicions were not unfounded. At the time, Syria viewed Turkey as an instrument of U.S. policy in the region, while Washington considered Syria a Soviet client and a base for the buildup of Soviet arms in the area.[6] About thirty years later, Israeli author Samuel Segev described the top-secret "Trident" program of intelligence cooperation among Turkey, Israel, and Iran during the 1950s. Segev refers to this program as the "peripheral alliance."[7]

The strong anticommunist sentiment of the Turkish government and the Turkish perception that the Soviet Union had expansionist designs in the region played a major role in shaping Turkey's policy toward Syria. This policy served as confirmation of Syria's belief that Turkey was a "gendarme of American imperialism" in the Middle East. To both Syria and the Arab nationalists in Egypt and elsewhere, the Baghdad Pact of February 1955 was another such confirmation. Syria was internally weak at the time and one of its greatest fears was that the pact would be used not simply as an instrument with which to undermine the cause of Arab nationalism, but also to encircle and hurt Syria.

Turkey's disapproval of the Anglo-French-Israeli invasion of Egypt in 1956 did not allay Syria's fears and suspicions. One year later, the Turkish government of Adnan Menderes strongly supported the U.S. and British operations in Lebanon and Jordan respectively. This support gave more force to the Syrian belief that Turkey was too closely identified with U.S. policy. From Syria's perspective, that policy was hostile to Syria, and to seek protection and save itself from internal disintegration, Syria chose the path of unity with Egypt.[8]

Since May 1960, when General Cemal Gürsel and his National Unity Committee seized power from the Menderes government, Turkey has followed a more neutral policy toward the Arab-Israeli conflict. Gürsel promised to improve relations with the Arab countries, extending diplomatic support to the cause of Algerian independence.[9] Later, in May 1967, when Egypt closed the Gulf of Aqaba to Israeli shipping, Turkey remained silent, and even declared that it would not allow NATO powers to use its bases in the event of war.[10]

Furthermore, Turkey declared that it was opposed to the acquisition of territory by force. Following the Six-Day War, Turkey opposed Israel's annexation of East Jerusalem and its subsequent annexation of the Golan. During the 1973 October war, Turkey did not allow the United States to use its facilities to ship supplies to Israel. Viewing the Arab world as an important source of economic and political support after the 1973 war, Turkey tilted toward the Arabs, thus improving its diplomatic and trade relations with the Arab states, particularly the Gulf countries. In 1979, Turkey allowed the PLO to open an office in Ankara, and when Israel invaded Lebanon in 1982, Turkey opposed the invasion.

Syria and the other Arab countries appreciated the new Turkish position, at the same time remaining suspicious of its intentions. Syria, for example, was unhappy over Turkey's refusal to label Israel an aggressor during the Six-Day War. Syria was also concerned about the upgrading of airfields in eastern Turkey in the early 1980s, believing that they would be used as a possible base for a rapid deployment force in the Middle East.

In this regard, the Syrian fear was that Turkey's bases would be used by the U.S. government to punish or intimidate Syria. Believing that the Reagan administration had connived with Israel to punish it in Lebanon, Syria was unsettled to see a closer military relationship between the United States and Turkey at a time when the U.S. government was hostile toward Syria, and also at a time when Ariel Sharon, Israel's defense minister, was trying to impose by force of arms a "Pax Hebraica" over the Levant.

Syria believed that Sharon had the support and encouragement of the Reagan administration, not only because of the ideological affinity between Washington and the Likud-led government in Israel, but because Reagan regarded Syria as a Soviet surrogate that should be punished and contained. When the nineteenth Palestine National Council declared the creation of a state of Palestine in the West Bank and Gaza, with East Jerusalem as its capital, in November 1988, Turkey was the first state to recognize it.

To Arab opinion, this decision was a welcome step. Syria, however, was unimpressed by Turkey's decision, partly because of the personal animosity between Asad and Yasser Arafat (who was declared president of the Palestinian state), but more importantly because Asad wanted Arafat to subordinate his movement to Syria's regional policy. Thus any move that granted more autonomy to Arafat, especially at a time when he was in alliance with Iraq and Egypt, was not viewed with favor by Syria.

Of course, it is necessary to put the Syrian attitude in the larger context of Syrian misgivings about Turkey's relationship with Israel. Even after the launching of the Middle East peace conference in November 1991, Syrian politicians reacted with suspicion to Turkey's new role in the region, as can be seen from the political literature published by the Damascus-based rejectionist Palestinian groups.

An autumn 1993 editorial in *Ila al-Amam* (*Forward*), a magazine published by Ahmad Jibril in Damascus, had this to say about Turkey's role in the region after the Gulf War: "The Turkish government, thus, views its political position as a regional line parallel and complementary to the Zionist one within the new security arrangements drawn by the United States, and the West in general, for the Middle East."[11] Although this is not an official Syrian position, the fact that the Syrian authorities have not discouraged the dissemination of these views suggests that they still view with deep suspicion Turkey's relations with Israel. Turkey's agreement to cooperate with Israel in the area of security after the Gulf War reinforced the Syrian suspicions.

THE IRAN-IRAQ WAR

During the Iran-Iraq war of the 1980s, Syria entered into an alliance with non-Arab Iran against Arab Iraq. There were strategic reasons for this move, but it was also rooted in the background of Asad and the poor bilateral relations between Damascus and Baghdad. From a strategic perspective, Syria welcomed the fall of the shah and regarded the advent to power of Iranian *mullahs* as a positive step that ended Iran's partnership with Israel and its subservience to the United States.

As viewed by Syria, revolutionary Iran was an anti-imperialist, anti-Zionist force whose friendship was an asset for the cause of Arab independence. From this point of view, Syria regarded Iran as a natural replacement for Egypt after the Camp David Accords. Thanks to the Khomeini revolution, Israel lost Iran, a big plus for the Arabs, especially since Israel was more dangerous than ever by virtue of the consolidation of its strategic alliance with the United States and of the "Greater Israel" vision of the Likud-led government in power at the time.[12]

In this light, Syria viewed Iraq's invasion of Iran as a waste of Arab resources and a dangerous diversion from the issue of occupied Arab land. Furthermore, in claiming Iran as a friend, Syria hoped to extract concessions from the Gulf states. The negative side of this policy was the cessation of aid to Syria, from the Gulf states and from Iraq itself.

Syria's reaction to the Iran-Iraq war was also influenced by Asad's own background as an Alawite whose community derived from Shi'ism, and as a man whose rural and minority origins made him sympathize with the oppressed Shi'a community of Lebanon, who had themselves won the support of revolutionary Iran.

On the question of Shi'ism, in Iran or Lebanon, Syria and Iraq held opposing views. Just as Asad valued the Shi'a community and welcomed the Khomeini revolution, Saddam saw both as a lethal threat to the security of his regime and to the territorial integrity of his country, which had never been a homogenous state. The antagonisms that this situation created were greatly sharpened by the personal animosity of Asad and Saddam, and by rivalry between the Ba'th factions in Baghdad and Damascus, at the heart of which lay competing claims to legitimacy and to inter-Arab preeminence.

Turkey, on the other hand, adopted a position of neutrality in the Iran-Iraq war. By showing no preference to either party, Turkey demonstrated its strategic commitment to the West, which wished to prevent a marked shift in the regional balance of power. The United States and its allies believed at the time that a victory by either country was not strategically desirable, because it could result in regional turmoil and increase the scope for Soviet influence.

By remaining neutral, Turkey improved its relations with Washington, strained in the wake of the 1974 invasion of Cyprus and the subsequent congressional embargo. Although the U.S. government had lifted the arms embargo against Turkey in February 1978 and begun negotiating the U.S. Turkish Defense and Economic Cooperation

Agreement, the Soviet invasion of Afghanistan and Turkey's neutral position during the Iran-Iraq war did much to accelerate the improvement of relations between Turkey and the United States.[13]

Turkey's neutrality also helped it in suppressing secessionist Kurdish groups. In May 1983 and October 1984 Turkish troops crossed into northern Iraq, with Iraq's knowledge and approval, to kill and capture Kurdish rebels. There are reports that Iran also cooperated with Turkey against Kurds who used Iranian territory as a sanctuary. The governments of Iran, Iraq, and Turkey have always been fundamentally united in opposing Kurdish independence even if, for tactical reasons, they supported Kurds in each other's territory.

There were financial dividends as well; indeed, neutrality helped Turkey implement the export promotion policies it had introduced in 1980. The most important were the liberalization of the foreign exchange regime, tax rebates, access to preferential export credits, foreign exchange allocation, and temporary import permits.

During the war, Turkey became a major trading partner of both Iran and Iraq. Turkey's exports to the Middle East flourished in the 1980s, jumping from 12.1 percent of its exports to the world in 1976 to 40.0 percent in 1985. In 1985, Iran was Turkey's largest customer among Middle Eastern countries and Iraq was its second most important source of exports. The four largest groups of Turkish exports to Middle Eastern countries were animal products, vegetable products, textiles and clothing, and iron and steel.[14]

THE WATER DISPUTE

The most immediate problem between Syria and Turkey is the water problem; indeed this problem is paramount on the political agenda of the two countries. This problem also has a direct bearing upon the question of Syria's support for Kurdish secessionist groups, most notably the PKK.

Controversial water schemes in Turkey have created serious difficulties not only between Turkey and Syria, but between Turkey and Iraq. One of these schemes was Turkey's building of two big dams on the Euphrates—the Keban, which was built between 1964 and 1974, and the Karakaya, which was started in 1976 and completed in 1987. The World Bank helped finance the two dams, and during the process of building, Turkey assured the Bank, but not Iraq or Syria directly, that Syria would receive at least 450 cubic meters of water per second from the Euphrates.

Both Syria and Iraq reacted angrily to the building of the two dams, charging Turkey with diverting major portions of Euphrates water for its own use. Iraq chose to confront Turkey over this problem, deciding in November 1977 to cut off its oil supply to Turkey and insisting that Ankara pay its oil debts of $330 million. This Iraqi step, which came at a time when Turkey was going through an economic and financial crisis, forced Ankara to go to other oil suppliers who insisted on cash payments.

At the time, Turkey received about two-thirds of its oil needs from Iraq, most of it through the Kirkuk-Yumurtalik pipeline, completed in 1977. One year later, Iraq allowed the resumption of oil supplies after Turkey promised to satisfy Baghdad's water needs.[15] Later, during its war with Iran, Baghdad chose not to take up the Euphrates problem with Ankara because it needed Turkey's cooperation to fight Kurdish secessionists. Both countries shared the strategic objective of curbing Kurdish separatism within their borders, and their cooperation in this regard culminated in the signing of a security protocol on October 15, 1984.

Such cooperation derived from an underlying fear, in both Turkey and Iraq, that Kurdish separatism poses a formidable threat to the territorial integrity of both states. The Kurds in Turkey number about 12 million, while in Iraq there are about 4 million. The number of the Kurds, their strong sense of political identity, and their geographic concentration make their assimilation particularly difficult.[16]

Syria's response to the Euphrates problem was in some important respects different from Iraq's. In this regard, Damascus followed a two-pronged strategy. On the one hand, it joined Baghdad in its lobbying efforts at the World Bank, which decided that Iraqi and Syrian water concerns were legitimate. On the other, Damascus continued to provide sanctuary to Armenian and Kurdish separatists and to left-wing Turkish activists who had fled Turkey after the military coup of September 1980. Unlike Iraq and Turkey, Syria does not have a Kurdish problem. The Kurds of Syria, whose estimated number ranges from 100,000 to 500,000, are not agitating for autonomy. Thus Syria can play the Kurdish card without inviting any serious threat to its territorial integrity.

Another water project which has posed serious difficulties for Turkey's relations with Syria and Iraq is the Southeast Anatolia Project (GAP), begun in 1983. GAP consists of the giant Atatürk dam; twenty-two smaller dams; and nineteen hydroelectric stations on the Euphrates and Tigris rivers, as well as two huge concrete tunnels that will carry water for irrigation.

Slated for completion by the year 2000, GAP is designed to be a multipurpose project which would generate 26 billion kW of energy per year and irrigate close to 4 million acres of land on the Urfa, Mardin, Hilvan, and Harran plains. The project reduces the discharge of the Euphrates, thus further reducing the flow of river to both Syria and Iraq. The current flow of the Euphrates is 500 cubic meters a second at the Syrian border. Syria wants 700 cubic meters per second for irrigation purposes.

Turkish statements on the water question, particularly those made by Prime Minister Süleyman Demirel shortly before inaugurating the Atatürk dam on July 25, 1992, created a lot of unease in Damascus. "The water resources are Turkey's," Demirel said. "The oil resources are [theirs]. We do not say we share their oil resources; they cannot say they share our water resources."[17] Syria's response to this argument is that oil stays underground until drilled and pumped by human intervention. River water, on the other hand, is a resource that naturally flows to downstream riparians unless its course is changed by human design. Asad expressed Syria's concern about Demirel's statement to Egyptian President Hosni Mubarak, and the Syrian press urged Turkey not to "monopolize" water resources, "denying Syrians drinking water and water to irrigate their crops."[18]

Several considerations shaped Syria's estimate of the danger of Turkey's water policies and the intentions behind them. Economic considerations relate to Syria's program of economic recovery. This is a most immediate priority for Syria, even more since its involvement in peace negotiations with Israel.

Peace with Israel will require more than just the return of the Golan to Syrian sovereignty. To be stable, peace also requires economic dividends. In pursuit of this goal, Syria has accelerated the process of economic reform it had launched in the 1980s to encourage foreign investment. As part of this reform program, the Syrian government passed Law Number 10 in June 1991 to promote investment in all sectors of the economy. The law offers incentives to local and foreign investors, including duty-free privileges and a tax holiday for the first five years of operation. One main goal of the new law is to attract the capital of Syrian expatriates, estimated at $30 billion.

Furthermore, Syria has launched a new five-year plan, ending in 1995, with a targeted total investment of around 295 billion Syrian pounds. Officials of the Supreme Planning Commission have stated that agriculture and irrigation are to receive top priority as well as industry, so Syria's ability to increase its electrical power generation is crucial if the country's program of agricultural and industrial growth is to succeed.

Yet despite the fact that the government has embarked on a major expansion program in power generation, power shortages and outages have been a familiar feature of Syrian life in recent years, and Syrian officials put much of the blame on Turkey's water policies.[19] From the Syrian viewpoint, Turkey is using the Euphrates water schemes to put direct pressure on Syria in the hope of forcing Damascus to enter into an agreement that legitimizes Turkey's annexation of the Alexandretta region.

This Syrian view of the water question gave added weight to the belief that Turkey does not harbor good intentions toward Syria. Particularly disturbing to the Syrians is their belief that Turkey is playing the water card at a time when Syria is launching a program of economic reform and revitalization, and when it is engaged in delicate negotiations with Israel.

The second consideration is Syria's interest in placing an exceptionally high premium on negotiating with Israel from a position of strength. Lacking Israel's military and political resources, Syria's main recourse lies in making its regional alliances the counterpoise to Israel's advantages. Thus Syria believes that it can hardly afford to be distracted by its water problems with Turkey. The view from Damascus is that Turkey's water challenge not only runs counter to Syria's interests, but is a foreign plot designed to encircle Syria and force it to make unacceptable concessions to Israel. Viewed in this light, Turkey's water policies serve a larger strategic purpose that goes beyond Ankara's own interests. Ankara, however, willingly applies these pressure tactics precisely because they serve its interests vis-à-vis the border question with Syria and the Kurdish dimension of its problem with Damascus.

Moreover, Syria views with suspicion Turkey's proposal to complete a "dream pipeline project" intended to carry water from the Atatürk Dam to Syria, Jordan, and Israel and across the desert to Saudi Arabia and the Gulf. It also views with deep mistrust the "Peace Canal on the Golan Heights" initiative, a peace plan based on a water project originating in Turkey. The plan was prepared by Wachtel and Associates, a consulting firm in New York City. In a confidential letter to the Syrian government dated May 14, 1993, its executive director had this to say:

> The Peace Canal plan calls for a diversion of 1,100 million cubic meters a year from Atatürk Baraji lake or from the Seyhan and Ceyhan rivers in southeast Turkey. Two underground pipelines would carry the 1.1 billion cubic meters per year through western Syria, where 275 million cubic meters/year would be diverted for Syrian use, and on to the current Syrian-Israeli border on the Golan Heights. The pipelines would then converge at a northern point of the border into an open canal, which is designed to double as an anti-tank barricade between Syria and Israel, to flow the length of the border to the southern edge of the Golan Heights. At that point, the canal would diverge into two to generate hydro-power at the proposed Maquarin dam on the Yarmuk in Syria and at the sea of Galilee in Israel. 275 million cubic meters/year would then be made available each to Jordan, Israel, and the Palestinians.[20]

The Syrians did not respond to Wachtel's proposal. They also did not view with favor all plans suggesting cooperation with Israel on the water issue before Israel commits itself to withdraw to the borders of June 4, 1967. From Syria's viewpoint, the aim of all such water proposals is to draw Syria into making concessions to Israel on issues related to the multilateral talks before Israel commits itself to a total withdrawal from the Golan.

The third Syrian consideration is Turkey's new role in the post–Cold War era. While many Arab diplomats have come more and more to accept Turkey's ascendance after the Gulf War, Syria holds a different view. The anxieties created by Iraq's invasion of Kuwait in 1990 made Gulf diplomats supportive of Turkey's ambition to act as a buffer against both Iran and Iraq and as a counterweight to Islamic fundamentalism. Egypt tends to share this view.

Syria, however, has a different perspective on the matter. It can be understood in the context of a mutual lack of confidence, as well as in the context of Syria's conception of Turkey's role and of its strategic desiderata in the region. From Syria's viewpoint, Turkey's ascendance translates into the marginalization of the Arab role, which means a serious limitation on the Arabs' ability to play a senior role in the game of regional politics. Any diminution of the Arab role is also a diminution of Syria's role and its ability to influence events.

Another aspect of Syria's misgivings about Turkey's new role is the long-standing relationship between Damascus and Tehran. As the Syrians see it, whatever role Turkey plays in containing Iran is primarily following a Western agenda, even though Turkey itself can reap some important benefits from this role, most notably a reaffirmation of its role as a dependable strategic friend to the West.

In Syria's view, it is convenient for the West to assign such a role to Turkey, if only because its quasi-Islamic identity provides the necessary cover. Israel, on the other hand, cannot play such a role because it is a non-Islamic power. Thus Syria's misgiving about Turkey's role is largely the product of strategic necessity. Syria views Iran as an asset mainly because it can serve as a counterbalance to Iraq and Israel, and as a lever on the Gulf states.

Because Syria's geostrategic vision extends beyond the Arab East to include non-Arab Iran, Damascus frowns upon the idea of employing Turkey as a buffer against a friendly Iran. Many Syrians believe that Turkey is the only Eastern gendarme of the Western alliance. The United States lost Iran and Ethiopia and is enhancing Turkey's role not simply to implement a policy of dual containment, but to act as an instrument of pressure against Syria.

MUTUAL INTERESTS

Despite Syrian-Turkish differences over major policy issues, both Ankara and Damascus have important common objectives, which make them careful not to allow themselves to be drawn into ill-considered moves against each other. In the case of Syria, this caution is strengthened further by its preoccupation with Israel. Syria and Turkey have in common three interlocking areas of policy concern.

The first has to do with the unity and territorial integrity of Iraq, a principle highlighted in the Asad-Demirel meeting in Damascus in mid-January 1993. This means that neither country would support the creation of an independent Kurdish state. Syria's support for this principle is particularly important for Turkey because an independent Kurdistan poses a serious threat to the integrity and authority of the Turkish state.

In this regard, it is important to note that the PKK seeks to carve out a Kurdish state from the eastern Anatolian provinces of Turkey and unite it with neighboring Kurdish areas, including the mountains of northeast Iraq. An independent Kurdish state could also destabilize Syria's friend, Iran, which has a Kurdish population of about 5 million.

Moreover, Syria opposes on ideological grounds the fragmentation of an Arab state, despite the Asad-Saddam animosity and the party schisms that divide Syria and Iraq. From the standpoint of strategy, Damascus appreciates the danger that the disintegration of Iraq would create, particularly considering that certain quarters in Turkey had in the past laid claim to the Mosul region there. Syria also understands that playing the Kurdish card can be a useful instrument of policy, but actually supporting a Kurdish state nothing but folly.

A second objective shared by Syria and Turkey is the containment of Saddam and the curbing of Iraq's ambitions in a post-Saddam era. The problems between Syria and Iraq are not new, nor are they confined to party splits and geopolitical rivalries. The two countries have quarrels over economic matters, water issues, and oil pipelines, one of which crosses Syrian territory.[21]

Thus a core aim of the Syrian leadership is to keep Saddam on a leash, even if it must therefore cooperate with Turkey. The containment of Saddam, even though it hurts Turkey economically, serves the country in a different way, reinforcing Turkey's position as a strategic asset for the West. Not everyone in the West is a subscriber to the Clinton administration's declared policy of dual containment. However, there is general agreement that the policy of punishing and curbing Iraq should continue, and that Turkey is a central pillar for this policy.

The third of these issues of common concern is the water question, where there have been for two decades intermittent diplomatic negotiations and technical discussions to address it. Iraq has also been engaged in these diplomatic activities, but so far no mutually acceptable long-term solution has been reached, and no permanent tripartite treaty ratified.

Turkey talks about "allocating" the waters of the Euphrates River, while Syria and Iraq talk about "sharing" them. Several steps, all having only limited utility, have been taken in this regard: the establishment of a tri-national Joint Technical Committee in 1980; the Protocol of Economic Cooperation concluded between Syria and Turkey in 1987; the doubling of Syrian-Turkish trade between 1988 and 1993 ($331 million by 1992); joint projects to develop Syria's recently discovered oil and gas reserves; and the intensification of high-level Syrian-Turkish diplomatic negotiations since the end of the Gulf War, including a summit meeting between Asad and Demirel.[22]

In these negotiations, the Syrians were interested in having Turkey help them meet their water needs in the name of equity and good neighborliness. Unpublished position papers prepared by Syrian officials indicate an inclination on Syria's part to conclude with Turkey an agreement modeled on the one concluded in 1959 between the United Arab Republic and the Sudan, setting out the rules for utilizing Nile water.

Turkey's officials, on the other hand, while expressing their desire to find a final solution for the water problem, were more interested in enlisting Syria's help in Turkey's fight against the outlawed PKK and its leader Abdullah Öcalan, who allegedly lives in Syria. For their part, the Syrians publicly deny that their country is behind PKK activities against Turkey. Privately, however, they suggest that if Turkey continues to play the water card against Syria, the Syrian government will not hesitate to use any kind of pressure that lies within its reach.

A position paper prepared for the Syrian Foreign Ministry suggests that Syria and Iraq should form "one united front" to confront the Turkish challenge. The paper also suggests that as long as Iraqi-Syrian relations remain unimproved, Turkey will continue to use the water of the Euphrates as a weapon with which to pressure both countries. In an attempt to induce Baghdad to cooperate with Damascus to cope with the water challenge, Syria signed with Iraq an agreement on April 16, 1990, under which Syria would receive 42 percent and Iraq 58 percent, regardless of quantity. It is difficult to expect an end to the Iraqi-Syrian conflict in the foreseeable future, but the situation may change with a change of leadership in either Baghdad or Damascus.

Syria's policy toward its water problems with Turkey will remain relatively subdued, in keeping with the general tendency of the Asad regime to eschew taking up the Turkish challenge while still in a state of war with Israel. The available evidence suggests that, for the time being at least, Syria is interested in resolving the water dispute on the basis of international law, including arbitration. Once there is peace with Israel, it is very likely that Syria will place a much higher premium on preparing itself to deal not only with its water problem with Turkey but also with the border question.

On the other hand, however, there is the alternative possibility that even in the event of peace with Israel, the leaders of Syria may shed their habitual suspicion of Turkey and the West. From Syria's perspective, this requires a transformation of Turkey's attitude toward the water dispute and the border question. It also requires a reorientation of U.S. policy toward Syria. An improvement in the bilateral relations between Damascus and Washington could go a long way toward changing Syria's perception of Turkey and its intentions. At least it will dispel a Syrian notion rooted in the past and shaped by past experiences, namely the belief that Turkey is a Trojan horse through which Western imperialism infiltrates into the Middle East in order to disrupt or weaken the defense of states that disagree with its policies.

This paper has benefited from interviews with Arab officials and from unpublished position papers. The officials requested that their comments not be attributed to them by name.

CHAPTER EIGHT

WATER POLITICS AS HIGH POLITICS
The Case of Turkey and Syria

Murhaf Jouejati

In an era of change, perhaps only continuity demands explanation. While technological advances, growing interdependence, and better communications throughout the world have changed international politics during the second half of the twentieth century, interstate relations in the Middle East continue to be dominated by power politics for a variety of reasons. First, most states in the Middle East— e.g. Turkey, Syria, Iraq, and Israel—aspire to regional hegemony. Second, many are embattled from within, through ethnic and sectarian conflict, and from without, through border conflicts. Finally, some are dominated by governmental structures in which the functions of the elite, the regime, and the state overlap to the point that they are almost indistinguishable. This is especially true of Syria, Iraq, Jordan, Saudi Arabia, and the Gulf states, where challenges to elite dominance are perceived as threats to national security, and vice versa.

The combination of these factors makes the political environment in the Middle East a conflictual one where almost every problem, including water rights, is perceived as a zero-sum proposition. Hence hydropolitics. Exploding rates of population growth and the depletion of the region's aquifers are aggravating the problem of water scarcity in the Middle East's arid and semiarid regions. By the end of the century, pressure on water resources will be so acute that wars may erupt as states seek to expand and secure their own supplies.

Tracing the origins and evolution of the water crisis between Turkey, Syria, and Iraq can help locate the obstacles to cooperation among the three riparians and identify practical solutions to help resolve the otherwise escalating dispute.

THE PROBLEM

How can the water dispute between Turkey, Syria, and Iraq be explained? Given the prevailing conflictual environment, states in the Middle East do not trust the intentions of other like-minded states. Each seeks to be self-sufficient. The problem lies in the fact that, unlike oil, river waters flow across boundaries.

Until World War I, the question of water rights did not appear in the long list of grievances between Turkey and Syria. The Euphrates and Tigris rivers flowed within territories under Ottoman control. However, with the dissolution of the Ottoman Empire at the close of the Great War and the redrawing of the region's political map, the emergence of new political entities in the Middle East created a complex situation. Syria and Iraq became co-sovereign over the two rivers by the terms of the treaties negotiated between the mandatory powers—France and Britain acting on behalf of Syria and Iraq respectively—and Turkey. These negotiations culminated in a series of treaties, protocols, and agreements including two in 1920, the 1921 Ankara Treaty with France, the 1924 Lausanne Treaty, the French-Turkish Treaty of 1926, the French-Turkish Agreement of 1929, the 1930 French-Turkish Treaty, and the 1946 Friendship and Good Neighborliness Treaty with Iraq. These arrangements regulated the use of the Euphrates and Tigris and explicitly protected the acquired rights of the downstream riparians. They worked as long as the waters were used at a minimal level.

Turkish interest in the exploitation of Euphrates waters began in the 1950s when Syria launched a development scheme on its segment of the river. However, riparian rights became a source of interstate friction only in the 1970s, when Turkey began the Southeastern Anatolia Project (Güneydogu Anadolu Projesi, or GAP) for domestic political reasons. By launching the massive project—GAP includes a total of twenty-two dams, nineteen hydroelectric power plants, and seventeen irrigation schemes on various scales in thirteen different projects with an estimated cost of $32 billion, covering an area of 73,863 square miles[1]—the Turkish elite, responding to leftist domestic criticism over the economic exclusion of the Kurdish minority, set out to develop the southeast of the country where the Kurds are concentrated. The transformation of the backward local economy from subsistence to commercial agriculture would, in addition to muting political criticism, dilute potential Kurdish national aspirations for an independent homeland.[2]

THE IMPACT ON SYRIA

Though Turkey had explicitly recognized the acquired rights of the two downstream riparians, it failed to live up to its international agreements, and its increased consumption of the Euphrates waters resulting from GAP affected Syria and Iraq adversely.[3] The average annual discharge of the river is 31.8 bm^3 (billion cubic meters).[4] Whereas Turkey consumed around 10 percent of the river's average annual discharge prior to GAP, its use jumped to an estimated 53 percent. This causes problems because Syria relies heavily on the Euphrates, which alone represents as much as 86 percent of its available water resources. One-third of the country is steppe, and more than half gets less than 250 millimeters of rainfall per year and consists of desert and semi-desert regions. Less than 10 percent receives enough precipitation for rain-fed agriculture.

Furthermore, Syria's ability to generate its own hydroelectric power is curtailed by the depleted water levels. The 800 megawatt-generating Tabqa Dam, completed in 1977, was supposed to meet Syria's energy needs well into the next century. In 1993, however, of the eight turbines only one was operational. Although inefficiency, mismanagement, and inadequate maintenance partly account for this state of affairs, the major reason is the low level of the Euphrates. The reduction in the flow of Euphrates waters also affects water supply available for Syria's agriculture, in terms of quality as well as quantity. Increased use of fertilizers and pesticides upstream has caused pollution levels downstream to increase. Of the 640,000 hectares of steppe that the dam was supposed to irrigate, less than 10 percent has come on stream.

THE BACKGROUND

Turkish insensitivity to downstream needs and concerns is a by-product of traditionally bitter relations between the two states. At the turn of the century, Arab nationalists, resentful of Ottoman rule, aligned themselves with Britain. Subsequently, Turkey, the successor state to the Ottoman Empire, has come to view the actions of the Arab National Movement, in which Syrians played a leading role, as a stab in the back. The competing aims of Turkish and Arab nationalisms shaped the future course of Turkish-Syrian relations.

In the years following the Ottoman collapse, Turkey and Syria were set to have different foreign policy orientations, with Turkey looking to the West and Syria to the Arab world. The border between them represented more than a political boundary; it was the dividing line between two cultures. Adding to the complexity of the situation and to the conflictual nature of emerging Turkish-Syrian relations was the fact that the French mandatory power ceded Iskenderun—a Syrian province—to Turkey on the eve of World War II. The Syrians have never accepted the mutilation of their country, and, to this date, Iskenderun is included in all Syrian maps. No Syrian regime has had the will or the inclination to recognize the status quo.

In this charged political environment, Turkey and Syria were predisposed for future conflict. This state of affairs explains the lack of knowledge of each other which, until the advent of the Asad administration in 1970 and the ensuing *infitah* (opening) of Syrian diplomacy, was exacerbated by the low level of official contact between the two states.[5] That Turkey ignored the harm its massive development project was causing downstream, especially in Syria, is therefore not surprising.

OBSTACLES TO BASINWIDE COOPERATION

What explains the lack of cooperation between Turkey, Syria, and Iraq? Miriam R. Lowi identifies several obstacles to basinwide cooperation in arid and semi-arid regions. First, given the condition of anarchy in the international system, states are motivated by fear and distrust, and their principal concern is with their security and survival. In terms of interstate water disputes, central decision makers choose less than optimal solutions in order to secure their own supplies.

Second, in a regional system where the only supranational authority—the Islamic Conference—is ill-equipped, if not altogether unable, to sanction or enforce rules, it is the combination of superior riparian position and power capabilities that determine a state's behavior. In

the absence of enticements, what induces a superior riparian to cooperate with downstream riparians? To be sure, there is nothing unusual
about Turkey's self-interested behavior. Its superior riparian position
and power capabilities enable it to pursue its self-interest. Third, the
existence of political conflict alongside a water dispute between upstream and downstream riparians is another obstacle to cooperation.
For Syria and Turkey, water is not the only source of conflict; important political differences separate them. Syria and Iraq are locked in
conflict, although theirs is motivated by ideological differences.

Fourth, cooperation among riparians is hampered by the perception that water-sharing is a zero-sum affair. "The concern that a division of gains from joint endeavors may favor others more than one-
self acts as a barrier to cooperation; as relative gains concerns
increase, cooperation becomes more difficult."[6] In the case of Turkey,
for instance, the relative gain it stands to obtain as a result of cooperation is less than the absolute gain without it. It is this perception of
relative gain that acts as the major impediment to cooperation. In
brief, an equitable solution of riparian disputes in arid and semi-arid
regions is impeded by the upstream riparian, which typically drags
its feet on the subject of a binding agreement.

By contrast, downstream riparians are eager for cooperation. The
vital issue of water is understandably perceived as one of national
security. Evidence from other riparian conflicts suggests that, in the
absence of cooperation, powerful downstream riparians have traditionally resorted to the use or threat of force to secure their supplies.
For example, when Syria attempted to divert the Banias stream in the
mid-1960s so that its waters would not discharge into Lake Huleh
and benefit Israel, Israel responded by bombing the Syrian construction sites.[7] Israel resorted to even more drastic action in 1967 when it
occupied the Syrian Golan Heights, where the Dan, the Hasbani, and
the Banias streams converge at a location near Jisr Banat Ya'coub to
form the headwaters of the Jordan. Similarly, in 1975, when Syrian
authorities began filling Lake Asad, which reduced the flow of the
Euphrates downstream, Iraq moved its army to the Syrian border and
threatened to bomb the Tabqa dam. Only third-party intervention
was able to defuse the situation. However, no agreement was signed
and the water dispute remains unresolved. Even Turkey, who had
been procrastinating on an agreement with Syria and Iraq, when the
shoe was on the other foot warned Bulgaria of "a serious crisis"

between the two nations "if they [the Bulgarian authorities] attempt to sell water once more and hold water."[8] Turkey faced a water problem with Bulgaria, which refused to let the Maritsa river flow to Turkey unless a certain amount of money was paid. Under such circumstances, it may well be that, rather than being a catalyst for regional cooperation, water disputes may instead become catalysts for future conflict.

BILATERAL AND TRILATERAL TALKS

The conflict between larger and more moderate gains offers a major impediment to cooperation. The benefits that Turkey derives from GAP, including domestic political stability and economic advancement, far outweigh the benefits of joint cooperation. In contrast, a bilateral or a trilateral agreement would reduce Turkey's share of water. It is this cost-benefit analysis that dictates Turkey's behavior, which, according to the evidence, has consisted of foot-dragging on the subject of a binding agreement that Syria and Iraq had been calling for to gain time for the completion of GAP.

Serious bilateral and trilateral talks began only after the establishment of the "Syrian General Establishment of the Euphrates Project" in 1961. Initially, these discussions seemed promising. The first bilateral Turkish-Syrian talks began in 1962 and were related to information-sharing in the Euphrates basin. The two sides met again in 1964 and agreed to form a Joint Technical Committee (JTC) whose task was to define the "equitable and reasonable" distribution of Euphrates waters. They also agreed to include Iraq in the committee.

However, talks quickly bogged down in the 1965 trilateral meeting in Baghdad. At issue was whether the JTC's jurisdiction was to be limited to the Euphrates basin—the Iraqi position—or whether it encompassed both the Euphrates *and* the Tigris basins—the Turkish proposal. Iraq and Syria consider the Euphrates an international river, to be treated as an integrated system. Both contend that the basic injunction against causing "appreciable harm" bars upper riparians from reducing the natural flow to established downstream users without their consent. On the other hand, the Turkish position is that international rivers are only those that form the border between two or more riparians. Turkey views the Euphrates as a "cross-boundary waterway," whose water is under Turkey's exclusive sovereignty until it flows across the border into Syria. It is only after the Euphrates joins the Tigris in lower Iraq to form the Shatt al-Arab, which serves as the border between Iraq and Iran, that it is to be regarded as an international river. This new twist implicitly meant that Turkey no longer recognized the co-sovereignty of the downstream riparians. Its obligations toward the two downstream riparians would henceforth consist only of unilaterally guaranteeing them a certain amount of water.

To buttress the argument that Turkey is sovereign over its share of the Euphrates and the Tigris rivers, Turkish officials cite the Harmon Doctrine, named for the U.S. attorney general who, in a late nineteenth-century dispute with Mexico, asserted a similar absolute American sovereign right to utilize the Rio Grande (Rio Bravo). However, by 1942 the legal advisor of the State Department acknowledged that a review of treaties regarding international rivers failed to find any one still supporting the Harmon Doctrine. Dante Caponera, the international legal authority who in 1966 drafted the International Law Association's Helsinki rules on the "Uses of the Waters of International Rivers," has pointed out that no international arbitrage decision has ever supported the Harmon Doctrine.[9]

The International Law Commission (ILC) of the United Nations, which, after many years of work, in September 1991 provisionally adopted a set of "Draft Articles on the Law of the Non-Navigational Uses of International Watercourses," defines an international watercourse as "a watercourse, parts of which are situated in different states."[10] The ILC does not distinguish in this regard between international and transboundary rivers. This definition clearly applies to the Euphrates and the Tigris. Moreover, Turkey considers the two basins one integrated entity. Turkey's position reflects its self-interest, for less water would have to be released to the downstream riparians if the two basins were considered one.

The imminent use of the Euphrates and Tigris by Turkey created new demands for cooperation. Under Iraqi pressure, Turkey reluctantly agreed in 1980 to form and participate in a new JTC related to the regional waters. Though Turkey's agreement to take part in such talks indicated once again its recognition of Syrian and Iraqi riparian interests,[11] its opposition to a binding trilateral agreement remained unchanged. Turkey's foot-dragging was reflected in the fact that despite sixteen JTC meetings, the parties could not agree on what was equitable. Turkish officials participating in the subcommittees went into excessive but unwarranted scientific detail. Turkey reiterated its interpretation of the controversial single entity issue. Again, Syria and Iraq interpreted Turkey's actions as buying time in order to complete GAP unhindered.

The lack of political will in Turkey and the consequent futility of the talks caused Syria to boycott the seventeenth JTC meeting. Even the interstate ministerial meetings intended to dissipate the mounting crisis ended in disagreement.[12]

THE ATATÜRK DAM CRISIS AND DOWNSTREAM CONCERNS

Tensions reached their peak in January 1990, when Turkish authorities began to fill the reservoir of the $1.6 billion Atatürk Dam, the linchpin of GAP. The river was diverted for one month, resuming its normal flow in February. During this time, the flow was sharply reduced. Turkey was implicitly asserting upstream riparian proprietary rights. The calculation in Ankara was that Iraq, recovering from its war with Iran, was in no position to react forcefully against Turkey. Similarly, it was assumed that, distracted by events in Lebanon, where part of its army was stationed, Syria would refrain from reacting.[13] Turkey did, however, take Syrian and Iraqi interests into account, first by warning them in advance of its intentions and second by releasing more water than usual in the month following the diversion in order to compensate for the loss.

However, the harm was done. A stretch of seventy miles from the Turkish border to Lake Asad could no longer be used because of the environmental damage the diversion had caused. Furthermore, farmers were not able to irrigate their crops because of the drop in the level of the river.[14] Turkey's *fait accompli* was even more flagrant when, in November 1991, another diversion reduced the flow into Syria from 500 m^3/sec to just under 165 m^3/sec. This time, however, Syria had not been forewarned of the cutoff.[15]

Of greater concern to Syrian planners were the prospects of future cutoffs. An erratic flow over the next decade could have serious implications for Syria, which is planning to supplement its hydroelectric power and its irrigation potential by the further exploitation of the Euphrates.[16] With the rising demand for food from a population growing at a rate of 3.6 percent a year, Syria is planning to expand the irrigated areas between three and four times.

THE SYRIAN RESPONSE

Because of the scarcity of its water resources and its heavy reliance on the Euphrates waters for irrigation, power supply, industrial, and domestic use, Syria is eager for a binding agreement with Turkey that would secure its future water supplies. This situation has forced the Syrian government to adopt two strategies, first to reduce Syria's dependence on Euphrates waters by increasing the efficiency of its water-resource management and second to increase the costs of Turkish noncooperation.

In order to reduce its dependence on the Euphrates, Syria has undertaken to diversify the sources of power generation. Natural gas is being exploited as a substitute for hydroelectrical power. A 200-megawatt power plant went on line in 1993 to meet the needs of Damascus, and the government has signed several contracts with Chinese companies to build other plants. The government also concluded an agreement with Mitsubishi to build a 600-megawatt station outside Homs.[17] Moreover, policy has been relaxed to encourage the private sector to participate in activities previously reserved for the state. The private sector can now, in some instances, generate and market electrical power to consumers. Second, the government seeks to improve irrigation methods and to increase agricultural productivity. In this context, agricultural institutions are working with international nongovernmental organizations (NGOs) like the United Nations Development Program, the International Center for Agricultural Research in Dry Areas, and other specialized agencies to improve water management techniques.

However sound these efforts, they are nonetheless dwarfed by the extent of Syria's reliance on the Euphrates waters. To make matters worse, demand for electrical power is increasing at a rate of 20 percent a year due to a boom in manufacturing occasioned by the economic liberalization of the early 1990s. The Syrian economy is suffering as a result of the electricity cuts that in many cities range between four and nineteen hours per day. To buffer themselves most manufacturers have bought expensive industrial-capacity generators.[18] But the sudden plethora of generators has caused its own problems. Heavy-duty industrial generators run on diesel fuel; the result has been a severe and prolonged diesel shortage. As far as drinking water is concerned, authorities have cut consumption in most cities by 40 percent, spreading the pain by choking off supplies to various neighborhoods on a revolving basis.[19]

Syria's heavy reliance on the waters of the Euphrates shapes its approach toward Turkey—usually a classic carrot and stick approach. The carrot included Syria's support of Turkey's rejection of the establishment of an independent Kurdish state in northern Iraq. The foreign ministers of Turkey, Syria, and Iran met five times to underscore their opposition to the partition of Iraq.[20] Second, Syrian central decision makers have opened the Syrian market to rapidly increasing Turkish exports, and Turkish contractors have won important projects in Syria.[21]

The stick has consisted in increasing the financial and diplomatic costs to Turkey of its lack of cooperation on the water dispute. In this regard, Syria blocked Western financial assistance to donor funding of GAP by withholding its consent, forcing Turkey to rely on its own financial resources since the World Bank's policy is to withhold financing of projects until riparian disputes are settled.[22] Furthermore, Syria's linkage of the water issue to the larger concept of Arab food security, which dominated Arab strategic thinking during the 1980s, and its pressure on Arab League member states to consider Turkey's self-interested behavior in the water dispute a threat to Arab national security on a par with Israel's has denied GAP potential Arab funding.[23]

The stick has been successful. In 1987 Turkey signed a protocol guaranteeing to Syria a flow of 500 m^3/sec (cubic meters per second). However, it falls short of Syria's intended goal, which is a binding agreement rather than a unilateral Turkish pledge. Syria's declared need for 700 m^3/sec prompted the signatories to declare this protocol merely an interim agreement.[24]

MUTUAL PERCEPTIONS OF THREAT

The danger lies in the fact that the water dispute may escalate as mutual perceptions of threat exacerbate an already tense situation. On the one hand, the Syrian state has traditionally perceived Turkey, a NATO member, as an instrument of Western power in the Middle

East. This is what Syria's foreign minister alluded to when he declared that what worries Syria "is not the quantity of water which flows to Syria and Iraq, but the fact that no firm accord has been reached concerning the sharing of water."[25] Furthermore, the Turkish diversion of the Euphrates waters has exposed the limits of Syrian and Iraqi power.[26] Although the Arab world rallied behind Syria and Iraq, Syrian central decision makers understood that there was little the downstream riparians could do beyond anti-Turkish media campaigns.[27] Moreover, Turkey demonstrated its ability to play one downstream riparian against the other—a reduction in the flow of the Euphrates waters downstream increases the pressure on Syria to reduce the flow to Iraq.

On the other hand, Turkey accuses Syria of supporting the Kurdistan Workers Party (PKK) in its anti-Turkish campaign, possibly as leverage in the water talks. It is difficult to ascertain whether this allegation is specifically linked to the water dispute or whether it is part of the overall political conflict.[28] If the link exists, Syria's behavior would be in line with that of downstream riparians in other river basins.

Whatever the case may be, Turkey and Syria seem to be on a collision course. If left to their own devices, the two states will not be able to defuse the increasing intensity of the dispute. Turkey has threatened retaliation against any government, including Syria's, that supports the PKK.[29] The Turkish government may make good on its threat of retaliating against suspected PKK targets in Lebanon's Bekaa valley.[30] In this event, the dispute threatens to turn into a real crisis.

IS COOPERATION POSSIBLE?

Three competing schools of thought differ on the ways in which cooperation might be attained. Hegemonic stability theorists posit that cooperation is possible if one of the riparians is endowed with overwhelming military capability that enables it to impose its rules on other riparians. However, despite obvious strategic disparities, no state in the region possesses such an overwhelming capability.

Functionalist theorists argue that an interstate agreement over water-sharing is possible (and could even become a catalyst for future regional cooperation) if riparians were to give up some of their sovereignty in favor of a supranational authority to manage the water resources. Accordingly, a solution could be achieved by functional cooperation across national boundaries and the creation of such apolitical organizations—the principal agents of cooperation—as supranational task-related organizations, specialized agencies, transgovernmental policy networks, and epistemic communities. Cooperation is possible if perceived as cost-free. States in non–zero-sum situations can collaborate with the assistance of institutions. Evidence from elsewhere shows that issues can be delinked and that cooperation in one field may spill over into others.

But precedents show that this optimistic view is not applicable in a conflictual context such as that in the Middle East. It is a functionalist line of thinking that drove the Eisenhower administration to formulate the Johnston Plan, intended to get the belligerents in the Arab-Israeli conflict to cooperate over the Jordan river, in the 1950s. The hope was that cooperation on this low politics issue would spill over and have a positive impact on the larger political conflict. It did not, however, and the Johnston Plan failed precisely *because* of the larger political conflict. Arab riparians feared it would enable Israel to absorb more Jewish immigration; Israel feared that this would guarantee the Arabs future claims to Upper Jordan water and encourage demands for territorial changes.[31] Another illustration of interstate conflict's impeding cooperation is provided by the Syrian rejection of a 1965 Turkish offer to conclude a binding water-sharing agreement over *all* rivers crossing their joint boundaries, including the Orontes river. The Orontes originates in central Lebanon and flows through Syria and Turkey before emptying into the Mediterranean. Syria rejected that proposal because the river flows through the disputed Iskenderun province, and from a Syrian perspective, agreement over the Orontes would imply Syrian recognition of Turkey's occupation of Iskenderun.[32]

For a basinwide agreement between Turkey, Syria, and Iraq, the three riparians must have the political will to sacrifice part of their national sovereignty. They would have to bypass politics and neutralize ideological issues. In addition, success of institutional arrangements are dependent on "elite value complimentarity."[33]

However, this is not likely to happen in the present political climate. Elites in the Middle East guard their sovereignty very jealously, and the conflictual nature of the regional political environment precludes the possibility that they may give up any part of their sovereignty. Illustration of the importance that elites attach to sovereignty is provided by the proposals that each riparian has advanced. Each proposal, depending on the state's riparian situation, protects self-interest but provides only half solutions to others. Two Turkish proposals are cases in point. In 1988, Turkey proposed the concept of a "peace pipeline" to serve both Gulf and Middle East countries. The proposal was to channel fresh water from the Ceyhan and Seyhan rivers in southern Turkey through Syria, Jordan, and Saudi Arabia to the Gulf. Two massive pipelines were to supply water to these countries—one to Jordanian and Syrian cities, and the other to Bahrain, Kuwait, Oman, Qatar, Saudi Arabia, and the United Arab Emirates.[34]

However, the pipeline project had to be dropped. Over and above the fact that it was cost-ineffective, the major obstacle had to do with regional politics: Syria did not want Israel to "gain";[35] Saudi and Kuwaiti officials feared giving the Turks a role in and possible control over their water sovereignty.[36] Other fears were related to the potential use of the pipelines for political blackmail or sabotage—precedents of pipeline sabotage and cutoffs in the Middle East are numerous.[37]

Another proposal that Turkey advanced, called the "Three Stage Plan for Optimum, Equitable and Reasonable Utilization of the Transboundary Watercourses for the Tigris-Euphrates Basin," was rejected by Syria and Iraq on two grounds. First, the plan was a repetition of the two critical concepts that had already been rejected, namely the concept of "transboundary watercourses," which implicitly rejected the notion of co-sovereignty, and the idea of the "Tigris-Euphrates Basin," which referred to the rivers as a single system. Second, the plan's proposal to determine jointly the common use of the waters by all three countries and the suggestion that high technologies be applied to minimize the requirements for agriculture were seen as an infringement on their sovereignty.[38]

Political "realists," for their part, make a third argument—that cooperation on such issues of low politics as water-sharing could be attained if there are parallel high politics issues over which states collaborate. The only national security issue that binds both Turkey and Syria is their rejection of the establishment of an independent Kurdish state. To be sure, this attitude was not meant solely to cajole Turkey but to satisfy Syria's self-interest. Syria has a Kurdish minority of its own and also feels threatened by Kurdish national aspirations. Moreover, Syria's self-proclaimed role as a pan-Arab leader precludes the dismemberment of a fellow Arab country. If there is going to be an agreement between Turkey and Syria over water-sharing in the Euphrates basin, it is the Kurdish issue that is most likely to make that possible.

IS THERE A SOLUTION?

In the absence of an optimal basinwide agreement, the only framework with which the three riparians can cooperate is one that preserves their individual sovereignty over their respective internal segments of the rivers.

Of all the proposals that have been advanced to resolve the dispute over water rights, the only one that seems flexible enough to be implemented is the Syrian proposal, which was also the most interesting because it was the most practical and because it had common ground elements.[39] The Syrian proposal consists of the following: First, it calls on the JTC to calculate the flow of the two international rivers. Second, the JTC is to estimate *grosso modo* the quantity of water needed by each riparian for ongoing and future projects. Third, the JTC would determine the quota of water to which each riparian is entitled, emphasizing the right of each to utilize its share according to its own social and economic circumstances. Since the quantity of available water is not sufficient to satisfy the needs of all three riparians, each country would have to prioritize projects.

Like all proposals, the Syrian one has its limitations. The drawback is that dividing a scarce resource is hardly either a scientific or an optimum solution and "does not alleviate scarcity, irrespective of how equitable the allocation procedure is."[40] Nor does the proposal take the seasonality of the Euphrates into account. Its flow varies considerably on a seasonal and annual basis, and historically, the river has been prone to regular and severe flooding.

What is interesting about the Syrian proposal though is its attempt to be scientifically based and hence apolitical. It attempts to secure the rights of all riparians in a manner both equitable and reasonable. And if taken to its natural conclusion, the proposal has the merit in taking conservation and economics into account. The first encourages riparians to choose projects that require less water, enabling them in the process to export excess water to other riparians who have exceeded their quota.

The Syrian proposal is to some degree similar to the India-Pakistan agreement over the Indus waters. Although India and Pakistan were divided by political and confessional conflict, and the balance of power tilted markedly in India's favor, the World Bank, acting as the mediator, formulated an agreement on the basis of non-interdependence. The mediator appreciated that cooperation via integrated development was unrealistic in this particular case, and in essence the plan extended the process of partition.[41]

CONCLUSION

Several factors impede a basinwide agreement between the three riparians over the use of the waters of the Euphrates. The existence of political conflict between Turkey and Syria on the one hand and between Syria and Iraq on the other, and the lack of trust among the three, render functional cooperation very difficult to achieve. It is unlikely that their security-conscious elites would give up any part of their sovereignty to transnational organizations. The mistrust and suspicion that generally characterize interstate relations are more prominent in the Middle East because bitter memories coexist with perceptions of threat held by narrowly based regimes. Turkey, Syria, and Iraq share many commonalties: contiguous political boundaries, ambitions to dominate the region, internal instability fueled by ethnic and/or sectarian conflict, and external challenges. The authoritarian nature of the regimes and their perceptions of threat aggravate this situation. In this highly charged political environment, it is hardly surprising that the competing elites use all available means to advance their self-interest.

The conflict over riparian rights between Turkey, Syria, and Iraq must be seen in this context. The dispute over which the three riparians are deadlocked cannot be isolated from the larger political context. Like everything else, hydropolitics will be conducted according to the rules of power politics, and any attempt to narrow regional political differences through a water-sharing agreement is likely to fail. Although cooperation along rational lines is desirable, it is unlikely given the present political state of the area. The Middle East has shown a remarkable capacity to resist change. The fact that democratization has swept many states of the Third World during the 1980s and 1990s, but not those in the Middle East, is one case in point. States in the Middle East will not yield to transnational forces easily, or soon. The creation of epistemic communities is dependent on a political will, which at present does not exist. Nor should we be made too hopeful by the promise of interdependence. As one Turkish official put it, "in this region, interdependence is understood as the opposite of independence. Every country here seeks a kind of self-sufficiency in every field, because they don't trust the others."[42]

In the immediate future, the initiative to solve the water dispute must be facilitated by a third party, preferably an NGO like the World Bank, with prior experience in riparian disputes. The impartial mediator must build on the Syrian proposal, determine the needs of the riparians, and apportion the waters accordingly.[43] While dividing up a scarce resource is hardly the ideal answer, it appears to be the most attainable. Each state must devise priorities in its development schemes. Although prioritization requires difficult political decisions, the subject can no longer be ignored.

CHAPTER NINE

ISRAELI-TURKISH RELATIONS
A Turkish "Periphery Strategy"?

Alan Makovsky

The post–Cold War era in Turkey has been marked by an assertiveness in foreign policy thought impossible in the first sixty-five years of the republic that rose in 1923 on the ashes of the Ottoman Empire. Gone are the reticence about asserting Turkish interests outside the republic's borders, the fear of contact with the so-called "outside Turks"—indeed, the passivity and insularity implied by the Atatürk dictum "peace at home, peace abroad."

Turkey was one of the first states to recognize the independence of the former Soviet republics of Central Asia and the Caucasus, and with the exception of Armenia, it has determinedly pursued relations with them ever since. In the Balkans, Ankara moved boldly to establish close ties with the new states of Bosnia and Macedonia, and with post-communist Albania. In addition, the Turks have established ties, of varying degrees of formality, with Tatars and other Turkic and non-Turkic Muslim groups in the Russian Federation. A nascent organization of Black Sea states, the Black Sea Economic Cooperation Zone, was born of Turkish initiative. Turkish ties with former Warsaw Pact enemy Bulgaria have also improved.

Two main factors account for new Turkish activism throughout the region: its growing self-confidence, based on an expanding economy and an improved and more experienced military, and changed regional circumstances that, among other things, have weakened Turkey's neighbors.

To Turkey's south, in the Middle East, however, its foreign policy remains largely reactive, somewhat in the old mode. Relations with

Syria are deeply troubled, with Iraq frozen, with Iran uneasy; the borders of all three have been a source of attacks by the Kurdistan Workers Party, the PKK. When Foreign Minister Deniz Baykal reviewed Turkey's foreign policy for the parliament in November 1995, virtually his only references to the Middle East dwelt on the terrorism and instability that Turkey endures and must combat.

The irony is that not too long ago the Middle East was the one area where Turkey acted with greatest policy initiative. Once the great hope of Turkish economic recovery and diplomatic support, the Middle East today provides few opportunities for Ankara. Turkish efforts to increase exports began in the late 1970s with a Middle Eastern focus, primarily oriented toward Libya, Iraq, and Iran. By 1982, more Turkish exports went to the Islamic world (47 percent of all exports) than to Turkey's Organization for Economic Cooperation and Development (OECD) partners (44 percent).[1]

That experience helped charge Turkey's export batteries, but it was short-lived. Libya quickly proved an unreliable customer, usually delinquent in its payments. Iraq, once the second leading market for Turkish goods (after Germany), today is virtually closed to international business because of UN sanctions. Even before the 1990 Gulf crisis, however, exports to cash-strapped Iraq, impoverished by its war with Iran, were largely financed by credits from the Turkish Central Bank. Trade with Iran is also in steep decline from highwater marks of the 1980s. Among potentially significant Islamic trading partners in the Middle East, only Saudi Arabia has increased its purchases of Turkish products in recent years.

As a percentage of Turkey's total exports, trade with Islamic countries is in steady decline. By 1994, exports to Islamic countries accounted for only 12 percent of total Turkish exports.[2] An end to the UN sanctions against Iraq—formerly Turkey's second largest export market—would boost that figure, but the major trend in Turkey's trading patterns—more toward the West and less toward the Arab world and Iran—appears steady. With Turkey's admission to the customs union with the European Union (EU), which took effect on January 1, 1996, the trend will almost certainly accelerate.

Diplomatically, Turkey's long-standing effort to garner Arab support on the Cyprus issue has come to naught. Beginning in the mid-1960s, Turkey progressively cut back its support for Israel— in 1949, Turkey was the first Muslim state to recognize Israel, and it remained so until the 1979 Egypt-Israel peace treaty—and increasingly adopted Arab positions on the Arab-Israeli and Palestinian issues. As Henri Barkey has written, Ankara was convinced that the litmus test of its relations with the Arab world was its stand on the Palestinian issue; it hoped Arabs, in general, and Palestinians, in particular, would respond in kind on Cyprus.[3]

But the Arab world persisted in seeing the Cyprus issue not so much as a matter of Muslim solidarity as one that recalled Israeli occupation of Arab land and thus required Arab opposition to the Turkish occupation of northern Cyprus. The Arabs roundly condemned the Turkish Cypriot declaration of independence in 1983—to this day, only Turkey recognizes the Turkish Republic of Northern Cyprus—and the Islamic Conference Organization has never accorded the Turkish Cypriot community more than observer status.

Its efforts at courting its Muslim neighbors having proved largely unrequited, Ankara has recently changed its policy in the region, focusing again on improving relations with Israel even more vigorously than before. Begun in earnest only in late 1993, Ankara's initiative toward Jerusalem has been bold, creative, and, so far, effective in pursuing an initiative intended to produce strategic, diplomatic, and economic results.

The flowering of Turkish-Israeli relations over the past two years marks the coming of age of a relationship long desired by both parties. It is noteworthy for reasons beyond bilateral relations, however. It brings together the United States' two strongest military allies in the Middle East, both secular democracies, and the two states with the most dynamic private sectors. Their cooperation could create a powerful axis of influence in the region. Pursued deftly, it could help lay the foundation for an alliance of moderate, pro-Western states in the Middle East; though handled clumsily, it could intimidate both countries' Arab neighbors, provoking a backlash and dividing the region along Arab/non-Arab lines. Second, Turkish-Israeli cooperation could create particular problems for Syria, already at odds with both. A Turkish-Israeli decision to coordinate strategies against Syria —or, more accurately, Syrian perception that such coordination might exist—would complicate Syria's own strategic planning and its approach to peacemaking with Israel, its support for terrorism, and perhaps other policies as well.

A note of caution: There has been considerable speculation over the years about covert cooperation between Israeli and Turkish intelligence agencies—rumors of it persisted even when relations were at a low ebb in the 1970s and 1980s. They were fueled still further by Prime Minister Tansu Çiller's open calls for intelligence cooperation[4] and the reported hurry-up visit that the chief of Turkey's National Intelligence Organization made to Israel during Çiller's visit there in November 1994. No attempt is made here to speculate on the nature of covert bilateral cooperation or to ferret out a "secret history" of Turkish--Israeli relations; that is better to left to historians who may one day have access to relevant archives.

Covert relations, by their nature, are limited to the security field; wide-ranging cooperation is possible only in the light of day. David Ben-Gurion reportedly once complained that "the Turks have always treated us as one treats a mistress, and not as a partner in an openly avowed marriage."[5] What makes the recent departure in Israeli-Turkish relations interesting and potentially important is that Ankara has been openly seeking Jerusalem's hand.

Israel welcomes the prospect of close ties with Turkey, but it is apparently the more reticent of the two parties. It has been particularly restrained, at least publicly, regarding Turkey's evident desire for cooperation against Syria and the PKK. Ironically—that is, to anyone who has monitored Israel's long and often unhappy pursuit of the Turks and its seemingly intractable dispute with the Arabs—it is Ankara, not Jerusalem, that has called for "strategic cooperation" and collusion against "Syrian-sponsored terrorism."[6]

Throughout its history, particularly in the 1950s and 1960s, Israel has sought to boost ties with Turkey as part of a more widely conceived "periphery strategy"—focused on Iran and Ethiopia, as well—in an effort to develop friends on the borders of a hostile Arab world.[7] After a period of close bilateral ties in the 1950s, relations began to sour after the 1956 Sinai War. In the 1960s and 1970s, as Turkey was driven by both economic and diplomatic reasons to improve ties with the Arab world, Ankara began to loosen its Israel connection. Trade with Israel dipped to almost imperceptible levels and diplomatic relations were downgraded at Turkey's initiative.

During the prime ministry of Turgut Özal, relations began to improve gradually. This mainly reflected Özal's desire to improve Turkish relations with the United States, particularly the Congress, and he hoped influential Jewish Americans would be friendly to the effort. By 1990, as it was becoming clear that Turkey had derived neither the economic nor the diplomatic benefit it had hoped from Islamic world ties—and after the PLO had implicitly recognized Israel in a November 1988 declaration of the Palestine National Council—the way was paved for a further improvement in relations.

With the October 1991 Madrid peace conference on the Middle East and the beginning of the peace process—in short, as the Arab world's own attitude toward Israel began to soften—Turkey finally took the long-awaited step of establishing full ambassadorial-level relations with the Jewish state in December 1991. Still, it was a step that connoted more necessity than warmth, since it was a de facto requirement for participation in the multilateral track of the Middle East peace process.[8] Moreover, rival Greece's recognition of Israel some months earlier—an action pressed upon Athens by its EU partners—had left Turkey in an embarrassing spotlight as the only NATO state without an ambassador in Israel.

The real breakthrough in Turkish-Israeli relations, which seems to have removed all obstacles to close bilateral ties, was the signing in September 1993 of the Israel-PLO Declaration of Principles (DOP), by which the two signatories formally recognized one another. From Ankara's perspective the DOP put to rest the Palestinian problem as a restraint on ties with Israel. Less than two months later, Turkish foreign minister Hikmet Çetin made Ankara's first-ever foreign ministerial visit to Israel, highlighted by his calls for wide-ranging bilateral cooperation.

The progress of bilateral ties and the change in tone of Turkey's public posture toward Israel is illustrated by two events. In December 1991, when the United Nations General Assembly voted to repeal its 1975 resolution equating Zionism with racism, Turkey could bring itself to do no more than abstain while the repeal resolution passed overwhelmingly: 111 to 25, with thirteen abstentions.[9] Yet less than three years later, in November 1994, when Turkish Prime Minister Tansu Çiller became the first Turkish prime minister to visit Israel, she showed no hesitation whatsoever about the Zionist philosophy that had led to the creation of the state of Israel and the displacement of hundreds of thousands of Palestinian Arabs. She spoke warmly of Israel's accomplishments and favorably of David Ben-Gurion, Israel's founding father, noting that both Israel and Turkey had been "blessed with unique and courageous founding fathers—Atatürk and Ben-Gurion—whose best achievements continue as guideposts for our respective nations today, leaders who[se reputations] have stood up in history." During the state banquet in her honor, Çiller even at one point referred to Israel as the "Promised Land"—provoking a political mini-firestorm back home. The willingness of a Turkish leader to praise Israel's origins—even to compare its founder with the revered Atatürk—shows how far Israel had come in achieving legitimacy in the eyes of the world and in the eyes of the Turkish government.

FACTORS SHAPING TURKEY'S ISRAEL INITIATIVE

Israel has long desired close relations with Ankara. Turkey's long borders with Iran, Iraq, and Syria are of obvious geopolitical interest for Israel, and relations with Turkey, a Muslim-majority state, have been useful in helping Israel dilute the religious component of its conflict with the Arabs and fend off charges that Zionism is somehow inherently anti-Islamic. But it had only modest success until a combination of circumstances and revised policy goals pushed Turkey itself toward closer ties. Three factors combined to encourage Ankara to boost its relations with Israel.

The most unambiguous was the conclusion of the Israel-PLO agreement. The Rabin-Arafat handshake freed Turkey to pursue the kind of relations with Israel much of the Turkish security and foreign affairs establishment had long desired and that, many believe, the two states already pursued in a quiet and limited way. In effect, the Declaration of Principles brought Israeli-Turkish relations into the light of day.

In addition, the Turkish government was disappointed in the state of its relations with the Arab states, having grown disaffected with a pro-Arab policy that failed to pay anticipated diplomatic and economic dividends. Meanwhile, disagreements over water are exacerbating Turkish-Arab tensions.

On the wider stage, the end of the Cold War has shaken Turkey's idea of itself in relation to both long-time allies and neighbors. In the late 1980s and early 1990s—that is, the period leading directly up to Turkey's 1993 initiative toward Israel—Turkey's stock as a NATO security asset appeared to be in decline. Ankara's Gulf War experience—when NATO responded to the danger of an Iraqi attack on Turkey only with great reluctance and then in a meager and nearly worthless fashion—had diminished its confidence in NATO security guarantees, particularly against Middle Eastern threats. In response, Turkey apparently felt it had to become more proactive in pursuing security policies in its Middle Eastern neighborhood.

For Turkish security planners, the Gulf War experience only confirmed what they had long suspected: that West Europeans saw NATO strictly as an organization for deterring or dealing with conflicts inside Europe and had no intention of sending soldiers to die in fending off a non-European attack on a peripheral NATO state—or, put another way, in a Muslim attack on Muslim Turkey. Thus, the need to seek Middle Eastern solutions to its Middle Eastern problems emerged as an important incentive to Turkish policymakers in pursuing ties with Israel.

GOALS

Turkey envisions potentially wide-ranging benefits from close ties with Israel. One is political-diplomatic in motivation, aimed at boosting support in the United States and, to some extent, Western Europe. In initiating its policy of close ties with Israel, Ankara hoped that it would score points with the U.S. government, particularly the Congress, which historically has been ambivalent toward Turkey. Although Turkey has been the number-three recipient (after Egypt and Israel) of foreign aid from the United States since 1980, it has also been subjected to repeated criticism and efforts to limit aid levels based on its human rights record, potentially embarrassing efforts to commemorate the "Armenian genocide," and, most seriously, the 1975–78 arms embargo that responded to Turkey's 1974 military intervention in Cyprus.

The process by which friendship with Israel may translate into support in the U.S. Congress is at best uncertain. Pro-Israeli lobbyists support foreign aid bills but do not advocate or support specific aid levels for other states (with the exception, perhaps, of Egypt, Jordan, and the PLO, the Arab parties that have entered into peace arrangements with Israel). Still, the goodwill that Ankara's good relations with Israel earns Turkey with the many pro-Israel members stand it in good stead when issues of importance to the Turks come up in Congress.

Good relations with Israel have already paid a handsome dividend for Turkey in its efforts to integrate with Western Europe. Israeli diplomats were very active in support of Turkey's bid to have its customs union agreement with the EU ratified by the European Parliament in December 1995. Drawing on his Socialist International contacts, Israeli Prime Minister Shimon Peres telephoned such leading European socialists as Spanish Prime Minister Felipe Gonzalez, German socialist leader Rudolf Scharping, and British socialist leader Tony Blair to lobby on Turkey's behalf. Prior to the ratification vote—which ultimately passed by nearly 200 votes in the 636-seat body—the socialists were widely viewed as holding the balance of power in what many thought would be a close vote. Çiller publicly thanked Israel for its efforts and sent Peres a personal note of gratitude.[10]

Israeli-Turkish cooperation is also shaped by certain common strategic characteristics, interests, and views: U.S.-supplied military inventories; loyalties to the West and to such Western values as democracy and secularism; mutually perceived enemies such as Syria; and, more generally, terrorism and Islamic fundamentalism. In her call for "a strategic relationship" with Israel, Prime Minister Çiller probably envisioned at least three dimensions to bilateral security cooperation: materiel, cooperation against Syria, and cooperation against the PKK.

Because both states' military inventories are based on U.S. equipment, Turkey sees Israel as an alternative and at times cheaper source of supply—and as a source that, unlike the U.S. Congress, will not raise quibbles about human rights when considering arms sales. Thus Turkey decided to turn to Israel for an upgrade of its aging fleet of F-4 Phantom jet fighters and considered buying an in-air refueling tanker from the Israelis. This is probably the area of bilateral security cooperation with the most potential. In addition to sales and upgrades, arrangements for arms training and joint production are also possible in the future.

Cooperation on dealing with the PKK and Syria is problematic because of the parties' differing strategic aims vis-à-vis different terrorist groups. Still, Israel and Turkey share a fundamental similarity of approach toward terrorism, as was revealed during debate over the final communiqué from the Euro-Med Conference at Barcelona. The Israeli-Turkish approach prompted Syrian Foreign Minister Faruq Sharaa to complain, "Israel and Turkey insist on defining resistance movements as terrorism as well. In citing excuses such as the

PKK and the opposition movement in Southern Lebanon respectively, Israel and Turkey attempt to present all armed movements as terrorism. Syria cannot accept this."[11]

Çiller has publicly raised the prospect of common effort against Islamic fundamentalism, including "Hizbullah"; in itself, it is remarkable that the leader of a Muslim-majority state would publicly suggest cooperation of this type with Jewish Israel. Still, Turkish and Israeli concerns and interests diverge in this area as well. Behind-the-scenes intelligence-sharing about Islamic terrorism groups is possible, of course. For example, both parties are interested in the international terrorist threat, the role played by third-party states such as Iran in fundamentalist terrorism, and international funding of Islamic fundamentalism. But the fact that each faces different enemies—in Israel's case, Hamas, Palestinian Islamic Jihad, and southern Lebanon-based Hizbullah, and in Turkey's case, less well-known groups, such as IBDA-C and Turkey-based Islamic Jihad and Hizbullah, plus the PKK—in different circumstances makes meaningful, ongoing, active cooperation less likely.

Moreover, the primary problem Turkey faces from fundamentalism is not violence but the electoral challenge from the fundamentalist Refah Party, as December 1995 elections showed. Notwithstanding Çiller's public call for cooperation, any type of publicized joint effort against terrorism would provide rhetorical fodder for Refah and almost certainly would pose political problems for a Turkish government.

As noted, Turkey's desire for Israeli cooperation against Syria is something of a mirror image of Israel's strategy toward Turkey and other states on the Arab-world periphery in the 1950s. Israel, however, is ambivalent about close cooperation with Turkey if it appears too obviously aimed at Syria. Asked about this in summer 1994, Israeli ambassador to the United States Itamar Rabinovich said that Jerusalem did not want to give Asad the impression that Israel and Turkey are "ganging up on him."[12] With Shimon Peres as prime minister, Israel is probably even less inclined toward policies that appear confrontational toward Syria than was the Rabin government. Peres, who in any case generally puts emphasis on building Israel's relations with Arab states as part of his envisioned "new Middle East,"[13] is particularly keen to complete a peace agreement with Syria before he faces the Israeli electorate in elections scheduled for fall 1996.

Rabin, by contrast, appeared to have grown skeptical of the possibility for pre-election progress on the Syrian track prior to his assassination in November 1995.

Quiet intelligence and security cooperation against Syria is possible and, indeed, probably assumed to exist by Damascus. Even without touting it as such, Turkish-Israeli coziness sounds a powerful note of caution to Syria, which must contemplate the possibility of unprecedented and growing cooperation between the U.S.-equipped militaries of its northern and southern neighbors. Syria already has been given pause by reciprocal visits of Turkish and Israeli air force chiefs, rumors of a joint air force exercise, and the F-4 upgrade deal, as well as Israeli President Ezer Weizman's January 1994 aerial tour of Turkey's Southeast Anatolia Project (GAP). Sharaa's comment before the Barcelona conference about a common Turkish-Israeli view of terrorism further suggests that Syria senses collusion.

Turkey also intends to look out for its own interests in the ongoing Middle East peace process, about which it remains ambivalent. On the one hand, Ankara strongly desires Arab-Israeli peace, the lack of which has contributed to instability on its borders and, because of objections from Arab neighbors, limited its ability to pursue strategic ties with Israel. On the other, it recognizes that Israeli-Syrian peace contains potential pitfalls for its own strategic interests. Thus, Turkey hopes to influence Israel to support its interests regarding water and PKK terrorism in Israeli peace negotiations with Syria. Primarily, this means seeking assurances that the Israeli-Syrian water problem will not be solved by means of further demands on Turkish water and that Syria will be required to cease its support of all terrorist groups, including the PKK, when peace is signed with Israel.

Additionally, Ankara hopes Jerusalem will use its influence in Washington to ensure that Syria is not removed from the U.S. list of state-sponsors of terrorism until it ends its support for the PKK and to ensure that Syria is not too abundantly rewarded by the United States, particularly in military terms, for making peace with Israel. Given its current enmity with Syria, one of the last things Turkey would like to see is a U.S.-Syrian relationship on a par with those Egypt and, more recently, Jordan have developed with Washington in the wake of their respective peace agreements with Israel.

Reflecting its concern that a post-peace Syria will redeploy its Israel-focused military to the north and train its guns on Turkey instead, Ankara may also hope to influence Israel regarding whatever post-peace military arrangements are incorporated into an Israeli-Syrian peace treaty. Limited-force and limited-equipment zones will almost certainly be an element of a post-peace Israeli-Syrian security regime, however. The nature of the resultant Syrian redeployment could have a serious impact on Turkish security; Ankara will want to use its regular consultations with Jerusalem, called for in a November 1993 Memorandum of Understanding, to learn about and, insofar as possible, influence Israel's positions on this issue. It is possible that Ankara may even want to consider joining in a subregional security zone in an effort to put a cap on Syrian troop and equipment levels deployed on the Turkish border.

For both economic and security reasons, Turkey would like to form a partnership with Israel to support multilateral efforts at regionwide stability. Turkey sees potential commercial benefit in the variety of transnational projects, for infrastructure and otherwise, being discussed in the multilateral component of the Middle East peace process. And, like Israel, Turkey hopes that regional integration projects will increase the number of individuals and states with a stake in regionwide peace, help end the Arab-Israeli dispute, encourage the creation of regionwide security structures like those in Europe, isolate —or seduce into cooperation—those states that continue to oppose peace, and ultimately tame a region that has become increasingly unruly in recent years despite gains in Arab-Israeli peace. Regional cooperation—in the Turkish view—can forge a moderate alliance for peace and against terrorism, while isolating and neutralizing recidivist states.

As a strong supporter of regional integration projects, Ankara has been an enthusiastic backer of the multilateral negotiations component of the Middle East peace process, as well as such associated activities as the Middle East/North Africa Economic Summits held in Casablanca in 1994 and Amman in 1995 and scheduled for Cairo in 1996.[14] Prime Minister Çiller was one of the few heads of government to attend the landmark Casablanca summit. In her speech there, she set forth Turkey's vision of a regional peace based on security-related confidence-building measures and regional "economic interdependencies."[15]

Turkey was the first, so far the only, state to endorse an Israeli-Jordanian idea for establishing a Conference on Security and Cooperation in the Middle East (CSCME) as an analogue to the Conference on Security and Cooperation in Europe.[16] Foreign Minister Peres first publicized the CSCME proposal during his April 1994 visit to Turkey; Ankara immediately endorsed it. CSCME was endorsed in the Israel-Jordan Peace Treaty but is moribund at this time. Still, it appears that the Middle East multilateral negotiations and associated activities stemming from the economic summits may well evolve into something very much like a CSCME.[17]

Turkey's stake in Middle Eastern security—even a certain status as a quasi-Middle Eastern state—was implicitly acknowledged in the Conventional Forces in Europe (CFE) agreement of 1990. At its request, Turkey was granted a so-called "exclusion zone" in the southeastern portion of the country that borders Syria, Iraq, and Iran. Within this exclusion zone, there are no limits on the troops and equipment that Turkey is allowed to deploy. (Elsewhere in its territory, it is bound to limits imposed by the CFE agreement.) Ankara based its claim of an exclusion zone on the fact that it has neighbors that are not part of the CFE regime.

Given its concern about Middle Eastern security and its experience in European security regimes, Turkey takes an active role in the multilateral negotiations on Arms Control and Regional Security (ACRS), where it serves as chairman, or "mentor," of workshops on "exchange of military information and prenotification of certain military activities" and has hosted several meetings of the "operational basket" group. Both groups are devoted to discussing and devising conventional military confidence-building measures, of the sort that characterize European security arrangements, for the Middle East.

Although Turkey participates in the multilaterals as an extra-regional, a senior foreign ministry official, speaking in a background interview in 1994, said that Ankara would consider joining "the right kind" of Middle Eastern security regime, that is, one that protects Turkish security interests. Of course, that almost inevitably would require that Turkey's bordering Middle Eastern neighbors, Syria, Iraq, and Iran—none of which are currently part of the ACRS process —would join the regime.

Turkey and Israel have put forth similar views on important issues in the ACRS working group. One of the key disputes within ACRS has been the fundamental issue of what its agenda should be —specifically, whether it should focus first on arms control and

weapons of mass destruction, as Egypt and most of the Arab participants say, or on conventional military confidence-building measures,
as Israel insists with increasing backing from Jordan. With the background of its European experience, Turkey has quietly but consistently backed the Israeli view that ACRS should focus its energies
first on conventional measures for the sake of confidence-building, as
in the Helsinki process.

Turkey also has been somewhat active in the Refugee Working
Group, for which it served as host of a plenary meeting in December
1994. It has been little involved in the other three working groups on
regional economic development, the environment, and water resources. Its minimal level of participation has been most conspicuous
in the water resources group, since Turkey is one of the few Middle
Eastern states with abundant water resources and since many
observers believe that any regionwide solution to the water problem
will involve Turkish water. (Indeed, Ankara itself has proposed pip-
ing Turkish water as far south as the Arabian Peninsula to help with
Middle Eastern water shortages.) However, Turkish views on water
are currently a source of controversy in the region, and many pre-
sume that Turkey does not want to subject its water to discussion in a
forum that would almost certainly prove unfriendly.[18]

THE PALESTINIAN DIMENSION

As it has sought to improve its ties with Israel, the Turkish government has continued to support the Palestinians for the sake of enhancing Middle Eastern stability, maintaining its diplomatic standing
with the Arab world, and—not least important—satisfying domestic
political opinion. Turkish public attitudes on the Israeli-Palestinian
issue are complicated. As perceived by Turkish leaders, however, a significant portion of the public would not want Ankara simply to discard
its interest in the Palestinians for the sake of pursuing ties with Israel.

Turkey was one of the first states to recognize the state of "Palestine"
following its declaration by the PLO's Palestine National Council in
November 1988. Ankara had recognized the PLO and granted diplomatic status to its Ankara representative in 1979, and this recognition
remains intact today. Where the United States and most Western states
speak of "the Palestinian Authority," "the PLO," and "Chairman
Arafat," Ankara speaks of "Palestine" and "President Arafat."

When Turkey raised its diplomatic relations with Israel to ambassadorial level in December 1991, it did the same with "Palestine," later joining the international effort to aid Palestinian autonomy in the West Bank and the Gaza Strip mounted following the September 1993 signing of the Israel-PLO Declaration of Principles. Ankara donated $2 million to the Palestinians and pledged a further $50 million in trade credits.

During her November 1994 visit to Israel, Prime Minister Çiller visited Palestinian authority head Yasir Arafat in Gaza; she was the first head of government to do so. Arafat also has been a relatively frequent visitor to Ankara over the years, most recently in June 1995. At Arafat's request, Turkey also sent a delegation of four academicians to monitor Palestinians' first-ever elections in January 1996.

Following her visit to Gaza, Çiller touched off a diplomatic mini-flap in Israel by departing from her schedule to make an unannounced stop at Orient House, the PLO's unofficial headquarters in East Jerusalem, where she met with PLO official Faisal Husseini, who heads the Palestinians' "Jerusalem Committee." Orient House is a source of controversy in Israeli domestic and foreign politics, since Israel claims that the presence of a PLO institution in Jerusalem is a violation of the Declaration of Principles so long as no agreement has been reached on Jerusalem's final status.

Çiller's visit to Orient House annoyed and chagrined the Rabin government. Rabin himself was reportedly angry, but confined his remarks to saying that though he regretted the incident, it would not affect bilateral ties.[19] However, the Orient House incident demonstrated how Turkey's perceived obligation to maintain a semblance of balance in its ties with Israel and the Palestinians can create bumps in an otherwise smooth evolution of close relations with Israel.

Turkey has clearly been successful in retaining its credibility with both Israelis and Palestinians. Both parties requested Turkey to serve as part of the proposed Temporary International Presence (TIP) foreseen by the May 1994 Gaza-Jericho agreement (Article XXI) to observe implementation of the first stage of the Declaration of Principles.[20]

WIDE-RANGING TIES

Many elements have highlighted the growing Israeli-Turkish relationship since the signing of the DOP. These include the beginning of senior-level visits between the states. In 1992, Turkish Tourism Minister Abdulkadir Ates made the first cabinet-level visit to Israel in some two decades. Before 1993, there had never been a presidential, prime ministerial, or foreign ministerial visit. Since then, there have been four, with another scheduled for March 1996.

A private visit by Israeli President Chaim Herzog in summer 1992 had the quality of an official visit. On that occasion, a gala party was held at one of Istanbul's finest Ottoman palaces to commemorate the 500th anniversary of the arrival on Ottoman shores of Sephardim following the great expulsion from Spain. With Herzog the guest of honor, the private party was attended by President Turgut Özal, Prime Minister Süleyman Demirel, and other members of the Turkish establishment, and the Turkish press accorded the celebration heavy coverage. Although unofficial, that event constituted a "coming-out party" of sorts for Israeli-Turkish relations.

The signing of the Israel-PLO Declaration of Principles on September 13, 1993, turned the page to a new era of Israeli-Turkish relations. Israel's recognition of the PLO—and the PLO's of Israel—meant that Ankara no longer had to restrain its ties with Jerusalem in order to impress the Arab world. A series of "firsts" then ensued: Çetin's visit to Israel in November 1993;[21] Israeli President Ezer Weizman's visit to Turkey in January 1994 (official, unlike Herzog's); Israeli Foreign Minister Shimon Peres's visit to Turkey in April 1994; and Turkish Prime Minister Tansu Çiller's visit to Israel in November 1994. President Demirel is scheduled to visit Israel in March 1996.

It is noteworthy that the scheduling of Demirel's 1996 trip was finalized only after Refah's success in the December 1995 parliamentary elections. In addition, Deputy Foreign Minister Onur Oymen visited Israel in January 1996. Together, these facts suggest that the Turkish foreign policy establishment does not intend to let the election results deter it from vigorously pursuing ties with Israel, at least as long as Refah is not part of the government.

Ministerial and working level visits between Turkey and Israel have now become almost routine. Others, such as military officials, parliamentarians, and opposition politicians, have also joined the line of visitors. One sign of the wide acceptance that Israel has gained in Turkey was the 1995 visit of former prime minister Bulent Ecevit, currently head of the Democratic Left Party, which finished fourth in the 1995 elections. Ecevit, a populist-style critic of many of

Turkey's more pro-U.S. and pro-Western policies, nevertheless has pronounced himself a supporter of strong Turkish-Israeli ties.[22] Ultra-nationalist right-wing leader Alparslan Türkes also favors close bilateral ties and has reportedly expressed interest in visiting Israel.

Agreements

Since the breakthrough in Turkish-Israeli relations in 1993, Ankara and Jerusalem have signed three diplomatic agreements, with a free-trade agreement currently under negotiation. The three already signed are a Memorandum of Understanding (MOU), essentially a general statement of an agenda for future relations, signed during the Çetin visit; an agreement on cooperation in the areas of international crime, narcotics-trafficking, and terrorism; and a trilateral agreement signed with the United States on cooperation on development projects in Central Asia.

Taken together, these agreements amount to little substantive, at least so far. Their more important purpose is to signal commitment to and establish a framework for future cooperation. The "Memorandum on Mutual Understanding and Guidelines on Cooperation" signed during Çetin's November 1993 visit pledged interparliamentary contacts, regular foreign ministry consultations on "international, regional, and bilateral issues of mutual interest," and efforts to boost trade and economic and technological cooperation in a variety of areas. One of the MOU's few philosophical statements— one that probably speaks genuinely to a concern of both parties —embraces the notion that "peace-building through increased cooperation and in a spirit of regional solidarity, embracing all the peoples of the area, . . . [is] a historic mission of long-term global significance."

Despite its title, the agreement on terrorism, drugs, and crime does not appear to pack a lot of wallop. Although its preamble decries "terrorism which denies democratic values and human rights," its operative section pledges the parties only to "cooperate in the exchange of information and experience regarding the security measures taken for the protection of the public." This cooperation, it specifies, should be carried out by "police authorities."

The Central Asia agreement is focused on small projects and thus far has been slow to move toward implementation. The initial project is slated to be a $1.5 million model-farm effort in Turkmenistan and Uzbekistan. Among the several problems that have delayed the project has been the lack of funding from the United States. Nevertheless, Turkey's readiness to cooperate with Israel in Muslim Central Asia, which Ankara has seen as its own privileged sphere, is politically and symbolically important, a statement of Turkey's high regard for its ties with the Jewish state.

Economic and Trade Growth

The pending free-trade agreement is potentially the most important. Both sides stand to benefit significantly from a free-trade agreement. Economically, it would give a boost to already growing Israeli-Turkish trade, which had begun to increase before the 1993 DOP and has grown considerably since.

In general, Israeli-Turkish trade relations have marched in lockstep with bilateral political relations. Bilateral trade was significant in the 1950s, but began to level off and decline following the Suez war of 1956. It then slipped to negligible levels during the era of increasingly frigid relations that ensued in the 1960s, 1970s, and 1980s. It has grown steadily in the 1990s, however, with total trade volume of more than $200 million in 1993, nearly $300 million in 1994, and, based on mid-year projections, probably close to $400 million in 1995. In January 1996, some 170 Turkish companies displayed their wares in a week-long Turkish export exhibit in Tel Aviv. Continued growth is likely, particularly if a free-trade agreement is in place between the two most dynamic private sectors in the Middle East.

The free-trade agreement was announced as a goal during Çetin's November 1993 visit to Israel. Although officials on both sides announced in each of the subsequent calendar years that the agreement would be completed within the year, it has been delayed until Demirel's March 1996 trip. Based on interviews with officials of both states, it appears that the primary, but not sole, obstacle to completion of the agreement has been Israeli textile manufacturers' concern about competition from Turkish textiles. Some limit on Turkish textile exports, or at least a set of quotas to be phased out only gradually, is likely to be a feature of the agreement. A free trade agreement would be yet another step that creates strong bonds between two states—a fact that will not be missed by others in the region.

Military Cooperation

Thus far the most important manifestation of military cooperation has been the September 1995 initialing of a $590 million agreement for Israel Aircraft Industries to upgrade Turkey's F-4 Phantom fighter jets. Other, smaller projects are also in the works. An umbrella defense-industrial cooperation agreement to govern future joint projects is currently under negotiation.

Turkey also flirted with the possibility of purchasing an air tanker, for in-air refueling, from Israel, before the United States finally overcame its reportedly human rights–based hesitation and decided to sell a tanker to the Turks in 1994. This incident raised the possibility that Turkey might seek to use access to Israeli equipment as an alternative to equipment from the United States or as a means of exerting leverage on Washington regarding equipment availability, human rights or other conditions, or price. Still, the effectiveness of this gambit would be limited by the fact that virtually all of Israel's sophisticated military equipment includes U.S.-made parts and thus its sale to third parties requires Washington's approval.

Human-level Contacts

Even in the days when bilateral political relations were at their lowest ebb, human contacts between the two countries continued through the medium of Turkey's 20,000-plus Jews. Many Turkish Jews have relatives in Israel and travel there frequently—there are an estimated 80,000 Israelis of Turkish origin in Israel, mostly located in the Mediterranean coastal town Bat Yam.[23] Turkish-origin Israelis tend to retain fondness for and interest in developments in their former homeland—a set of feelings more akin to that of Western-origin Israelis than to that of most other Israelis originally from Muslim-majority states. When Prime Minister Çiller visited Israel in November 1994, the Bat Yam Turkish-origin community hosted her at a Sabbath meal.

Recently the level of human contact has increased considerably, as Turkey has become a choice destination for Israeli tourists. In 1993, there were reportedly some 100,000 Israeli tourist entries to Turkey. That figure tripled the following year, when Turkey became the number-one tourist destination for Israelis. The 300,000 level appeared likely to be achieved again in 1995. Israeli tourists are attracted by the modest cost of holiday packages as well as Turkey's cultural attractions, its landscape and beaches, and its casinos—gambling is legal in Turkey but not in Israel.[24] In 1994, experiencing their worst economic year since an economic restructuring plan was put into place in 1980, most Turks were particularly grateful for the infusion of badly needed foreign currency.

By contrast, there has been no wave of Turkish tourists in the other direction. Reportedly there were 8,000 Turkish tourist entries into Israel in 1993, mainly by Turkish Jews. [25] Approximately 5,000 Turks are working as laborers in Israel, many of them illegally. Poor treatment of Turkish workers in Israel was an object of protest by Turkish Ambassador Onur Gökçe in early 1995. Israeli Labor Minister Ora Namir publicly joined the ambassador's complaint, affirming the need for improvements in treatment of Turkish workers and thus helping defuse a potential source of bilateral tension. Despite these problems, the willingness of Israelis to recruit Turkish workers, like the Israeli tourism to Turkey and the increased trade, is a sign of the growing comfort level between the two nations.

POTENTIAL OBSTACLES

Whether this rapid pace of improvement in relations can continue is open to question. Major policy considerations on both sides could have a significant effect on the pace and scope of that improvement.

In the case of Israel, that consideration is the peace process, which complicates the pursuit of any alliance against Syria. Insofar as Turkey is interested in pursuing a common front against Syria, Ankara will find Israel a reluctant partner. Israel has little desire to alienate Damascus or otherwise further complicate an already immensely complex peacemaking effort. Giving Asad some pause for thought as he reckons with the implications of Turkish-Israeli friendship is one thing. Implicitly threatening Damascus through overt cooperation with Turkey in an anti-Syrian alliance is quite another.

Perhaps indicative of Israeli Prime Minister Peres's determination not to let ties with Turkey interfere with peace efforts on the Syrian track was his response to a question at a National Press Club briefing in Washington in December 1995. Asked whether Israel would insist that Syria expel the PKK as part of a peace agreement and whether there had been any contact between Turkey and Israel on that issue, Peres acted baffled. He asked, "I am sorry, where did Turkey come in in the story? . . . I wouldn't like to speak about a situation which I am not sure that I am fully aware of. . . . [A]s far as we are concerned, there are ten refusal [i.e., Palestinian rejectionist] organizations in Syria, and we say repeatedly that Syria must put an end to it."[26]

The PKK issue constitutes a particularly thorny problem for Turkish-Israeli relations. It is widely believed that Ankara seeks Israeli support and help in its struggle against the PKK. In an interview with an Israeli journalist in early 1994, Prime Minister Çiller called for bilateral cooperation against terrorism, charging that Syria "abet[s] terrorism in Turkey,"[27] almost certainly a reference to Damascus' support for the PKK. At least publicly, however, Israel has shown no inclination to involve itself on this issue. Indeed, Israel thus far has never condemned the PKK nor labeled it "terrorist."[28]

Any number of reasons may explain Israeli reticence. First, many Israeli officials feel they have no business involving themselves in what is essentially an internal fight and a problem created at least in part by limitations on freedom of expression in Turkey and exacerbated by the heavy-handed manner in which the Turkish military has waged its war against the PKK. One Israeli diplomat, speaking on background about his government's reluctance to involve itself against the PKK, referred to the Turkish fight against the PKK as "a dirty business."

Second, whatever the merits of the Turkish case, some Israeli decision makers apparently feel that Israel, not heretofore a target for PKK terrorists, should hardly be seeking to add the PKK to the mix of Islamic fundamentalists and Palestinian extremists that already threatens the security of Israeli diplomats, private citizens, and establishments. Moreover, they may wish to avoid creating a new point of friction with Damascus, which supports the PKK.[29]

Third, there is some pro-Kurdish sentiment within the Israeli public and security establishment, though the Kurdish Jews in Israel are mainly of Iraqi origin, and Israeli political support for the Kurds has been limited to covert aid for Mustafa Barzani and his Kurdistan Democratic Party–led revolt against the Iraqi government in the 1970s. And there is little support for the PKK itself. But popular sympathy for the situation of the Kurds in general might be a factor in dissuading open government support of Ankara against the PKK. Over time, Israeli reluctance to satisfy the Turks on the PKK issue could dampen Ankara's enthusiasm for bilateral ties.

For Turkey, the major restraint on developing bilateral relations with Israel is domestic: the rising popularity of the pro-Islamist Refah Party. Refah gained international headlines in December 1995 when it emerged the winner, by a slight plurality, of national elections in Turkey. Although it appeared Refah probably would be unable to parlay its showing into a place in the government, the party's popularity appears to be rising inexorably; it has increased its vote in six consecutive national elections (parliamentary and municipal). Thus, Refah and its religious sentiments could have a strong impact on Turkish political discourse, and Turkish-Israeli relations could be significantly affected. As a result, secular politicians may become inclined to play down the more public aspects of Turkey's ties with Israel, particularly arms deals and high-level visits.

Israeli ambassador to Turkey Zvi Elpeleg spoke to this point in a post-election comment, warning that the results might "harm ties with Israel, because the secular politicians who make the decisions will tend to take the new realities into account and lean toward religion." Elpeleg made a harsh judgment on Turkish political leaders: "Political officials in Turkey look over their shoulders and try to meet the public's expectations. Now they will concede more to Islamic religious circles. . . . For years the secular parties' reaction to the growing strength of the Islamic radicals has been to attempt to appease them."[30]

Refah's own policy toward Israel is harsh and virtually uncompromisingly rejectionist. Refah leader Necmettin Erbakan frequently blames Israel and "Zionist conspiracies" for problems in Turkey. He has implicitly rejected the Israel-PLO agreements and seems never to have acknowledged Israel's right to exist. He bitterly criticizes Turkish politicians who support strong ties with Israel, accusing Tansu Çiller of being "Israel's puppet."[31] In his 1995 campaign speeches, Erbakan pledged that a Refah government would "liberate" Jerusalem, as well as Sarajevo, Nagorno Karabakh, and Chechnya. In summer 1995, the Refah mayor of Sanliurfa refused to meet with the visiting Israeli minister of agriculture. (However, in contrast, when the Refah mayor of Ankara gave a dinner for all embassies based in Ankara, he invited the Israelis, even including an Israeli flag at the placesetting.) In an interview with Israeli radio after the Turkish elections, Refah deputy chairman Abdullah Gül avoided direct answers to questions about the future course of Turkish-Israeli relations under a prospective Refah government. Asked about the attitude of a Refah-run Turkey to the Israeli-Palestinian peace process, however, Gül said, "It's up to the people over there. . . . I mean, if they are happy, well, we have to accept this."[32] He thus both indicated Refah's displeasure with the peace process (presumably because of Palestinian acceptance of Israel's existence) and signaled that while in government the party might have to resign itself to the fact of the process.

Still, while the Refah electoral victory creates an element of uncertainty in bilateral ties, it need not have a decisive effect. It is not at all clear that Refah owes much of its success to its foreign policy statements or that its foreign policy message has a wide resonance. Following Refah's strong showing in nationwide local elections in March 1994, for example, Turkey—and Israel—faced the dilemma of whether to proceed with Israeli Foreign Minister Shimon Peres's official visit to Ankara scheduled for the following month. Rather than cancel or postpone the visit, the parties let it proceed on schedule. The visit not only went forward without a hitch; it received high-profile and positive coverage in the mainstream Turkish press, with no visible sign of public opposition.

Even with Refah leading in public opinion polls throughout 1995, Israeli-Turkish ties saw no apparent decline in either the most important symbols of close ties—senior-level visits—or in substance. Indeed, the $590 million deal for the Israeli upgrade of Turkish F-4 fighter jets, announced in September 1995, was the boldest and most significant Israeli-Turkish agreement ever. Whether Turkish leaders, having now seen that Refah's 1995 showing was neither a fluke nor confined to the local arena, will be sufficiently self-assured to continue their vigorous pursuit of ties with Israel remains to be seen.

A freezing—or dramatic slowing in the pace—of the peace process, particularly on the Palestinian track and if it caused a serious erosion in the process of Arab world normalization with Israel, also could have a significantly restraining effect. In the case of a stalemated peace process, Turkey would take its cue from the Palestinians and the moderate Arab world, perhaps staying one step ahead of them in its public approach to Israel.

One additional domestic political factor in Turkey could affect bilateral ties: the mere departure from office of Prime Minister Çiller (which, in the aftermath of the December 1995 elections, appears to be a real possibility). A policy of close ties with Israel now appears to enjoy such across-the-secular-spectrum support in Turkey that it is often forgotten—or thought irrelevant—that all the dramatic improvements of recent years have taken place under the Çiller regime, which began in June 1993. Her warm regard for Israel appears to be personal as well as strategic.

Domestic politics would not constrain any Israeli government, either Labor or Likud, from pursuing close ties with Turkey. Only peace with Syria, or the quest for it, could alter somewhat the Israeli calculus of ties with Ankara, if Jerusalem feels it must modify some aspects of its relations with the Turks in order not to alienate Damascus, particularly under the Labor Party government. A Likud government would probably be much less concerned about the impact of close ties with Turkey on prospects for peace with Syria. Likud is deeply mistrustful of Syria, and its staunch opposition to returning the Golan Heights would make an Israeli-Syrian peace agreement unlikely. Indeed, given Ankara's misgivings about the potential impact of Israeli-Syrian peace on Turkish interests, Ankara may well welcome the election of a Likud government.

Even if Refah's rising popularity and Israel's approach to the peace process do not obstruct the Turkish-Israeli attempt to build a regional partnership, some bilateral policy divergences are likely, limiting the prospects for full "strategic cooperation." For example, both states oppose terrorism and Islamic fundamentalism, but the enemies against which they fight are different and must be fought in different ways, rendering cooperation difficult. Disagreements also could emerge about regional water-use planning, the best approach to preparing for a post-Saddam Iraq, the nature of the threat from the Islamic Republic of Iran, and various issues related to Syria.

A "COMMON SENSE OF OTHERNESS"

Notwithstanding potential restraints, the long-term outlook for Turkish-Israeli relations is bright, since the fundamental requirements of cooperation are in place. Both states are pro-West and pro-U.S., are committed to democratic and secular values, have similar views toward terrorism and Islamic fundamentalism, and are militarily based on U.S.-made equipment. Perhaps most important, Israel and Turkey share a "common sense of otherness" in a region dominated by Arabs and nondemocratic regimes. Even an Israel eager to build bridges to the Arab world, as it tries to overcome long-enduring animosity, is likely to find itself more comfortable working with the Turks.

Unlike its pro-Arab tilt of the 1960s through 1980s, Turkey's relations with Israel square comfortably with its Western self-image and its European integration efforts. In some ways, partnership with Israel allows Turkey to pursue a Middle East–focused policy, should it choose, without cost to its image in the West. And, as Israel's acceptance in the Arab world grows, there is little cost to its relations with moderate Arabs, either.

Broadly speaking, Turkey and Israel together could form the backbone of a moderate, pro-U.S. consensus in the region—along with such states as Morocco, Tunisia, Jordan, Egypt, and some of the Gulf states—for diplomatic and eventually security purposes. Particularly in partnership with Jordan, which shares their enthusiasm for regional cooperation, Israel and Turkey could provide greater energy for Middle Eastern multilateral efforts, including both economic projects and security-related confidence-building measures.

For Turkey, the benefits of close ties with Israel are many: trade, a close security relationship, enhanced ties with Washington, influence on the peace process, and, possibly, enhanced regional stability. Indeed, in view of these benefits, Turkey may want to take other unilateral initiatives to boost the cause of moderation in the Middle East. These might include closer ties with Jordan, including an effort to coordinate policies on the future of Iraq, about which both Turkey and Jordan are likely to have an important say. Ankara also might consider making a proposal about water that would help to resolve one of the most difficult issues facing Israeli and Syrian peace negotiators. In doing so, Ankara could help shape the contours of an Israeli-Syrian peace agreement, which has such high stakes for Turkey in terms of its war against the PKK and its future relations with its traditionally resentful neighbor Syria. Shaped appropriately, such a proposal also could strengthen Turkey's leverage in its water dispute with Syria. In taking such initiatives, Turkey would also fortify its much-improving ties with Israel.

CHAPTER TEN

IS THERE A NEW ROLE FOR TURKEY IN THE MIDDLE EAST?

Mehmet Ali Birand

Since the 1920s, Turkey has generally sought only stability in its Middle East policy. Thus, it has made no effort to improve either bilateral or multilateral cooperation, although its historical disposition and geographic location would seem to compel it. On the whole, the constant in its foreign policy in this region has been to wait and see rather than be directly involved.

Turkey's seventy-year history has not been long enough to erase the memories of being back-stabbed by the Arabs as the Ottoman Empire was nearing its end. Although it is not quite said in those words, this deep-rooted mistrust still survives in Turkish public sentiment.

Though the Turks share a religion with the Arabs, they nonetheless have always considered the Middle East to be a kind of quicksand that they would prefer to avoid. Turkish policy has thus been to observe events in the Middle East rather than be involved in them. Publicly Turkey was on the Arabs' side whenever it was necessary. However, the Turks offered timid practical support, and only when there was absolutely no alternative. However, the economic and political importance of the Middle Eastern countries makes efforts at closer relations necessary for Turkey. Still, no significant improvement can be detected, and Turkish foreign policy in this regard remains rather awkward.

Nevertheless, there have been some changes of late. With the collapse of communism, one can detect an element of vivacity in Turkey's relations with the Middle East. This is only a beginning, however, and there still remains a great deal of ground to be covered before genuinely good relations can be reached. Ever suspicious, Ankara still prefers to keep clear of Middle Eastern political problems and international intricacies. This desired aloofness, however, does not extend to an avoidance of economic cooperation.

The view from the other side is not all that different; in fact one could argue that the feeling of distrust is quite mutual. The Middle Eastern nations still regard Turkey as a successor of the Ottoman Empire, reminding them of the imposing power of a bygone era. After all, the days when the Arabs fought for their independence are not so far in the past, inspiring in them a rather wary approach toward Turkey. This does not mean, though, that the Arabs believe that relations with Turkey ought to be avoided altogether. Close contact with Turkey ought be established and maintained within certain well-defined and respected limits. Perhaps the most vivid example was the cool reception given by Saudi Arabian officials to Turkey's offer to send troops during the Gulf War. By accepting Egyptian and Pakistani troops, and turning a cold shoulder to a Turkish military presence, the Saudis demonstrated that they were not completely free of old resentments. During the Cold War era, that old resentment had been buttressed by a newer one: as an American stronghold and a shield ready to protect Israel, Turkey was a country that Arab nations could approach only with prudence.

Yet Turkey can hardly be ignored by Middle Eastern countries. As a secular state with a pluralist democracy and a liberal economy, it remains the only model of its type in the Muslim world, and as such, exists under the watchful eyes of its Muslim neighbors. The success or failure of this model will have a bearing on the whole of the Middle East.

Despite their cautious approach, most Middle Eastern countries nonetheless respect and have confidence in Turkey's efficiency. If Turkey were to choose a more active foreign policy and a different image, the Middle Eastern countries might take steps to establish stronger ties. At any rate, in the short term, any intensification in relations will be limited to economic issues.

Generally, Turkey is considered a significant player in the Middle East due to its geographical position, relative power, and close contacts with the West. Turkey is now entering a period when its role will become increasingly important.

A NEW ERA FOR TURKEY AND THE MIDDLE EAST

As the Cold War era fades into history, and especially as peace is forged between the Arab states and Israel, a new opportunity is emerging for Turkey in the Middle East. Even if Turkey wanted to resist these changes and hold on to its ancient antagonisms, the developments in the region as a whole give Turkey a pivotal part to play. For Israel in the past, Turkey was important as a non-Arab Islamic country, with no real hostility to Jews. Turkey was also strategically located and backed by the U.S. military.

Even though Turkey's approach to the Middle East has undergone fundamental changes, it still lacks a definite overall orientation. The main source of this vagueness can be seen in Turkish diplomacy's failure to adapt itself to the new international dynamics, that is, to a multipolar system in which nuances that hardly existed before are now determinant. Turkish foreign policy is still characterized by a hesitancy resulting from an inability to pinpoint the new parameters and variables in world politics. The fact that Turkish diplomacy matured in, and is still very much accustomed to, a world of only two super powers is the root cause of its present difficulties. Turkish policy in the Middle East suffers particularly from the fact that, unlike the West European countries, the states of the Middle East do not form a cohesive block united by common principles and policies; as a result, Turkish diplomacy routinely encounters confusion and uncertainty.

The collapse of the USSR, followed by the Gulf War, in essence encapsulated Turkish attitudes toward and evaluations of the Middle East. As Russia pulls itself together and tries once again to have influence in the region, pressure on Ankara to find for itself a more substantial policy toward the Middle East increases.

COUNTRY BRIEFS

A brief overview of each of the neighboring countries provides a clear demonstration of the problems facing Turkish policymakers.

The Gulf War created a major dilemma for Turkey. On the one hand, by opposing the Saddam Hussein regime, Turkey took the side of the allies and stopped the vital flow of Iraqi oil through Turkish pipelines. In providing the United States with unlimited support in the conflict, Turkey was the first to administer a severe blow to the

Iraqi regime. On the other hand, Turkey now faces an intensification of its domestic Kurdish problem, resulting in serious discomfort for both Turkish diplomats and the public. In siding firmly with the allies, Turkey also played an important part in protecting and providing food for the northern Iraqi Kurds escaping Saddam's wrath in the aftermath of the Gulf War. An increasing number of Turks believe that Ankara itself virtually helped to establish a Kurdish state on its border with Iraq, thus exacerbating Turkey's own Kurdish problem. Turkey continues to hope that Iraq will be able to hold together its territory, and that the Iraqi regime will reach a consensus with the Kurds. Ankara firmly believes that the only power strong enough to stop the Kurds from establishing a state in the region is either Saddam Hussein's or that of another Iraqi regime carrying out Saddam's policies on this issue.

Furthermore, because the embargo against Iraq has hurt its once booming and lively economy, Turkey's southeastern region has now become a virtual desert. Unemployment is increasingly feeding the activities of the Kurdistan Workers Party (PKK), the Kurdish separatist group that since the 1980s has adopted terrorist methods to achieve its aims. This, together with an estimated total economic loss of $20 billion since the beginning of the Gulf War, has created a bleak picture for Turkey, and further undermines its resolve to continue its support of the allies' policy toward Iraq. Turkey would prefer to make a deal with Saddam—or anyone else in charge in Baghdad— in the belief that the time has come to ease sanctions on Iraq, which has been sufficiently punished. Each day the sanctions continue is a further tax on Turkey's fundamental interests. Conflicting pressures from the allies, and Turkey's basic need to have good relations with Iraq, give rise to a perplexing foreign policy dilemma.

Turkish-Iranian relations have entered a relatively calm period following one of turbulence. Unfortunately, however, few expect the relative calm to last, since this period is imbued with an ever-present sense of mutual distrust. Iran has been isolated by the West, Turkey's allies, and has, as a result, suffered economically. Though Iranian support for religious radicals in Turkey has been increasing rapidly, Iran, perhaps for the first time, has understood the vast proportions of the Kurdish problem and accepted the need for a limited degree of cooperation with Turkey. The fact remains, however, that the PKK is still using Iranian territory from which to send its guerrillas into

Turkey. Therefore, it would be naive to believe that Turkish-Iranian cooperation will genuinely deepen in the near future.

Russian efforts to return to the region through its former ally Syria have increased Ankara's worries. In some respects, Syria could be an almost perfect neighbor for Turkey if a situation could be devised that addressed each other's needs, as they appear to complement each other well: Turkey needs Syrian natural gas and oil and, in return, Syria needs Turkish electricity, know-how, and water. However, disagreement over the PKK has turned this potential complementarity into a state of hostile relations. The perception in Ankara is that in the aftermath of the Arab-Israeli peace agreements, Syria will be left with one political card to play: the Kurdish one, one that it is determined to hold on to and exploit to the fullest. Not unsurprisingly, this situation lies at the heart of Turkey's discontent with Syria and, in the absence of a resolution, it is difficult to conceive of a permanent solution to the tense relationship between Turkey and Syria.

As the most important country with a leadership claim in the region, Egypt is very cautious toward Turkey. Egypt sees itself not only as the natural leader of the Arabs, but as leader of all the Muslims in North Africa and the Middle East more generally. Therefore, it does not view any wider Turkish economic and political influence in the region with enthusiasm, and unhesitatingly says so in public. There is a direct relationship between Egypt's perceived diminishing role and importance in the Middle East following the Arab-Israeli peace process and its increasingly cold attitude toward Turkey. This is despite the fact that Egypt and Turkey mirror each other with the very important problem of growing religious radicalism.

Saudi Arabia, which, like Egypt, considers itself the natural leader of an Islamic world, faces a dilemma in its relations with Turkey. The Saudis support the Islamic revivalist movement in Turkey while at the same time not wishing them complete success in the form of outright political victory. What Saudi Arabia hopes to see is an increase in Turkish influence and activity in the Balkans and the Caucasus without a similar engagement in the Middle East. Not surprisingly, it tends to avoid closer contact with Turkey. These two states resemble distant relatives who are not exactly enamored with one another but who are yet unable to stop observing the other with curiosity and suspicion.

Jordan, the Gulf countries, and a large part of the remaining states of the Middle East are cautiously watching Turkey as the Islamic revivalist movement picks up speed inside Turkey and the Welfare (Refah) Party augments its share of the national vote. These countries know well that fundamentalism is a crucial issue that can easily spread into their territories as well. Although technically not part of the Middle East, the countries open to a fundamentalist challenge include the Central Asian and other Islamic republics in the former Soviet Union and even in some African states.

The cases discussed above not only show the limitations of Turkish policies but also provide a hint to the new role Turkey could assume in the future, not just in the Middle East but in other regions of the world as well.

THREE KEY ISSUES FOR THE FUTURE

Three key issues for Turkey's future role in the Middle East are secularism, water, and stability. On the whole, in many Islamic countries, radical Islam-based movements are becoming more and more intense and entrenched in their struggle. Especially following the collapse of communism, the poor in these countries have tended to listen to the promises of religious radicals rather than the slogans of old-time, now discredited, leftist political leaders. In many cases, religious revivalists have taken old slogans and made them their own. Today, religious radicals lead the bandwagon in opposition to dictatorship, protest against poverty, and the struggle against injustice. With such slogans and a clear-cut ideology, they have garnered the support not just of religious fanatics but also of the otherwise neutral masses.

The worldwide increase of a trend toward religious radicalism is accompanied by increased risks of religion-based competition. The only obstacle in the face of the Islamic fundamentalist movements is the example of Turkey as a secular, Islamic country, and as a result, all eyes seemed to be turned toward it. Turkey's importance in today's world does not derive from its strategic location or its heralded role as a gateway to the East, but from its perceived role as a bellwether for secularism.

A model of an Islamic country with a democratic political system and a liberal economy is the antidote for radical religious movements. If Turkey can control the gains of the Refah (Welfare) Party and incorporate them into the political system, it will have played an unquestionably important role not only in the Islamic world, but the rest of the world also. In fact, because this is well known to the Islamic radicals, they are doing their utmost to destabilize Turkey and gain the upper hand. However, they fail to recognize that Turkey is not the shah's Iran, much less Algeria. Unlike those two countries, Turkey has had an established secular middle-class for the past seventy years. Another advantage is that Turkey's democracy is much more mature than those of its peers in the Islamic world. In spite of all Turkish democracy's shortcomings, the people in Turkey are able to speak their minds rather freely, and it is this atmosphere of free speech that is the strength of secularism in Turkey.

Viewed from the outside, Turkey's secular system may appear to be in grave danger. However, this view should be tempered by an analysis of the percentage of votes the Welfare Party has received in the past. Compared with the party's historical performance, its recent success should be interpreted more as a timely warning than an imminent danger of systemic collapse. The Welfare Party's sudden rise and notoriety could easily be curbed if the mainstream parties managed to organize themselves better. Turkey is all Islam's "flagship" and its only fortress with regard to a secular political system in the Islamic world. Seeing it keep that system standing in the twenty-first century will certainly leave its imprint on Islamic countries and administer a blow to religious radical movements. This simple reality will have an impact on all developments in the region, with regard to the Arab countries as well as Israel.

Water will continue to be a crucial issue in the twenty-first century; as many have said, water may become even more important than oil. The lack of water in the Middle East leads many countries in the region to consider Turkey a water reservoir. Ongoing negotiations between Turkey and its neighbors on this issue are a clear indication of the sensitivity of this matter. The other countries in the region increase Ankara's unease by claiming that Turkey should not hoard but share its natural wealth. Turkey does not consider itself a reservoir, and recognizes that its resources may not be sufficient even for its own needs in the near future. The seed for future conflict has been sown, and Turkey is bound to be a primary protagonist in this drama.

The third and the most important role Turkey can play in the Middle East is to preserve its own stability. Despite—and because of—all the turmoil that surrounds it, Turkey's continued stability will undoubtedly contribute to the stability of other countries in the region.

No matter how painful it might prove, the Israeli-Palestinian peace process will work. All countries in the region have sensed the comfortable prospects of peace and started to prepare themselves accordingly. The beginnings of a period of peace between Israel and the Arabs have already had a positive effect on Turkey. When economic obstacles are overcome, Turkish-Arab relations will blossom. Turkish-Israeli relations will improve along all dimensions—economic, political, and military—beyond all expectations and forecasts. In general, these long-neglected relations will prove to contribute considerably to the stability of the entire region.

CONCLUSION

Turkey has tried hard to avoid taking an active part in the affairs of the Middle East and done its best to stay off the slippery ground where intrigues blossom. However, the years to come are about to bring a change and a golden opportunity regarding Turkey's role in the region. The main challenge for Turkey in the future was best summarized by Israel's foreign minister Shimon Peres, "Turkey has one million graduates, one million mosques, and one million soldiers. It will choose one of these three."

CHAPTER ELEVEN

AVOIDING THE QUESTION

Philip J. Robins

Since 1960 Turkey has been a diffident and tentative actor in the Middle East. Initially, this was a reaction against the foreign policy failures of the 1950s when Turkey adopted an active role toward the region. The 1958 national revolution in Baghdad, the defeat of the Baghdad Pact, and the rise of Egyptian and Soviet power in the Middle East all contributed to a sense that regional dynamics were stronger than the Turkish will or means to mold them. The early 1960s marked a turning point in Turkish policy toward the Middle East. Turkey reacted to the zealotry of its 1950s foreign policy by avoiding involvement in intraregional disputes; seeking correct bilateral relations with all the states of the area regardless of ideology and regime; and scrupulously avoiding interfering in the domestic affairs of Middle Eastern states.[1]

After 1964, and the American rebuff to Turkey over Cyprus in the form of the Johnson letter, Turkey came to appreciate the value of supporters wherever it could find them. It pragmatically set about building support in the region for its policy toward the island, thus delinking its membership of the Western alliance and its ideological predilections from its pursuit of regional support. In the late 1970s Turkey belatedly set out to benefit from the financial windfall that came to the region through the massive increases in income of the oil producers. In doing so, Turkey adopted what might be called a Japanese approach. Though never entirely turning its back on Israel, Turkey did not allow politics to interfere with its overriding aim of material benefit. Turkish neutrality during the Iran-Iraq war was the apex of success for this approach, with politics sublimated to commercial opportunity.

By 1989 and the end of the Cold War, Turkish policy toward the Middle East was routine and well understood. In substance it was materially oriented and politically noninterventionist. In style it was low key and predominantly incremental. In essence it was Kemalist; that is to say, intrinsically uninterested in and comparatively aloof from the Middle East, while studiously concerned not to appear to be projecting power beyond its borders.

The changes in the international context at the end of the 1980s might, in the fullness of time, have prompted Turkey to reassess its policies toward the Middle East. The Iraqi invasion of Kuwait on August 2, 1990, the first revisionist move since the collapse of the old international order, deprived Ankara of the luxury of a measured and strategic response to changing world circumstances. The Iraqi invasion was, instead, a sudden and exceptional development, even by the unpredictable and shambolic standards of the post–Cold War period, in turn obliging Turkey to improvise in its response. Moreover, Turkish policy toward the Gulf crisis was made by a leader, President Turgut Özal, unrepresentative of the Turkish elite in the foreign policymaking domain. Bold, vain, and supremely self-confident, Özal was not only willing to overturn the substance of past Turkish policy toward the region, but even prepared to glory in it. Indeed, he acted in a way that was resonant of the turbulent phase of the mid- and late 1950s.

Despite the end of the Gulf crisis and Özal's death, Turkey is still living with the consequences of the crisis and of Özal's legacy. Though the crisis was resolved, the situation in Iraq itself was not. In policy terms, though the Gulf crisis and Özal were untypical, Turkey is being judged as if the substance and style of its actions during the crisis were the new norms of its changed approach to foreign affairs. In the Middle East itself, Turkey is regarded once again as a regional power with an interventionist predilection; a close ally of the West's, willing to do its bidding. In the West, Turkey is seen as an important ally in the Middle East theater and as providing important ballast for the moderate camp in the region.

CAPABILITY

Turkey's potential to be an influential actor in the Middle East is constrained by its limited capability. First, there are structural constraints, that is to say constraints that may be assumed to be enduring and beyond the current power of Turkey or other actors to rectify. Second, there are policy constraints; in other words, constraints that are dictated by other policy domains. These are to a much greater extent within the ability of Turkey to change, though the difficulty of doing so should not be underestimated.

Though "political culture" is a difficult term to define and apply, its appropriateness in describing the differences between Turkey and both the Arab World and Iran is compelling. While the method and form of conducting politics in Turkey is far from perfect, it approximates far more a southern European model than that which prevails in the Middle East, Israel excepted.

Two examples illustrate the point. In Turkey, as in most European countries, the formal domain is preeminent in politics. The powers and roles of different institutions are relatively clear both through regulation and convention. The Ministry of Foreign Affairs (with the exception of the brief Özal interlude) is an important vehicle for the collection and analysis of information, and for advice on policy. Making policy and passing laws involve complex bureaucratic processes, but once a policy has been adopted it is relatively easy to find out what it is. There is an independent judicial process for testing and refining new laws. An active and independent media gives transparency and adds accountability to the process.

In the Middle East, the situation is very different, with informal politics dominant. Decision making is highly centralized, with even relatively minor issues having to await cabinet involvement. With the notable exception of a country like Egypt, the Ministry of Foreign Affairs is of far less importance than it is elsewhere, either in terms of information gathering or policymaking. Policy is made in the presidential or royal palace. Foreign ministers are little more than spokesmen, information ministers with an external portfolio. It is often very difficult to discover what policy is and, indeed, whether it exists on certain issues. The press, let alone the media in general, is usually heavily circumscribed in terms of what it can report, and is often uncritical.

Again, Turkey's political institutions are differently arranged than those of its Middle Eastern neighbors. In Turkey formally constituted political parties compete for power through national elections involving universal suffrage. The process of coalition building, once completed through a process of informal bargaining, is then formalized through a coalition agreement. The coalition government rules, subject to parliamentary scrutiny. When the life of a government ends, it must resubmit itself to the will of the people. The office of the president is filled through election by the members of the Turkish parliament.

This institutionalization of politics has in the past—as in other southern European countries—been interrupted by military intervention. While this has weakened the institutions of state, the Turkish military (in contrast to those of Greece, Portugal, and Spain) has allowed for the re-civilianization of politics within a relatively short period, facilitating the reemergence of vigorous institutions.

In most of the Middle East, political institutions either do not exist or have very little real power. Parties are only permitted in a handful of countries, and even then find it difficult to operate freely or gain real access to power. Legislatures often do not exist, but even when they do their role is usually only marginal. The judiciary in most countries does not function independent of the regime in power. There is rarely an institutionalized process for political succession.

The formal and institutionalized nature of politics in Turkey tends to make for policy continuity. In the Middle East, the personalization of power, the absence of checks and balances, and the hidden conduct of politics can result in apparently sudden changes in policy.

The difference in political culture in the nature and conduct of diplomacy often makes Turkish diplomats ill at ease with the Middle East. They are in any case poorly prepared for dealing with the region, with postings to the Middle East regarded negatively and few opportunities in Turkish higher education in area studies. Consequently, for example, the Turkish Foreign Ministry, like those in most Western countries, is routinely uncertain in its comprehension of Iranian political dynamics.

This difference in political culture has also resulted in the Turkish foreign policy establishment's rushing to embrace Israel since 1992. Turkey's political elite has often responded to Israel with a sense of recognition, as the one country in the region with a political culture much like its own. In its desire to bolster relations with Israel over the last couple of years, Turkey has shown the limitations of its understanding of the rest of the region. For Israel, which has a more sophisticated understanding of the Middle East born of time and location, the Turkish embrace has been welcome, but too claustrophobic to be fully reciprocated. As it seeks a breakthrough in relations with Syria in an attempt to expand the Arab-Israeli peace process, Israel has not deemed it prudent to agree to all of the Turkish agenda for cooperation, especially those with implications for the Syrian-controlled Bekaa Valley. Israel is also uneasy at the prospect of having to turn its back on the Kurds, who were for so long a valued ally against the Arabs. Though Turkey has on the whole reaped the benefit of improved relations with Israel, it has been at the expense of heightened Syrian suspicions, which could further impair relations between Ankara and Damascus.

POLITICAL GEOGRAPHY

The geographical location of Turkey is both its blessing and its curse. It is an attribute in that Turkey cannot be ignored as an international actor in a number of different subsystems: the Balkans, the Caucasus, the eastern Mediterranean, the Black Sea, and southern Europe are all subregions where Turkey's location and size have an impact. Yet, in spite of the important role that it periodically plays in such areas, Turkey is not central to any of them (save arguably the Black Sea through its control of the Straits). It has therefore been Turkey's fate to be consistently ignored or to have its regional importance downplayed by policymakers and foreign policy analysts alike.

The Middle East is no different for Turkey. From an international relations perspective there can be no doubt that Turkey is a regional actor. Its territory lies adjacent to that of Syria, Iraq, and Iran. The strategic rivers, the Euphrates and Tigris, both rise in Turkey and flow into Syria and Iraq. Demography pays no respect to international boundaries, with significant Kurdish populations in Turkey, Iraq, Iran, and, to a lesser extent, Syria. More practically, during the Gulf crisis Turkey's role as part of the international coalition and, more specifically, as a base for air raids into Iraq, was more important than the largely symbolic role of all but a handful of the other members. More generally, Turkey's ties with the region are solidified through the historical experience of empire and the sharing of the Muslim religion.

In spite of these strong and enduring connections, Turkey remains located on the periphery of the Middle East. Geography, not to mention ethnicity, has meant that Ankara has never been an actor of substance in the Arab-Israeli dispute. In the other leading conflicts of the last decade, from the Lebanese, Yemeni, and Sudanese civil wars to the shipping war in the Persian Gulf, Turkey was without significance. Even in the Iran-Iraq war, where Turkey was a more proximate and active player, its involvement owed more to economic geography than political geography.

Even if one takes into account the intellectual fashion of the last two years to say that the boundaries of the Middle East now encompass Central Asia, Turkey's marginality is not changed. For Turkey also lies on the periphery of Central Asia, without even the benefit of territorial contiguity.[2] Indeed, this deficiency as much as any other has been responsible for the disappointingly limited potential that Turkey's stuttering relationship with Central Asia so far has fulfilled.

Geopolitics therefore clearly sets limits on the nature and potential of Turkish involvement in the Middle East. Turkey is a critically important state for its immediate Middle Eastern neighbors, as they are for it. Turkey in turn has some secondary benefit for the southerly neighbors of Syria, Iraq, and Iran, notably Jordan, Kuwait, and Saudi Arabia. If drawn further into the politics of the region, Turkey could act as a counterweight to these three regional powers in the Levant and the northern Gulf. Beyond this, its regional role is circumscribed.

THE COMPETING AGENDA

Since 1989 Turkey's foreign policy agenda has been a long one, consisting both of enduring areas of interest and new concerns born of the upheavals in the international system sparked by the fall of communism and the end of the Cold War. In both fields Turkey has had little leeway in choosing its priorities.

Existing priorities, such as the Cyprus issue and Turkey's aim for a more organic relationship with the European Union (EU), have had to remain the subject of close and continuing attention. Turkey's European vocation is one which remains dear to the values—not simply the aspirations—of its Kemalist elite. Since early 1993, the EU[3] and Turkey have conducted intensive discussions in preparation for the establishment of a customs union by 1995. Since the November 1992 meeting of the Association Council, the two parties have entered into a more intensive political dialogue.[4] The implementation of closer economic and political relations offers the possible prize of some form of Turkish membership in the EU in the next century. Cyprus too continues to be an important, though only periodically pressing, issue. The presence of nearly 30,000 Turkish troops on the island,[5] together with the emotional importance of the issue to public opinion in Turkey, means that Ankara's active and continuing engagement in the issue is unavoidable.

New priorities have presented themselves in consequence of the collapse of the communist regimes in Eastern Europe and the Soviet Union. For Turkey's foreign relations, three new related areas have demanded attention. First, new relations have had to be forged with the newly independent republics of the old USSR and its former Eastern European surrogates. This involved the initial dispatch of fact-finding delegations from the Foreign Ministry and the hosting and subsequent reciprocity of high-level political visits. Many new embassies had then to be established, with the accompanying burden of acquiring and furnishing appropriate buildings. Diplomats were then assigned to serve in the new posts. With the new missions in the former Soviet south containing only a couple of diplomatic staff, the process of developing contacts and stabilizing relations with the new republics has been and will remain a long one.

Second, attention has been focused on new areas of conflict which have arisen out of the rapid changes in the Balkans, the Transcaucasus, and Central Asia. The two leading and most enduring conflicts have been the war between Armenia and Azerbaijan over control of Nagorno Karabakh and the conflict in Bosnia-Herzegovina. The former has been of particular concern to Turkey, because of the proximity of the fighting to its borders. Though Turkey has adopted a restrained and non-interventionist posture toward the conflict, it has not remained a bystander; it has become involved indirectly, both in giving guarantees to Nakhichevan against the perceived possibility of attack from Armenia and in implementing a blockade against the Armenian Republic. Moreover, Ankara has spasmodically played a mediatory role, both in attempting to galvanize the involvement of the great powers and, latterly, in the form of multilateral diplomacy through the Minsk group.

Though not as pressing an issue for Turkey, the Bosnian issue has commanded attention from Ankara, which played a tireless role within Western institutions in favor of a more interventionist policy to bolster the position of the Bosnian government.[6] It has also adopted a leadership role within the Islamic Conference Organization contact group. Furthermore, Turkey has been prepared actively to contribute to the peacekeeping and peacemaking intervention of the international community. It has supplied aircraft to the NATO air contingent based in Italy, which has been on standby to aid the enforcement of UN Security Council resolutions on Bosnia, and has sent a contingent of peacekeeping troops, which have been deployed between Bosnian government and Croat forces at Zenica.

On the larger stage, Turkey has been obliged to participate in the international debates as to how best to respond to the changed international circumstances. This has ranged from Ankara's arguing for an expanded Security Council in the context of UN reform[7] to fighting a rearguard defense for the retention of NATO in the form that it took before the end of the Cold War. Turkey has also sought to gain entry to the emerging European security institution, the Western European Union;[8] has been an active member of the Conference on Security and Cooperation in Europe; and has played a role in the development of the Partnership for Peace formulation to give the old communist countries a closer relationship with NATO.[9]

These new areas of interest, together with long-standing ones, have imposed a great strain on the resources, manpower, and organization of the Foreign Ministry. Two organizational restructurings—one major and one minor—have been undertaken within the ministry since 1992.[10] For example, the old office of vice directorate-general dealing with Eastern Europe and Asia (including the USSR) has been divided into two. Instead of being covered by one department, together with such other Asian countries as China, the new states of the old Soviet Union are now the exclusive charge of two departments, interestingly divided between two different vice directorates-general. Moreover, a new body, affiliated with the Foreign Ministry and called the Turkish International Cooperation Agency, was established in August 1992. Its brief was to coordinate the cooperation between Turkey and the so-called Turkic republics.

However, these new geographical responsibilities have not been matched by new resources. Much of the increased workload has been borne by diplomatic staff working longer hours, the promotion of diplomats above their level of competence, and the posting abroad of junior diplomats before they have completed their mandatory initial two years' home posting in Ankara. Coordination has suffered as senior staff travel more frequently and have fewer opportunities to hold business and planning meetings with one another. Increasingly, the Foreign Ministry has sought the assistance of academics, journalists, and retired ambassadors as sources of new ideas and analysis to help compensate for the shortage of adequate manpower at the center.[11] However, a developing relationship between academics and diplomats has been disrupted by Turkey's financial crisis and the subsequent April 1994 austerity measures.

In short, since the onset of the Gulf crisis in August 1990, Turkey's foreign policy priorities have been largely determined by external contingencies. This has left little time or resources for strategic planning. The chief aim of the Turkish government has been to bring stability to those areas close to its borders that have experienced turmoil. With the prospect of continued conflict in Bosnia and the Transcaucasus, the future of Central Asia uncertain, and the outlook for central and southeastern Europe far from assured, the preoccupations of the recent past are likely also to be those of the immediate future. This leaves little time or resources for the development of a new role in the Middle East.

THE PROBLEM OF RUSSIA

Almost continuously for around 280 years the Soviet Union and its predecessor states have presented a direct threat to Turkey (and before it the Ottoman Empire). There was therefore no reason why the collapse of communism alone should have freed Turkey from the threat from the north. Initially, however, this did appear to be the case. A belt of independent states provided a buffer between Turkey and the newly constituted Russian Federation. Moscow appeared to enter a period of introspection as it began a phase of radical economic adjustment, and different groups and personalities wrestled for political influence.[12]

Despite this initial appearance it was not long before Russia began to reassert itself in its "near abroad" to the south. The Russian authorities feared that Turkey would expand its influence in these buffer states while Moscow was distracted. It also feared the growth of political Islam and of consequent instability on its southern borders. Russia therefore moved once more to project its power. First, Russia received the agreement of the new states in Central Asia to continue its role as guardian of external border security, thereby allowing Moscow to maintain its forces in the area. Moscow also forged a close relationship with the post–civil war regime in Dushanbe, as a way of trying to consolidate stability in Tajikistan.

Second, and more critically for Turkey, Russia moved to reassert its authority in the Transcaucasus, where it was most alarmed by the apparent growth of Turkey's influence. Russia, at the very least, declined to restrain the Armenians as they scored successive battle-field victories over Azerbaijan in early 1993. Thus Moscow approvingly watched the steady undermining of the Elchibey regime in Baku, which had hitherto been stridently pro-Turkish. Having publicly spurned Ankara's attempts to galvanize a Russo-Turkish mediation of the Armenian-Azerbaijani conflict in spring 1993, Russia was presumably content with the fall of Elchibey in June 1993.

A second way of reimposing its influence over the Transcaucasus was for Russia to oblige the two recalcitrant states of Georgia and Azerbaijan to recognize its power. Georgia's will to resist Russia's influence was broken by the rebellion in Abkhazia, and Georgian President Eduard Shevardnadze was obliged to travel to Moscow in an act of deference to Russia, and to permit Russian peacekeepers to enter his state. Azerbaijan has more successfully resisted Russian pressure, though indirectly at the price of the occupation of more than 20 percent of its territory (including Karabakh). In summer 1994 Baku came under pressure to accept the deployment of Russian servicemen as peacekeepers. Russia has also objected to the Azerbaijani government's decision to sign a major oil deal with a foreign consortium for the exploitation of hydrocarbon resources in the Caspian Sea.

For Turkey, such developments have been troubling. In contrast to the expected withdrawal of the military, Russian troops can now be found in two states that border Turkey to the north, Armenia and Georgia. Ankara has resisted continuing efforts to bring about a revision of the Conventional Forces in Europe Treaty, which would allow Russia to increase its military presence in the Transcaucasus. Blunt signals have periodically emanated from Moscow indicating that Russia disapproves of Turkey's attempts to improve relations with the newly independent republics, and Moscow's contempt for Turkish diplomacy in the Transcaucasus has been perceived as both alarming and insulting.

Moreover, two further issues have emerged to exacerbate the atmosphere of antagonism. The first is the issue of shipping access through the Turkish Straits. The Russian authorities are seeking to maintain their control of the economies of Kazakstan and Azerbaijan through the establishment of transit routes for future oil exports from these two states. In order to do so, the Russians want export oil to be transported to the Russian Black Sea port of Novorossirsk and then by tanker through the Straits, claiming the right to free passage under the 1936 Montreux Convention. Turkey objects because of the potential environmental and safety consequences for Istanbul, should there be an accident involving one of the new generation of supertankers, and because such a route would deprive Turkey of the economic and strategic advantages of a land-based crude oil pipeline from Azerbaijan.

The second issue is that of Bosnia and the increasing role of Russia in the diplomacy surrounding the conflict. Turkey was concerned that the expanding role of Russia would make it harder to mount international pressure on Serbia, the Turks perceiving the conflict as one essentially of Serbian expansionism rather than a civil war in Bosnia. In particular, Ankara smarted at the role of the Russian government in brokering the ceasefire around Sarajevo in spring 1994, and the deployment of Russian troops to help oversee it, especially since, in the past, Turkey's repeated offers of troops were rebuffed on the grounds that states perceived to be too closely connected with a conflict should not be called upon to play a role in UN efforts.

The existence of direct or indirect problems over Central Asia, the Transcaucasus, the Straits, and the Balkans illustrates the extent to which the interests of Turkey and Russia continue to collide. It also points to the enduring legacy of bilateral suspicions. It is of course not inevitable that any one of these problem areas will lead to a spiraling of tension and even conflict. To date, in a variety of ways (not least the acquiescence of Turkey), these issues have been managed sufficiently well to ensure that this has not happened. In addition, there are areas of common interest that give both sides a strong incentive to keep relations harmonious. Chief among these is the growing level of bilateral trade, with Turkey importing Russian gas and exporting consumer goods and contracting services.[13]

What is beyond dispute, however, is that for Turkey its relations with Russia are of primary importance. Ankara must devote considerable attention to managing ties with its northern neighbor over a range of problems. Policy must be developed sensitively in order to ensure that ties remain as stable and cordial as possible. With relations with Russia likely to remain the single greatest preoccupation of the Turkish foreign policy establishment, the Middle East will continue to be of subordinate importance. Furthermore, with the Middle East itself close to Russia, and Moscow enjoying a long historical relationship with two of Turkey's neighbors, it is firmly within Ankara's interests to ensure that a strong Russian-Syrian and/or Russian-Iraqi alliance does not reemerge.

POLICY CONTRADICTIONS

Policy constraints on Turkey's playing a new role in the Middle East are not confined to the issue of competing priorities. Policy problems also exist in developing Turkey's position toward a number of questions related exclusively to the Middle East, principally regarding contradictory aims and interests that make consistent and cohesive policy difficult to achieve.

The most obvious example is the attempt to develop policy toward the Kurds in northern Iraq. The Turkish state is deeply suspicious of the safe haven that has been created in northeastern Iraq by the resolutions of the UN Security Council. Through the activity of Operation Provide Comfort, a coalition effort that has guaranteed its existence, the safe haven has since 1992 begun to take on the characteristics of a politically autonomous area. This security has enabled the Iraqi Kurds to hold elections for a national assembly with legislative powers, establish an executive committee to govern the area, and begin the admittedly difficult transformation of the peshmerga into a national force.

From the perspective of many in the Turkish establishment, the developments in Iraqi Kurdistan have been deeply troubling. On the one hand the safe haven appears to be increasingly taking on the trappings of an embryonic Kurdish state. This, it is feared, will act as an incentive and an example to Turkey's large, alienated Kurdish population in parts of the southeast, inspiring them to try to create a similarly semi-independent entity. On the other hand, the strength of the Kurds in northeastern Iraq has not been sufficient, always presupposing that the political will existed, to police the border areas with

Turkey. Thus the Kurdistan Workers Party (PKK) has been able to prosecute its insurgency over the border into Turkey with only inter- mittent restraint by the Iraqi Kurds. Turkey is thereby the double vic- tim of a policy of the international community with which, in view of the fact that Operation Provide Comfort operates from its territory, the Turkish state openly cooperates.

Many in the Turkish establishment, notably the military, may be in favor of both ending Operation Provide Comfort and snuffing out the safe haven, preparing the way for its reintegration into the Iraqi state. In addition to ending the possibility of Kurdish statehood, this would also help to contain fears of the fragmentation of the Iraqi state. The disaggregation of Iraq is a particularly worrying scenario because of the open competition for influence in the newly truncated entities among Iran, Syria, and Turkey that could result. However, those in Turkey attracted by the reassertion of Iraqi sovereignty are deterred from contemplating such an end by the knowledge that as long as Saddam Hussein remains in power in Baghdad the reincor- poration of the safe haven into the Iraqi state is likely to precipitate the sort of mass flight that saw around 800,000 Kurdish refugees on the Turkish-Iraqi border in spring 1991. As in the wake of the Iraqi defeat in Kuwait, a second flight would be potentially costly both to Turkey's international image and its exchequer and could further exacerbate Turkey's own Kurdish problem.

With these conflicting aims, Turkish policy toward northern Iraq has become entangled in contradiction and muddle. As long as the current political situation prevails in Baghdad, Turkey seems resigned to a status quo from which it is currently unable to extract itself with- out unacceptable consequences.

A second example of policy contradiction surrounds Turkey's rela- tions with Saudi Arabia. Philosophically, the prevailing political ide- ology in both states could hardly be more contradictory. In Turkey, secularism is a core value of the Kemalist elite. In Saudi Arabia the Wahhabi sect prevails,[14] with its "root and branch" notions of strict piety. In Turkey, Sufi sects are many and influential; in Saudi Arabia the prevailing puritanism is deeply hostile to Sufism. In Turkey, the Kemalist elites identify with European values and aspirations; Saudi Arabia has in turn chosen to develop an Islamic solidarity.

In spite of this ideological opposition, Turkey considers Saudi Arabia one of its best allies in the Middle East.[15] Both are widely identified as being in the "moderate" camp of Middle Eastern politics. Both have developed a close and often strategic relationship with the United States, which, for Turkey, goes back to the Korean War, and, in the case of Saudi Arabia, began with the commercial exploitation of oil. Furthermore, both were on the same side during the Gulf crisis, and their territory was the main launchpoint for the U.S.-led coalition attack on the Iraqi forces. Both states had a strong interest in the defeat of Iraq and an end to the occupation of Kuwait.

Yet this apparent convergence of interest does not tell the whole story. At best Saudi Arabia appears ambivalent toward Turkey. Over recently suggested cooperation with Turkey toward Central Asia and the Middle East, the Saudi state has been equivocal. Regarding Turkey's domestic politics, Saudi Arabia has been interfering. Groups inside Saudi Arabia have consistently pursued a course aimed at undermining the values and orientation of the Turkish state, with the Riyadh government standing passively by at best. During the 1980s, large sums of money poured into Turkey from Saudi Arabia to fund a range of activities from mosque building, to religious schools, to the provision of scholarships for Islamist youth. There have also been repeated accusations that Saudi Arabia has financed the Welfare (Refah) Party, Turkey's main Islamist party.[16] In other words, Saudi Arabia has injected vast resources into Turkey to help undermine the very authorities who have been responsible for helping to confront Iraq and support the United States, the guarantor of the Saudi state.

TURKEY IN THE MIDDLE EAST

Russia may be the top issue in Turkish foreign policy, Azerbaijan the scene of the conflict closest to its borders, and Bosnia the issue that most frequently engages its foreign policy establishment, but there can be no doubt that Turkey also has interests in the Middle East. Turkey is clearly a member of the Middle East subsystem of states; that is to say, the actions and perceptions of Turkey are taken seriously in the calculations of the other principal actors in the region. Indeed, it is because of this view from the region that, whether it likes it or not, and regardless of the vision of Atatürk, Turkey has no choice but to be an actor in the Middle East.

Political Islam has emerged over the last decade and a half as the ideology of protest and opposition in the Middle East. Islamist regimes now hold power in Iran and Sudan. In Algeria, civil war is taking place between the military and the forces of political Islam. In Egypt, Jordan, Oman, Saudi Arabia, and Tunisia, and among the Palestinians, Islamist groups present the greatest threat to the political status quo.

Turkey is not immune to Islamist ideas and movements. Though its political institutions make for more stable politics, and its tradition of laicism provides a bulwark against the growth of political Islam, Turkey remains a country populated by Muslims who show increasing signs of personal piety. The ground exists for the growing importance of Islamist ideas. Moreover, the long existence of influential and widely supported *tarikats*, or Sufi religious orders, increases the potential receptivity of Turkish society to Islamic ideas and movements.

Indeed, there have been important signs in recent years that the attraction of political Islam is growing. In the March 1994 local elections, the Refah Partisi (widely known as the Welfare Party, sometimes translated as the Prosperity Party), Turkey's self-consciously Islamist party, polled 17.98 percent of the popular vote. This made it the third largest party, with its main rivals receiving 22.64 percent and 21.19 percent of the vote.[17] Its strong organization, its popular reputation for being free from corrupt practices, and the absence of any party rival to it in the domain of political Islam means that Refah's electoral prospects are good, with a strong possibility that it will emerge as the main opposition party at the next general election, and there is even a chance that it may have an opportunity to form a coalition government.

Mindful of such a prognosis, the Kemalist establishment in Turkey, which includes the career military, secular intellectuals, and Westernized women, is extremely concerned. They see their values, indeed their way of life, as potentially threatened. Yet, despite this, there have been relatively few instances when political Islam has been an issue in Turkish relations with Middle Eastern states. This issue has, in fact, been largely confined to relations with Iran and has more to do with the issue of Islamist terrorism than Islamism as a political movement. For instance, there have been periodic allegations that the Turkish journalist and investigative writer Ugur Mumcu was assassinated by Islamist militants trained in Iran.[18] Of late, Turkey and Iran seem to have accepted each other's very different worldviews, and resolved to cooperate (or at least to stabilize relations) due to the many areas where they have common interests.[19] Ankara's desire to keep ideological problems out of its foreign affairs with Middle Eastern states, in spite of the emergence of political Islam as a critical domestic issue, is evidence of the Turkish government's continuing commitment to keep relations with the region on a stable and low-key footing.

The Kurdish insurgency, which has engulfed southeastern Turkey over the past five years, presents the greatest challenge to the Turkish state. In addition to presenting a threat to the territorial integrity of the state, the insurgency has been a colossal financial drain and has had negative consequences for Turkey's foreign relations. These have on the one hand taken the form of growing criticism by Turkey's Western European allies of its human rights record. On the other, it has given those of Turkey's immediate neighbors with which it enjoys mercurial relations a way of gaining political leverage against Ankara.

Those countries that have made the greatest use of the PKK-led insurgency are Turkey's Middle East neighbors Syria, Iran, and Iraq. Syria has been the most important sponsor of the PKK, allowing it to establish training bases in the Syrian-controlled Bekaa Valley in Lebanon, and permitting its leaders to reside in Damascus. Since 1987 Turkish leaders have been trying to forge an accord with Syria that would end Damascus' support for the organization.[20] Such attempts have worked only fitfully at best, as Syria has appeared keen to retain its PKK card as a quid pro quo for a definitive Turkish agreement to guarantee the flow of water from the Euphrates across the border. More recently, however, Damascus appears to have significantly reduced its support for the PKK, closing down its main training camp in Lebanon, and obliging the organization's leader, Abdullah Öcalan, to lower his profile in Syria. The chief reason for this appears to be a concerted Syrian effort to have itself taken off the U.S. State Department's official list of states sponsoring terrorism.

Iraq and Iran too have periodically given support to the PKK as a function of their relationship with Turkey. The most recent example of Baghdad's apparently aiding the PKK came in the wake of the Gulf crisis, when the Iraqi regime seemed keen to show that it still had some leverage over Turkey. Iranian support for the PKK appears to have been even more recent. It seems to have been motivated by anger in Tehran at the fact that the Mojahedin-e Khalq Organization

(MKO), the most violent of the various Iranian oppositionist groups, was being allowed to operate freely in Istanbul. During extensive bilateral security cooperation visits in 1994, Iran appeared willing to devalue its links with the PKK in return for a tougher Turkish policy toward the MKO.[21] The Iranian authorities even went as far as to hand over fourteen PKK members to Turkey in March 1994.[22]

With the PKK insurgency continuing to be the top issue for Turkey in its relations with its three immediate regional neighbors, Syria, Iraq, and Iran, all know what they have to do to improve their ties with Ankara. In turn, a more accommodating approach from the region over the PKK, as is currently the case, requires an appropriate response from Ankara.

WEAPONS OF MASS DESTRUCTION

Until the late 1980s, Turkey adopted a relaxed approach with respect to military threats from the southeast. Turkey was a country that had a population more than three times as numerous as either Iraq's or Syria's. Only Syria, with its continuing but low-key territorial claim, seemed to hold irredentist designs. Turkish membership in NATO offered the security, whether real or illusory, of alliance protection in the event of attack. When the Turkish government became increasingly agitated about the perceived military threat from Syria in the late 1950s, it was not because of any direct threat, but because of a general concern that the Soviet Union might be able to use it as a base for operations. Last, and perhaps most pertinently, the sheer size of Turkey's physical geography, with its main population and economic centers in western Anatolia or on the Aegean coast, seemed to give it an unassailable strategic depth.

The increasing importation of medium range missiles and the local modification of such delivery systems to reach targets even further afield appear to have undermined this traditional approach to defense. In spring 1990, just weeks before the Iraqi invasion of Kuwait, the Turkish authorities were therefore happy to cooperate with the British government in intercepting parts of the so-called Iraqi Supergun, which was to have been transported across Turkey. Iraq's Scud attacks against Saudi Arabia and Israel during the Gulf War in January 1991 caused panic among Turks, who believed, not unreasonably, that their state might too become a target. Gas masks were distributed in the southeast of the country. Indeed, there were even somewhat more hysterical fears that Istanbul might become subject to attack. The revelations about the extent of the development of Iraq's weapons of mass destruction, in the wake of the expulsion of Iraqi forces from Kuwait, ought to have come as a sobering surprise to Turkey.

Turkey therefore has a stronger interest than most states in ensuring that Iraq's program to develop weapons of mass destruction has been eradicated, and that a rigorous mechanism for continued verification is introduced. Curiously, this aspect is often absent from public discussions of whether the UN sanctions against Iraq should be lifted, and even the Turkish military appears to have become rather blasé about the issue.

Turkey also has an interest in ensuring that Iran and Syria do not develop weapons of mass destruction. Iran's apparent desire to acquire such weaponry has been a matter of considerable speculation over the past several years. It seems that Iran already possesses chemical weapons; it also appears to have a biological weapons program and has been trying to develop, in part through imports, a nuclear capability. The latter may take up to ten years to develop without significant outside input. Iran, however, lacks an effective delivery system either for its chemical capability or in the expectation of developing its other areas of nonconventional weapons.[23] Syria, too, is believed to have chemical weapons, although there appears to be little international concern that Damascus might seek to acquire a nuclear capability.

To date, justified concerns about the proliferation of weapons of mass destruction in the region do not appear to have translated into the Turkish military's strategic doctrine. This is difficult to comprehend, especially as, in the absence of a clear common enemy, the NATO commitment to Turkey's defense looks increasingly shaky. The apparent lack of concern in the Turkish military is perhaps partly explained by its inability to take sufficiently seriously the prospect of threats from its Arab and Iranian neighbors. Threat perceptions to the east of the country are, in contrast, dominated by the position of Russia and the PKK-led insurgency in the Kurdish southeast of Turkey.

Whether Ankara's relaxed attitude to regional proliferation is calmly measured or irresponsibly complacent, it does not appear that the issue is likely to be a central determinant of strategy toward the region, at least for the foreseeable future.

WATER POLITICS

Turkey is beginning to near the end of an ambitious program of civil engineering aimed at exploiting the waters of the Euphrates River. When combined with the consequent expansion in hydroelectric power and the agricultural sector, this comprises the Southeastern Anatolia Project (known by its Turkish acronym of GAP). The largest dam, the Atatürk Dam, has been built and much of its reservoir filled. In November 1994 the first of the Urfa irrigation tunnels were opened. Through this network the Harran Plain will be irrigated, and the total irrigated area of Turkey increased by 19 percent.

As Turkey has increasingly begun to exploit the Euphrates waters for its own use, so alarm has increased on the part of the downstream riparian states, Syria and Iraq.[24] In the past, they have used the resources of the river at will, without any incentive for using optimal irrigation or damming methods. Now they face the possibility of three unpalatable consequences of Turkey's recent exploitation of the river—first, that in the future the waters flowing across the Turkish border will be insufficient for their use; second, that water quality will decline due to the heavy use of agricultural chemicals; and third, that they will have to overhaul their own water-harnessing techniques to husband the increasingly scarce resource. This could be extremely expensive, especially for Syria, which has already experienced severe technical problems in utilizing the dam at Lake Asad for electricity generation.

A fourth fear, and an intention that Ankara has repeatedly denied, is that control of the Euphrates could be used strategically to apply political pressure to the downstream riparians. For both Syria and Iraq this fear was made tangible in mid-January 1990 when for thirty days Turkey diverted the flow of the Euphrates into the Atatürk Dam reservoir.[25] It mattered little that Turkey had already sought to compensate the other two states by releasing water over most of the previous two months from its two other largest dams, or that Turkey chose to undertake the operation during the winter when the level of precipitation would be at its height.

To date all attempts to arrive at an agreement acceptable to all three sides have failed. A trilateral technical committee has met periodically since 1980 to discuss the issue. In 1987, Turkey and Syria concluded a protocol under which Turkey agreed to release a minimum annual average of 500 cubic meters per second "until the ultimate allocation" of the flow between the three states is made. Iraq objected to this formula because it was omitted from the agreement, and Syria was only partly assuaged by the accord due to its temporary nature. Turkey has in turn been reluctant to commit itself to a permanent, open-ended agreement because of long-term uncertainty about the future volume of water flow. The Turkish government appeared to pull back from an undertaking to negotiate a final accord by the end of 1993. The best that Turkey appears able to contemplate is a twenty-five-year agreement on water flows.[26]

For Turkey the river issue is, as with the related question of the PKK insurgency, a difficult and sensitive problem, but only in its relations with its immediate neighbors rather than the wider region. The management of such critical problems with Turkey's immediate neighbors is therefore always likely to take precedence over less crucial regional issues.

THE MIDDLE EAST MARKET

It is only over the last fifteen years or so that Turkey has come to value and exploit the Middle East as a market. It was the large successive jumps in the price of crude oil and the effect that such increases had on Turkey's balance of payments and its debt profile that obliged Turkey to do more business with the region. Turkey sought to export goods and contracting services to the region to ensure something approaching balanced trade, primarily with the oil-exporting countries, notably Iran, Iraq, Saudi Arabia, and Libya.

The high point of Turkey's trade with the Middle East came in the early 1980s. In 1982 Turkey exported $2.5 billion worth of goods to the Middle East, more than 44 percent of total exports. By 1985 this figure had risen to $3.2 billion, although the profile of the region in Turkey's foreign trade had slipped to 30 percent as the new export-led growth strategy began to prosper. Today the Middle East market accounts for around 20 percent of Turkish exports; far from the heyday of the first half of the last decade, yet nevertheless a significant proportion. There seems little reason why this trend should not continue.

Indeed, if anything, over the longer term it should increase. As already mentioned, a key element in the GAP project is agricultural expansion. With Turkey largely self-sufficient in farm produce and the southeast being host to a relatively small part of the total population, much of the new agricultural output will be for export. The Arab world, which has fought a progressively losing battle for food security, is envisaged to be a major market by the time the GAP project is scheduled for completion in 2005.

Turkey is also looking forward to developing important trading relations with other parts of the region. The Turkish government is very interested in economic opportunities springing from the Arab-Israeli peace process, especially, in the short run, for its contracting sector. Turkey also sees the Middle East as providing a good market for its expanding defense industries, with the Gulf Cooperation Council states and Egypt perceived as being at the top of the list of potential purchasers. The development of new trade links will not be a one-way street, with growing imports of gas likely to favor Middle Eastern exporters. Turkey has recently added purchases of Algerian liquid natural gas (LNG) to the liquefied petroleum gas (LPG) which it has been buying from the North African state for over one year.[27] The construction of a further LNG processing plant and Turkey's general strategy of developing its gas power sector should mean a growing trading relationship with Algeria.[28] The desire to develop its use of gas while not becoming overdependent on Russia as a supplier could result in closer trading relations with Qatar as well. At the end of 1993, following nearly three years of discussions, it was agreed that Turkey would buy an initial 2 million tons of LNG from Qatar.[29]

The main reason for Turkey to develop improved relations with the Middle East as a whole is therefore economic. It has proved in the past that it is capable of trading with a variety of Middle Eastern countries, regardless of regime. The expectation is that this approach will continue to prevail in future, with the pragmatic criterion of economic complementarity being the decisive factor in the establishment and pursuit of commercial relations.

TOWARD A LIMITED ROLE IN THE REGION

It has become a cliché to say that the end of the Cold War and the fall of communism have provided both new threats and new opportunities for Turkey. These threats and opportunities do not for the most part lie in the Middle East. The main threats for Turkey today are to be found in the shape of Russia; in the uncertain relationship between Turkey and its traditional friends, both institutionally and bilaterally; in the West; and in the enduring possibility of widespread instability on its borders. Only in relation to the future of Iraq is instability an immediate concern for Turkey's Middle East policy. As for opportunities, the large Turkish contracting and trading companies appear most absorbed by the economic potential of a clutch of members of the Commonwealth of Independent States (CIS) . Turkey's small entrepreneurs and tradesmen favor such countries as Romania, Azerbaijan, and Turkmenistan.

With many more immediate concerns in the Balkans and various parts of the CIS making continuous demands on its foreign affairs resources, the need for stability and the defusing of potential conflicts in the Middle East has never been more pressing for Turkey. In view of such an objective, Ankara has been well served—and would be so again—by having recourse to some of its traditional principles of engagement. For example, it should establish, continue, and, if possible, deepen relations with all states in the region, regardless of ideology or orientation. Second, it should steer clear of intraregional rivalries and tensions, regardless of which states are involved; and third, it should not become, wittingly or unwittingly, the surrogate for the policies of any Western countries toward the region, unless they conform with the interests of Turkey.

Clearly, however, a Kemalist "do nothing" approach to the Middle East is no longer either possible or advisable for the Turkish state. A number of issues require a mixture of firm assertion and careful management. The top priority for Ankara must surely be to minimize outside influences over its own internal affairs, especially those that have a key importance for the future of the country. This issue is important in relation to two areas. Any attempts by Middle Eastern states, through material or practical means, to interfere in the domestic political process must cease. This would apply to the external funding of political movements in Turkey, as it would to training or assistance given to those groups that seek to use violence to further their cause. It would also apply equally to those states suspected of such interference, whether they were a difficult neighbor like Iran or a supposed friend such as Saudi Arabia.

Second, the harboring or support of the PKK as it prosecutes its secessionist campaign of violence in southeast Turkey must also cease. Here Ankara has met with considerable understanding and assistance from the United States, which has helped to deter Syria from its sponsorship, direct or indirect, of the organization.

Another priority must be to manage a small number of potentially explosive issues that affect both Turkey and its immediate Middle Eastern neighbors. The most important and pressing is the future of Iraq. To this end the establishment of regular consultations at the foreign ministerial level involving Iran, Syria, and Turkey has been a positive step forward. Those countries that have expressed reservations about the initiation of this dialogue, notably the United States and Britain, have done so without the best interests of the Turkish state uppermost in their minds. Such sessions are important because of the need to avoid the potential suspicion, competition, or even conflict that could ensue in the event of the collapse or fragmentation of the Iraqi state.

All three states have a set of common interests in relation to Iraq: that the integrity of the Iraqi state should be maintained; that Iraq's program to develop weapons of mass destruction should be ended and adequate verification mechanisms introduced to ensure against recidivism; that a Kurdish state should not emerge in northeastern Iraq; that the borders of the states of the region should be inviolable and be recognized as such, Kuwait included; and that access to commercial opportunities provided by the Iraqi market should be restored as soon as possible, conditional upon the satisfactory implementation of Security Council Resolution 687.[30] These are, it should be noted, also the common interests of most of the international community as articulated at the Security Council by such states as France and Russia. It therefore does not seem unreasonable, from the perspective of the interests of Turkey, that such aims should be actively pursued.

A third priority must be to encourage the Arab-Israeli peace process as a way of seeking a broad-based and sustainable peace in the region. A significant by-product of such an objective would be the normalization of relations with Israel, the state with which the

Turkish foreign policy elite has the greatest affinity. Here, Turkey's involvement is likely to be low-key, but no less helpful for being so. Turkey's cordial relations with both Israel and the Palestine Liberation Organization (PLO) are an asset that could be useful in diplomacy and peacemaking. Ankara has also been prepared to offer Turkish troops to act as peace monitors in difficult circumstances.[31] With Turkish contingents recently in Somalia and currently in Bosnia, such a contribution will also help bolster Turkey's emergence as a responsible and impartial actor on a wider stage. It will also help Turkey position itself to take maximum advantage of the commercial and contracting opportunities that are expected sooner or later to accrue as a result of the implementation of the peace process.

But does all of this amount to a new role for Turkey in the Middle East? If an unequivocal answer is required, then it must be no. All talk of a new role should in any case be eschewed because of how it will be interpreted by the other powers in the region. A new Turkish role in the Middle East will, for Arab intellectuals and regional leaders alike, have all the resonance of the Menderes years of clumsy interventionism in the mid- to late 1950s. Those offering advice to the Turkish government need to be mindful of the exceptional circumstances of the Gulf crisis and the idiosyncratic nature of Özal's foreign policy with its most un-Turkish flourish. They need also to consider that it is such unrepresentative experiences that now dominate Middle Eastern perceptions of contemporary Turkey. To compensate for this distorted image, more effort must be invested in the presentation of Turkish foreign policy constraints than in loose talk of a new role.

Yet all of this is not to deny that the Middle East could be a better and more stable region, and that toward this end Turkey could play a part. Özal was always a zealous advocate of stability through interdependency. Turkey was, for example, a leading light in the idea of the integration of the electricity networks of the region. This aim is now on the way to being realized, and, as a result of the successful achievements of the Middle East peace process, may well in the not-too-distant future hook up Turkey and Israel's power lines via Jordan and Syria.

Turkey has also been a constructive (though cautious) participant in the multilateral track of the Arab-Israeli peace process and has provided the venue for a number of meetings related to it. From a low-profile beginning, the multilaterals offer the possibility of incrementally building a practical framework to foster peace and cooperation in the Middle East. The agenda of the multilaterals, covering as it does economic development and arms control issues, certainly holds an attraction for Ankara. However, as long as Syria, Iraq, and Iran all remain outside its structure, Turkey's involvement will be restrained. Ultimately, assuming that the peace process continues to take root and participation in the multilaterals is expanded, this process may provide the most efficacious vehicle for Turkish participation in the region's affairs: a low profile, yet effective contribution to the stability and prosperity of the Middle East within the context of an inclusive rather than an exclusive body of states.

CHAPTER TWELVE

ALTERNATIVE TURKISH ROLES IN THE FUTURE MIDDLE EAST

Graham E. Fuller

The events of the past decade have thrust Turkey to the geopolitical forefront of the Middle East. Many factors contributed to this event, foremost among them the unanticipated overnight collapse of the Soviet Union and the breakup of its empire. Turkey was the primary beneficiary of that momentous event, since the instant liberation of large areas from Soviet control gave Turkey sudden room for play in areas long closed to it: the Balkans, the Caucasus, the Black Sea region, and Central Asia. During the same period, Iraq was convulsed by Saddam Hussein's foolish gamble against Kuwait, which left Iraq prostrate and threatened by separatism, unleashing a new Kurdish political reality in the area, however precarious. Turkey is thus involved in Iraqi politics as never before, and must face its own long-postponed and fateful consideration of its Kurdish minority. In addition, the "Third Balkan War" in former Yugoslavia has raised new questions about the Muslim factor in southeastern Europe and new webs of alliance in that volatile region.

In the Arab world, growing fears of the spread of Islamic radicalism have created new and different ties between the many Arab states seeking security and the United States. Major progress toward a final Arab-Israeli settlement is setting to rest one of the most corrosive long-term issues of all in the Middle East, but its resolution will quickly open the door to new, long-unattended domestic issues in most countries of the Middle East that will severely affect their stability and perhaps even their ideological orientation.

In short, discerning the shape of Turkey's future in the Middle East and the world has become vastly more complicated with the emergence of a multitude of new factors; and this all comes in the context of a new and fluid world order in which the strategic lodestars of Cold War political navigation have vanished. There are several alternative scenarios of Turkey's future relationships in the Middle East —perhaps only dimly foreseeable today. Indeed, there can be no one single future assessed for Turkey, but small indicators in the present could, under changing circumstances, suggest very different kinds of prospects.

TURKEY'S ALTERNATIVES

Four different alternative courses suggest themselves for Turkey's future orientation in the Middle East. First is a straight-line projection of Turkey's familiar national characteristics and policies. But the seeds of several other options are also latent in the present political situation. Thus, second, there is the possibility of the assertion of an increasing Turkish nationalist orientation, moving in the direction of pan-Turkist policies and possibly bordering on chauvinism. Third is the possibility of a new Islamic orientation, in which Turkey places greater emphasis on its Islamic roots in the Middle East. Finally, there is a prospect of a new federative-style Middle East, in which many of the old borders and relationships will be reshaped, possibly within a more democratic context. The last three new directions in Turkish orientation are naturally less likely than a continuation of present trends. But this has been a decade of more than a few surprises; even if none of these alternative scenarios come to dominate in the first decades of the next century, they represent latent tendencies that will certainly be felt as minor undercurrents, even if they do not emerge as dominant. Nor are they mutually exclusive: the chances are that all will be present, to one degree or another, within the Turkish body politic.

Straight-line projections of present circumstances are, of course, always the most likely, anticipating as they do few major changes of direction. Turkey's policies since the end of World War II have been marked by a strategic commitment to the West, including an alliance against Soviet expansionism; avoidance of involvement in Middle Eastern politics where possible; and, in the last decade, a move toward a free-market economy and expansion of international trade in all directions. These policies have come in the context of increasingly democratic governance within Turkey itself. Ankara's policies toward the Middle East have been largely congruent with U.S. policies: opposition to Soviet client states; cooperation against Iraqi expansionism; working ties with Israel; distrust of Iran's intentions and role in the region; good ties with the Persian Gulf oil states and concern for their stability; and good ties with Egypt, Pakistan, Morocco, Jordan, and other moderate regional states.

A straight-line projection of these characteristics into the future implies a Turkey that will remain largely impervious to the major changes that are taking place. Greater Turkish interest in the Caucasus and Central Asia is certain, as are a wary eye on potential rogue policies of Iraq and Iran and a greater voice in the Balkans, but no significant change in world vision or ideological outlook. These themes are broadly known and discussed within a fairly narrow framework, even though shifts in Ankara's tactical policies can have considerable impact as, for example, in the degree of Ankara's cooperation in maintaining UN sanctions on Saddam Hussein's regime. This scenario under any circumstances suggests a Turkey of increased importance in the region, but moving within fairly familiar lines of interest and behavior.

Under any circumstances, however, Turkey's new interests in the former regions of the Soviet empire automatically converts Ankara into something of a bridge between Middle East politics and the new Muslim cultures and states of the Balkans, Caucasus, Central Asia, and China. The Middle East will now be more aware of and even involved in these new Muslim regions—in part via Turkey. Indeed, most of these regions are the Turkic world.

A NATIONALIST COURSE

The genius of Atatürk was to envision a finite and practical definition for a new Turkish identity to replace the collapsed Ottoman identity. This new identity also explicitly eschewed any kind of pan-Turkism or irredentist vision of the future Turkey—out of wise recognition that most of the world's Turks were enveloped within a threatening Soviet empire. With the liberation in 1991 of all these non-Russian ethnic regions of the former Soviet empire, however, the concept of pan-Turkism has emerged from seventy years of hibernation and is now an intellectually acceptable topic in both regions. The consequences of this change are still far from clear. Like all nationalisms, pan-Turkism can serve as an acceptable cultural bond of unity within a context of special relationships, or it can metastasize into a virulent, intolerant, chauvinistic force threatening to its neighbors.

First, there is the reality: some 50 million or so Turkic peoples in the former Soviet Union, mostly in Central Asia and in Azerbaijan, some also within Russia itself, especially in Tatarstan on the Volga. But there are also 8 million Uighur Turks in Xinjiang province in Western China. There are also up to 2 million Turkish minorities (Uzbek, Turkmen, and Kyrgyz) in northern Afghanistan and perhaps some 10 million Turks (mostly Azerbaijani, but also Turkmen) in Iran. There are, of course, Turkish minorities in Iraq, Greece, and Bulgaria, and a large minority in Cyprus.

Turkey now has at least the option to pursue a far more nationalist, pan-Turkist policy than ever before. There has long been a nationalist trend within Turkish politics, most notably embodied in the figure of Alparslan Türkes and his National Movement Party, whose views on pan-Turkish unity, seen as marginal (if not subversive) for many years, have now been vindicated by external events. This trend has been complemented by the emergence and public tolerance for greater ethnic expression within Turkey, including political expression by formerly "captive" Turks from the communist world who now press Ankara for policies more responsive to their brethren in China, the Central Asian republics, Tatarstan, the Caucasus, and the Balkans (including a large contingent of Bosnian Turks). These ethnic elements represent a new public pressure group in the formulation of Turkish foreign policy—a process that is increasingly less the sole preserve of an elitist Foreign Ministry.

The burgeoning character of the Kurdish dilemma in Turkey also serves to fuel nationalist flames. Popular anger at the Kurds has intensified Turkish nationalist feelings. Strong popular frustration grows out of the plight of the Bosnian Muslims as well, and from the losses Azerbaijanis have suffered at the hands of Armenian and Karabaghi forces inside Azerbaijan. In principle it may only be a matter of time before Turkish radical nationalists push hard on the status of Iranian Azeris, deprived of many cultural rights inside Iranian Azerbaijan, and the position of Uighurs in China, whose interest in national autonomy or even independence is certain to grow. In short, the raw material is there for a new nationalist departure in Turkish foreign policy. What would its consequences be?

First, Turkey could undertake a more aggressive stance toward the protection of Turkish minorities in neighboring countries—even moving toward irredentism. This policy would affect neighbors such as Bulgaria, Greece, Iraq, and Iran, as well as Armenia (insofar as it would affect Erevan's military policies and support for Armenian separatism in Azerbaijan). The confrontation with Iran would be the most serious since it would threaten Iran's territorial integrity in a key province and could very likely lead to war between Ankara and Tehran—even though Turkey would probably make no claims on Iranian Azerbaijan itself but would only support its union with Baku. These tensions and rivalries with Tehran would probably extend more vigorously to Central Asia as Ankara and Tehran would clash over the future of the Kurds in the region as well, which could affect the territorial integrity of both states as well as Iraq.

While Turkish and Kurdish nationalism are at odds with each other today, it is possible to conceive of some kind of "combined nationalism" in which Turkey, rather than running the risk of "losing" Kurdistan, would join forces in supporting a Greater Kurdistan that would include Iranian and Iraqi Kurdistan under Turkish aegis and protection. The Kurds in these areas would see Turkey as the best vehicle for their own ambitions and the safest political culture within which to exist, given the more advanced state of Turkish democracy. This scenario obviously leads to clashes with both Iraq and Iran.

Conversely, however, a Turkey whose nationalism verged on chauvinism would find it extremely difficult to accommodate any Kurdish demands for autonomy within its borders and might thus alienate the Kurds entirely, forcing their nationalist leaders to ally with Iran and Iraq against Turkey. The Kurdish issue is already the preeminent issue within the nationalist movement, which is already growing less flexible and more emotional on the topic. A failure of the Turkish state to accommodate its own Kurdish population could lead to civil war, with drastic impact on the Turkish social order and Turkish democracy, stability, and economy. It could bring Turkey into sharp conflict with Europe and the United States, further embittering Turkey against the West; indeed, the more nationalist (*ülkücü*) circles in Turkey are already permeated with a generally negative attitude toward the West, its power, and its "imperialist" tendencies, which they see as designed to weaken Turkey.

A nationalist, pan-Turkist Turkey would represent a sharp challenge to its neighbors in the Middle East. Apart from Iraq and Iran, whose territorial integrity is directly challenged, Syria would view itself as threatened, especially by Turkish control of Euphrates water. This scenario also implies a Turkey that would draw sharp lines of distinction between itself and the Arab world, for which Turks have historically had little respect. But it would not automatically exclude good relations with the Gulf oil states who themselves view both Iraq and Iran as threats and who might welcome Turkish counterpressure.

A nationalist, pan-Turkist Turkey would also represent a rival to Russia's own interests and influence in the Caucasus and Central Asia. A Russia thus challenged would probably seek allies in Iran and the Arab world to balance Turkish influence. The situation in some ways would therefore be reminiscent of the Cold War alignment of forces.

While some Gulf states might welcome a strong, even a nationalist, Turkey as a balancing factor in the Gulf, by and large the Arab world would be hostile to it. Turkism and Arabism would most likely be at odds rather than sympathetic, with the perceived Turkish threat waking memories of the unlamented Ottoman past. But for the first time in history, an active pan-Turkism would be large enough in geographical territory to rival pan-Arabism—two huge rival ethnic blocs. The key flash point would come primarily where Turkish and Arab states meet—that is, in Syria and Iraq. Iran, however, would probably find itself allied with Arab regional states against the expansion of Turkish influence.

It is important to note that a strong nationalist trend might emerge in conjunction with a return to military dictatorship by Turkey. These trends have largely been put to rest. But if Turkey is severely tested by internal separatism, ethnic strife, economic hardship, poor relations with the West, and hostility from Iraq and Iran, it is conceivable (though unlikely) that a strong national-chauvinist regime might indeed be military or authoritarian in character—until Turkey could at some time reclaim its positive experience with democracy. This combination of forces could push a military or authoritarian regime toward greater foreign adventure in a search for legitimacy and mobilization of the public.

These are all only theoretical formulations of power blocs. In the real world, despite a fundamental rivalry between Turkish and Arab blocs, some states within each would find interests with states in the other—such as in the Gulf—preventing the formation of "pure" ethnic blocs. Indeed, not all Turkic states in the world would wish to subordinate themselves to dominant Turkish influence, nor would Turkey necessarily seek the physical political union of all Turkic states.[1] Finally, a union of Turkic states in some form, even if achievable, involves for Turkey considerable trade-offs in its relations elsewhere and might not be a sufficient prize in itself. Its orientation would essentially be anti-Russian and anti-Chinese—two formidable adversaries. Even the greatest economic prize, Central Asian oil and gas, is hostage to geography: it is accessible to Turkey only via Russia or Iran—short of a risky pipeline scheme across the Caspian, Azerbaijan, and Georgia.

A nationalist, pan-Turkist Turkey would be in keeping with other broad international trends that emphasize ethnicity. As with all such movements, it need not be territorially irredentist or aggressively hostile to outsiders, but would complicate political cooperation in the region if it went much beyond the cultivation of special cultural and economic ties. Indeed, trends of ethnic separatism could also lead to some Turkic states' seeking to maintain full independence with no subordination to any other state, however ethnically similar. The Uzbeks, for example, might seek their own regional hegemony in a Central Asian world distant from the shores of the Aegean and Mediterranean. Turkey might limit its close political ties to Azerbaijan, and a politically isolated Kazakstan and Turkmenistan (where the oil and gas is), leaving the rest to the Uzbeks.

In terms of current Middle Eastern politics, such an ideological trend in Turkey would increase confrontationalism in the region. But despite the problems, the chances are excellent that a more assertive regional Turkish nationalism of some kind will emerge in the region under almost any circumstances. Turkey has a long tradition of geopolitical thinking and wide-ranging rule throughout the region at various times; it now has the options, and potentially the institutions, to exert greater influence where the rest of the region is still finding its way.

AN ISLAMIC IDENTITY FOR TURKEY

Turkey is not a likely candidate to adopt a full-scale Islamic identity. Indeed, the history of modern Turkey is the repudiation of this Ottoman past, associated as it is with military humiliation, failure, and collapse in the empire's last century. But several trends encourage a rethinking of the conventional wisdom about the "inherently secular" nature of Turkey. First, Turkey has not yet reached full intellectual or social accommodation with Islam in the contemporary period. Secularism was of course imposed upon the Turkish population by Atatürk—a move that was essential to Turkey's development as a modern, Western-oriented state. As important as this development was, a cost was associated: Atatürk's sweeping secularization cut Turkey off sharply from its past. Today, a Turkey that is fairly comfortable with its successes in modernization has begun to reexamine its long-reviled Ottoman past. Recollections are growing, even among staunch Atatürkists, that the Ottoman era was hardly all bad, indeed, that it had its periods of great glory as a high point of world Islamic civilization.

Islamists, of course, never once doubted the glory of the Ottoman era, and feel that the nation has at last begun to shed the particular cultural blindness of the Atatürk era and catch up with the correct historical perception. Even secular Turks are beginning to move behind the historical looking-glass to discover Ottoman history as an important part of the Turkish developmental experience. Many are deciding that they do not need to apologize for the Ottoman past, that Turkey had begun to find a path to modernization on its own— even before Atatürk's drastic measures in a severely truncated new nationalist Turkey. In short, Turkey does not have to owe all its modernization to Atatürk and the West alone, but can find strong elements of it within the Turkish tradition itself—a more authentic source. Ample intellectual and historical grounds exist to encourage the rediscovery of Turkey's Islamic past. This development facilitates a rapprochement with Turkey's Islamic identity, even from a secular point of view.

Second, Islam and nationalism do not have to be completely contradictory movements, as can be observed elsewhere in the Muslim world today. True, nationalism based on the nation-state is in many ways an ideology imported from the West. But in many cases Islamist and nationalist movements operate along parallel lines: both stress authenticity of culture as opposed to imported culture; both look askance at the colonial and imperial legacies of the past; and both encourage a thin-skinned, prickly kind of nativism that makes Western dealings with them more difficult. A Turkey that feels excluded from the European membership to which it aspires; that witnesses the disproportionate sufferings of one of the few Muslim populations in Europe, in Bosnia, that the West will not relieve; under Western pressure regarding human rights in Kurdistan; and seeking a full measure of pride in its own past can easily accommodate a healthy dose of Islam with its secular nationalism.

As Turkey finds new options open in the former Soviet empire and a more active role in Iraqi politics, the charge has been leveled by some in the Middle East that Turkey may aspire to some kind of "neo-Ottomanism." In the mouths of Turkey's opponents, such a term is redolent more of imperialism than Islam. It suggests a renewed Turkish domination of the region, including its old imperial lands in the Arab world (but never including Central Asia). It also suggests Western manipulation of Turkey as an instrument of Western strategy in the region, at the cost of Arab interests. To Arabs, neo-Ottomanism might not look any better than pan-Turkism, even though it is not by definition racially exclusivist. Turkish domination under any rubric is not welcome.

But the term "neo-Ottomanism" is not simply pejorative. The traditional Western nation-state concept is now somewhat under assault. A glance at the disorders and decline of so many (non)nation-states of the world, rent by neo-nationalism and separatism, suggests that the Western model of the nation-state may not necessarily be an ideal either. First, most countries are not true nation-states; therefore nationalism as a basis of state organization in a multiethnic state only encourages separatism. Second, nation-states seem to fall readily into patterns of ethnic conflict and discrimination and can make little claim to long-term superiority of international organization. The Ottoman era, to the contrary, presents a model of a multinational, multiethnic, multireligious state living together in what was unusual harmony by the standards of the time. (Naturally, even the Ottoman Empire began to suffer the contagion of nationalism by the nineteenth century, and its system of administration—however excellent by contemporary standards—also created many grievances among its disparate population, including among Turks themselves.) But in a Middle East rent by ethnic and religious conflict, with Arab states that are not nations and an Arab nation that does not have a state, there is time at least to rethink some kind of union of states based on something broader and more enduring than raw nationalism.

In the eyes of some Turkish intellectuals today, then, neo-Ottomanism suggests at least a new social glue, even within the confines of the modern Turkish state, by which diverse peoples—especially Kurds—can readily take part without feeling excluded.[2] The social glue of the Ottoman period can now be seen as two-fold. In the eyes of its contemporaries the glue was Islam, linking largely Muslim peoples in a nonnational order of theoretical equality. (Large Christian populations and a smaller Jewish population also were part of the empire in which they had genuine citizenship rights, though not as many as Muslims. It is difficult to find other social glue for the Ottoman period without turning to imperial Ottoman (secular) values of allegiance, which did not truly exist then outside of the Islamic context. Neo-Ottomanism, then, can suggest a society with greater inclusivity, without necessarily hinting at territorial expansionism. Will the new Turkey reconcile with the Ottoman past to find a more comfortable place in the Muslim world?

Whatever the historical circumstances, neo-Ottomanism represents an important element in any return of the Turks to an Islamic identity. Such an identity can never overwhelm the national Turkish identity, but it can complement it considerably and push the Turks toward a broader sphere of identification in the region. While Turks have historically looked down on their former Arab subjects—feelings intensified by the Cold War in which many Arabs looked toward Moscow—closer ties with the Arab world need not necessarily come at the cost of Western integration. Indeed, a Turkey with good communications in the Arab world would be a valuable partner to a forward-looking Europe.

In fact, this type of thinking is already present to some extent in Turkey's Islamist Refah (Welfare) Party. Refah desires Turkey to play a greater role in its "own" world of Islamic culture and to avoid a slavish identification with Western interests. Refah itself demonstrates a mixture of views, expressing warmth toward Saudi Arabia and the Gulf states (which most Islamist parties do not), and also believes in good ties with Germany—where many Turks live and work—a potentially important economic and political partner for Turkey.

A strengthened Islamic identity need not be Islamist in the sense of radical political Islam or "fundamentalism." It can suggest a coexistence in both the Western and Muslim world that would lend Turkey considerable cultural-strategic weight. Such a Turkey would be far more prickly toward Western assumptions that it should automatically pursue a Western agenda in the region. Sharp differences of interest on Islamic world matters would coexist with considerable overlap of interest on many strategic issues (especially related to Russia) and economic issues. An Islamic-oriented Turkey would likely pursue close relations with the Gulf oil states—partly out of economic interest—and would oppose nearly all Western intervention in the Muslim world. Ties with Israel would be nonexistent or pro forma at best. Turkey would react far more sharply on the issues of Turkish minorities in Greece and Bulgaria and would be actively interventionist on the question of Bosnian Muslims. It would also be inclined to support closer political ties in the Middle East, including certain kinds of federation or confederation schemes. Such a Turkey could also serve as spearhead for the cause of Islam in Russia and the former Soviet republics, putting it on a possible collision course with Russia.

Finally, an Islamic-oriented Turkey might serve as a moderating influence on Islamist policies in the region. Islamist movements often have only poorly evolved theories and policies about the application of Islamic ideas to modern policy questions. Turkey could well develop a more advanced model synthesizing Islamic ideals with the broader corpus of international law. It then could perhaps head a coalition of Islamic states interested in retaining the principles of Islam in governance without assuming the highly radical or narrow visions championed by many of the most radical or violent movements in the region. In this fashion, Turkey might again perform its classic cultural role of bridge between East and West, effecting a broader synthesis of Islam and Western political concepts.

GREATER MIDDLE EAST DEMOCRATIC CONFEDERATION

A Middle Eastern political confederation need not necessarily be based on Islam per se; it could rest on a more secular foundation of democratic values and moderation. Such a grouping would clearly imply commitment to a modernist and moderate agenda in which states sharing common political values find common cause against those that do not.

This idea is not completely new. Some ethnically unrelated states found common security interests for a period during the Cold War, especially Turkey and Iran (and, briefly, Iraq). Because of the East-West divisions of the Cold War, and domination of the region by the Arab-Israeli conflict, such moderate alliances were short-lived, over-shadowed by the dynamics of larger struggles. Today common security concerns about Iran and Iraq link the smaller Gulf states in the Gulf Cooperation Council, sharing a political moderation—but definitely not a liberal political vision for future reform and change.

While it might appear counterintuitive, both Iran and Iraq—especially Iran—have considerable potential for development of modern democratic institutions. Iran has had the experience of entirely home-generated parliamentary government starting at the turn of the century (though often at odds with despotic shahs). Even today it permits significant public debate in a lively parliament that matters highly in Iranian politics. Iraq, after the political firestorm and cataclysm of the Saddam Hussein era, may find it virtually impossible to preserve and manage a multiethnic, multireligious Iraq except through processes of democratic federalism—unless more Saddams appear to keep the country united by force and terror. These three states could be the nucleus of a broader grouping that will eventually emerge, concerned with bringing to an end the strong-man era of Middle East politics—characterized by arbitrary and despotic rulers who intimidate neighbors, build up massive arms depots, stoke radical ideologies, foster internal repression, and increase regional insecurity. It would be in the interests of these more politically advanced states to isolate and weaken nondemocratic, hostile, and destabilizing forces.

Such a policy suggests a Turkey that has grown more comfortable with its existence in the Middle East, a Turkey that need not defensively declare that it is "European." Turkey has generally acted as if its more advanced political development was somehow demeaned by any association with its geographical and geopolitical region. Of course Turkey is European in many aspects of its culture, institutions, and tastes; its political values need not be provocatively defined as European so much as described as enlightened, democratic, and sharing in contemporary universal values. A Turkey in which Islam was a more natural part of foreign policy might worry less about the implications of being a central player in Middle East politics, an involvement that has unquestionably made Turkey culturally uncomfortable up to now.

VARIABLES IN THE MIDDLE EAST

Turkey's options in the future Middle East cannot be determined by itself alone; developments in the region and the world will affect its inclinations and decisions. What are some of these determinants?

First, American and European policies will have significant impact. Will Turkey grow more integrated into Europe, or will it be rejected, causing it to look more closely at alternatives? Increasingly negative development of the Kurdish situation could draw Western opprobrium and further alienate Turkish opinion. Bosnia also has negatively influenced Turkish cooperation with the United States in several areas. What kind of future does the West perceive for itself with the Islamic world, especially an Islamic world that now lives increasingly inside the West as well, both in the Balkans and as immigrants in Western Europe?

Turkey's evolution will also be deeply affected by political change throughout the Middle East. If Islamist regimes are able to gain a major voice in the region in the next few decades, Turkey will find itself under considerable ideological onslaught as the bastion of secularism, betrayer of Islam, and lapdog of the West in the Middle East. It was Turkey after all that was once capital and leader of the Sunni world—until Atatürk abolished the Caliphate and left Sunnis without a commander of the faithful. Unless Turkey itself undertakes some bows in the direction of a more Islamic agenda, it will become more isolated from the Islamic character of the rest of the Middle East. Conversely, if democratic governance makes some progress in other Middle Eastern states in the next decade or so, Turkey will find natural allies and could be drawn into a new moderate and democratic grouping .

The security needs of many states in the Middle East will also affect Turkey. Will smaller Persian Gulf states seek a counterweight to neutralize Iran and Iraq? Will other Arab states seek a Turkish role in security cooperation? The past would suggest considerable Arab leeriness of any such Turkish role, linked as it was at one time with the Western strategic and security agenda in the Middle East. As the

218   ALTERNATIVE TURKISH ROLES

Cold War and the Arab-Israeli conflict fade, Turkey may become a more acceptable partner.

Turkey's acceptability in the region in part rides on the development of the Arabs' own perception of the aging concept of Arab nationalism. Arab nationalism is an entirely legitimate concept of aspiration toward greater commonness of purpose in the political, economic, and cultural arenas, based on shared cultural and linguistic heritage. Indeed, it is a cultural more than an ethnic concept. Unfortunately it has been exploited by many different leaders to many different ends, often to justify the ambitions of despotic rulers seeking regional domination. Arab unity as a term has thus become somewhat suspect, if not cynically received by many Arabs, because of the circumstances of its past invocation. Arab nationalism as a driving force needs to focus on the positive and universal features of Arab civilization and its relationship to world civilization, rather than being an instrument of exclusivism and even confrontation with other Muslim societies. Arab perception and use of Arab nationalism will therefore have great impact on the role of Turkey in the region in the future.

Arab interest in the "Islamic" character of the Ottoman experience will also be significant. To most Arab nationalists, Ottoman rule was the imperial embrace from which they were liberated by Arab nationalism. A more Islamically oriented Arab nationalism, however, could reach reconciliation with a greater Islamic vision that would implicitly include a sense of neo-Ottomanism, particularly with its reach into the Balkans and the Caucasus. How much will Arabs cheer a Turkish role of leadership in Central Asia as well, or will the issue be strictly one of competitive rivalry?

In sum, will the Arab world gradually move toward accommodation and cultural reconciliation with the West, or will it be driven more broadly by separatism or rivalry? This will, in turn, depend heavily on how the West comes to treat the Muslim world in the new post–Cold War, post–Arab-Israel era. The road may divide or converge, depending on the attitudes and events on both sides that will deeply affect Turkey's own options.

CONCLUSION

A conservative guess suggests that Turkey will not change its cultural and political orientation sharply in the next decades. However, outside that unchanging vision, the alternatives presented above are not entirely fanciful, and do, after all, have some roots in the present—even if they never gain prominence. Turkey under any circumstances will most likely find a greater degree of Islamic values creeping into its domestic and foreign policies, especially if its main Islamic party gains greater voice in government policies. But the Arab world is even less likely to undergo sharp revision of its historic suspicions of Turkey in the next decade—although over one or two generations quite significant changes in outlook could perhaps take place. Turkey is likely to maintain considerable rivalry with Russia in the decades ahead as well, which will cause it to look West if only for strategic support. Turkey's elites are strongly Western-oriented and not likely soon to replace that orientation with any other, regardless of the anger they may come to feel over many Western policies.

Turkey's role in the Middle East, therefore, will probably not undergo any of these major reorientations. But there has never been a time since the emergence of the modern Turkish republic when so many traditional factors have now been in flux. It is possible that the Turkey we have known since 1923 may itself be an aberration—born of the artificial circumstances of a world constrained by the rapid emergence of the Soviet Union, a loss of other options for Turkey, a cold war, and a ban on Islamist thinking. All those determinants are now gone. Will other historical attributes of Turkey, some of much greater scale and duration, reemerge to help form it for the new century? Has all that sunk into some dark hole forever? If dramatic change was ever likely to come in Turkey's role in the Middle East, it is likely to come in the new world (dis)order. These are the trends that Turkey will conjure with as it examines its future.

NOTES

1. CARLEY, "TURKEY'S PLACE IN THE WORLD"

1. The only exception was the relatively small numbers of Jews, Armenians, and Greeks recognized in the Lausanne Treaty as the only minorities in Turkey.

2. DERINGIL, "THE OTTOMAN TWILIGHT ZONE OF THE MIDDLE EAST"

1. Eric Hobsbawm, *Age of Empire* (London, 1987), p. 3.

2. L. Carl Brown, *International Politics and the Middle East: Old Rules, Dangerous Game* (London, 1984), p. 7.

3. Ehud Toledano, *State and Society in Mid-Nineteenth Century Egypt* (Cambridge, England, 1990), p. 22.

4. Robert D. Kaplan, "There Is No Middle East," *New York Times Magazine*, February 20, 1994.

5. Basbakanlik Arsivi (Prime Minister's Archives, Istanbul. Hereinafter referred to as BBA). Irade Dahiliye 97030/11 Muharrem 1309/August 17, 1891.

6. BBA Yildiz Hususi Maruzat (Y.A HUS) 243/33. 11 Cemaziyelevvel 1308/January 22, 1891.

7. BBA Irade Dahiliye 100010. 9 Receb 1309/February 10, 1892. Grand Vizier Cevad Pasa to the Municipality of Istanbul.

8. BBA Yildiz Mutenevvi Maruzat (Y.Mtv) 192/6. 2 Rebiyulevvel 1317/July 10, 1899.

9. BBA Y.A HUS 260/112. Ottoman Embassy in Bucharest to Sublime Porte. Telegram no. 15.

10. BBA Y.Mtv 181/22. 5 Rebiyulahir 1316/July 23, 1898. Sublime Porte Foreign Ministry, no. 157.

11. BBA Irade Dahiliye 4. 10 Muharrem 1317/May 21, 1899. The "Jewish language" in question here is more likely to have been Judeo-Spanish (Ladino) than Hebrew or Yiddish.

12. Robert Olson, *The Emergence of Kurdish Nationalism and the Sheikh Said Rebellion 1880–1925* (Austin: University of Texas Press, 1989), pp. 5–7.

13. Stephen Duguid, "The Politics of Unity: Hamidian Policy in Eastern Anatolia," *Middle Eastern Studies* 9 (1973), p. 146.

14. BBA Y.Mtv 57/38. 15 Cemaziyelevvel 1309/December 17, 1891. Ottoman Chief of General Staff Riza Pasa to Sublime Porte.

15. BBA Y.Mtv 138/92. 7 Evval 1313/March 23, 1896. Imperial General Staff. General in Charge of Cavalry forces Osman Ferid Pasa. It is interesting to note that a recent work on the topic, like all other works to date, only guesses that the *Hamidiye* were designed on the Cossack model, because of obvious similarities. See Ali Karaca, *Anadolu Islahati ve Ahmet Sakir Pasa 1838–1899* (Istanbul, 1993), p. 173. It is now clear from the evidence that the government took the Cossack example very literally, to the point of sending officers to be trained in Russia.

16. BBA Y.Mtv 186/82. 30 Kanun-u Sani 1314/February 11, 1898. Chief of Staff Riza Pasa to Sublime Porte.

17. Ronald Grigor Suny, *Looking Toward Ararat: Armenia in Modern History* (Bloomington and Indianapolis: Indiana University Press, 1993), p. 105.

18. BBA Y.Mtv 87/133. 19 Cemaziyelevvel 1311/November 28, 1893.

19. On the Tribal School, see Bayram Kodaman, *Sultan II. Abdulhamid'in Dogu Anadolu Politikasi* (Istanbul, 1983), pp. 110–119.

20. BBA Meclis-i Vukela Mazbatalari (Minutes of the Ottoman Cabinet) 72/82. 6 Kanun-u Evvel 1308/December 19, 1892.

21. BBA Y.Mtv 165/2. 3 Agustos 1313/August 16, 1887. Telegram from the Governor of Erzurum on the shooting of one *Hamidiye* officer by another.

22. BBA Y.Mtv 67/1. Telegram from Mehmed Zeki Pasa, Imperial Commissioner for the constitution of the *Hamidiye* regiments.

23. BBA Y.Mtv 68/21. 27 Eylul 1892/October 10, 1892. Telegram from Imperial ADC Sakir Pasa, Commissioner in charge of reform in the eastern provinces, concerning the formation of units from the Arab tribes around Urfa.

24. BBA Y.Mtv 68/28. Telegram from Hakki Pasa, Chief of the Commission for the Establishment of *Hamidiye* Regiments in Urfa.

25. BBA Y.Mtv 67/1. 25 Agustos 1892/August 25, 1892. Sakir Pasa to Yildiz Palace.

26. BBA Y.Mtv 73/46. 13 Kanun-u Evvel 1892/December 26, 1892. General Directives on the Rotation of the *Hamidiye* regiments to Istanbul.

27. BBA Y.Mtv 73/69. 17 Kanun-u Evvel 1892/December 30, 1892. Imperial ADC Sakir Pasa to Yildiz Palace.

28. Suny, *Looking Toward Ararat*, pp. 105, 106; and Olson, *Kurdish Nationalism*, p. 14.

29. BBA Y.Mtv 171/85. 22 Ptaban 1315/January 16, 1898. Imperial Chief of Staff Riza Pasa to Palace.

30. BBA Y.Mtv 187/46. 19 Sevval 1316/March 2, 1899. Imperial Chief of Staff Riza Pasa to Sublime Porte.

31. BBA Y.Mtv 188/88. 18 Zilkade 1316/March 30, 1899. Imperial Chief of Staff Riza Pasa to Sublime Porte.

32. BBA Y.Mtv 190/43. 7 Muharrem 1317/May 18, 1899. Imperial Chief of Staff Riza Pasa to Sublime Porte.

33. BBA Y.Mtv 191/155. 27 Safer 1317/July 6, 1899. Chief of Staff Receiver's Office no. 421. Report dealing with various complaints about the misbehavior of *Hamidiye* officers.

34. BBA Y.A RES 110/69. Selh-i Saban 1318/December 22, 1900. Council of State memorandum, no. 2390.

35. BBA Y.Mtv 253/111. 21 Tesrin-i Sani 1319/December 4, 1903. Yildiz Palace Imperial Secretariat.

36. Duguid, "The Politics of Unity," p. 15.

37. BBA Y.Mtv 252/363. 21 Saban 1321/November 12, 1903.

38. Olson, *Kurdish Nationalism*, p. 10.

39. Ibid., p. 12.

40. Some of the *Hamidiye* regiments were later to fight in the Balkan wars and the First World War. They would experience at first hand the challenge to Turkish power in the Balkans, and many would actually empathize with their Turkish fellow officers.

41. Ibid., p. 12.

42. Selim Deringil, "The Struggle Against Shi'ism in Hamidian Iraq: A Study in Ottoman Counter-Propaganda," *Die Welt des Islams* XXX (1990), pp. 45–62.

43. BBA Yildiz Resmi Maruzat (Y.A RES) 1/1. 22 aban 1293/September 3, 1876. Ottoman Ambassador to Tehran Munif Pasa to Sublime Porte. Tel. no. 104.

44. Deringil, "Struggle Against Shi'ism," p. 49.

45. Ibid.

46. BBA YEE. 14/88-11b/88/12. No precise date is given, but this anonymous assessment was most likely written in the early 1890s.

47. BBA YEE. 14/454/126/9. (n.d.). "Views on the preservation of Sunnism and the forbidding of Shi'ism in Baghdad." By the former Seyhulislam Hüseyin Hüsnü Efendi.

48. Deringil, "Struggle Against Shi'ism," p. 52.

49. BBA Bab-i Ali Evrak Odasi (BEO) 30919. Mosul Giden 336. 28 Zilkade 1311/June 3, 1894.

50. BBA YEE 14/1188/126/9. 9 Ramazan 1309/April 8, 1892.

51. BBA BEO. 272681. 1 Cemaziyelahir 1323/August 3, 1905. Office of the Seyhulislam, no. 56.

52. Deringil, "Struggle Against Shi'ism," p. 59.

53. *Zaman* "Belediyelerde Osmanli Modeli," April 8, 1994.

54. *Cumhuriyet*, April 9, 1994.

55. *Sabah*. Firat interview. March 6, 1994.

56. *Sabah*, March 20, 1994.

57. Cengiz Çandar, *Sabah*, March 8, 1994.

58. *Cumhuriyet*, April 9, 1994.

3. BARKEY, "TURKEY AND THE NEW MIDDLE EAST"

1. Anthony Lake, "Confronting Backlash States," *Foreign Affairs* 73, no. 2 (March–April 1994), pp. 45–55.

2. Alvin Z. Rubinstein, "New World Order or Hollow Victory?" *Foreign Affairs* 70, no. 4 (Fall 1991), p. 61.

3. Ghassan Salamé, "The Middle East: Elusive Security, Indefinable Region," *Security Dialogue* 25, no. 1 (March 1994), pp. 17–35.

4. Jack S. Levy and Michael M. Barnett, "Alliance Formation, Domestic Political Economy, and Third World Security," *The Jerusalem Journal of International Relations* 14, no. 4, 1992, p. 25.

5. Oles Smolansky, "Russia and the 'Near Abroad'—The Case of Nagorno-Karabakh," in Alvin Z. Rubinstein and Oles Smolansky (eds.) *Regional Power Rivalries in the New Eurasia* (New York: M. E. Sharpe, 1995).

6. Henri J. Barkey, "Turkey's Kurdish Dilemma," *Survival* 35, no. 4 (Winter 1993–94); and Philip Robins, "The Overlord State: Turkish Policy and the Kurdish Issue," *International Affairs* 69, no. 4 (1993).

7. Hamit Bozarslan, "La régionalisation du problème kurde," in Elisabeth Picard (ed.) *La nouvelle dynamique au Moyen Orient: Les relations entre l'Orient Arabe et la Turquie* (Paris: L'Harmattan, 1993), pp. 174–191.

8. Ibid., p. 184.

9. Graham E. Fuller, *Iraq in the Next Decade: Will Iraq Survive until 2002?* RAND, N-3591-DAG, 1993.

10. To further its cause, Turkey in fall 1994 blocked rival Iraqi Kurdish leaders from attending a signing ceremony in Paris, orchestrated by the

French presidency to put an end to their bitter squabbles, reorganize their polity, and schedule new elections.

11. Mohammad Noureddin in *al-Hayat, Mideast Mirror*, November 24, 1993, pp. 15–16. Noureddin also makes the point that Turkey's position on Cyprus will correspondingly degrade.

12. *Mideast Mirror*, November 30, 1993, p. 21.

13. Süha Bölükbas, *Türkiye ve Yakınındaki Orta Dogu.* (Ankara: Dıs Politika Enstitüsü, n.d.), p. 92.

14. For instance, Turkey expects to allow 35 percent of the used waters to flow into two rivers that directly feed into the Euphrates on the Syrian side. Elisabeth Picard, "Aux confins arabo-turcs: territoires, sécurité et ressources hydrauliques," in Picard (ed.) *La nouvelle dynamique au Moyen Orient*, p. 172.

15. Riyad Najib al-Rayyes, *Mideast Mirror*, November 30, 1993, p. 21

16. The Arab League's assistant secretary general went on record arguing that Turkish threats against Syria risked disrupting this country's relations with the rest of the Arab world. *Mideast Mirror*, November 4, 1993, p. 23.

17. See Abdallah al-Dardari, "Arab Role in the Euphrates and Tigris Water Issue: Syrian-Iraqi Apprehensions over Turkish Plans for Coming Phase," *Al Hayat* (London), January 3, 1993. JPRS NEA-93-019, February 8, 1993, pp. 9–10.

18. Michael Eisenstadt, *Arming for Peace? Syria's Elusive Quest for "Strategic Parity"* (Washington, DC: Washington Institute Policy Papers # 31, 1992), p. 99.

19. Sedat Sertoglu, "Yeni Dünya Düzeninde Ortadogu ve Türkiye," in Sabahattin Sen (ed.) *Yeni Dünya Düzeni ve Türkiye* (Ankara: Baglam Yayıncılık, 1992), p. 147.

20. Mustapha K. el-Sayyid, "'L'expérience turque' vue par la presse égyptienne et arabe (1985–1990)," in Picard, *La nouvelle dynamique au Moyen Orient*, pp. 46–60.

21. See, for instance, Mohammed Hassanein Heikal in *al-Quds al-Arabi, Mideast Mirror*, February 4, 1994; Abdelmon'em Said in *al-Ahram, Mideast Mirror*, October 22, 1993; and Riyad al-Rayyes, *Mideast Mirror*, November 1, 1993.

22. Abdelmon'em Said in *al-Ahram, Mideast Mirror*, October 22, 1993.

23. Riyad al-Rayyes, *Mideast Mirror*, November 1, 1993, p. 24.

24. Ruzbeh Buolhari, Commentary "Blackmail—Ankara Style," *Abrar* (Tehran) in Persian, February 9, 1993, FBIS-NES 93-034.

25. Selim Ilkin, "Les relations financières, commerciales et économiques de la Turquie avec les pays arabes," in Picard, *La nouvelle dynamique au Moyen Orient*, pp. 78–96.

26. Sabri Sayar, "Turkey: The Changing European Security Environment and the Gulf Crisis," *Middle East Journal* 46, no. 1 (Winter 1992), pp. 9–21.

4. MARR, "TURKEY AND IRAQ"

1. The Economist Intelligence Unit (EIU), *Iraq, 1st Quarter, 1994.* (London: EIU, 1994), p. 12.

2. Thomas Naff, interview, May 27, 1994.

3. Thomas Naff and Ruth C. Matson, *Water in the Middle East: Conflict or Cooperation* (Boulder, Colo.: Westview Press, 1984), p. 89.

4. EIU, *Iraq, Country Profile, 1993/94.* (London: EIU, 1994), p. 19.

5. EIU, *Turkey, 4th Quarter, 1992.* (London: EIU, 1992), pp. 19–20.

6. Naff and Matson, *Water*, p. 97; and Naff, interview, May 27, 1994.

7. EIU, *Iraq, 4th Quarter, 1993*, p. 9.

8. In 1975, Syria and Iraq moved to the brink of war when Iraq said the water level in the Euphrates fell from 920 m³/sec to 197 m³/sec and endangered the livelihoods of 3 million Iraqi farmers. The dispute was mediated by Saudi Arabia and an informal agreement was arranged on apportioning the Euphrates water—60 percent to Iraq, 40 percent to Syria. It is doubtful that the crisis was about water. Filling the dam the previous year had not caused a crisis because Syria released a compensatory flow to Iraq. It did not do so in 1975 for political reasons, including Syrian fears of Iraqi subversion in Syria. Water was released to Iraq after the mediation effort. (Naff and Matson, *Water*, pp. 93–95.)

9. Phebe Marr, *The Modern History of Iraq* (Boulder, Colo.: Westview Press, 1985), Table 9.6, p. 266; and EIU, *Iraq, Country Profile, 1993/94*, p. 9.

10. Marr, *Modern History of Iraq* p. 259.

11. EIU, *Iraq, Country Profile, 1993/94*, p. 22.

12. EIU, *Iraq, 1st Quarter, 1994*, p. 12. This figure, attributed to President Demirel, may be high. According to an oil analyst, Turkey charged $0.35 a barrel at full capacity; $0.85 a barrel for 300,000 barrels or less, plus 14 million tons of oil at preferential rates. At full capacity, 1.5 million b/d, the fees would equal over half a million dollars. (James Placke, Cambridge Energy Associates, interview, May 20, 1994.) Demirel also claimed that Turkey was losing 3 to 4 billion dollars a year in forgone trade. (EIU, *Iraq, 1st Quarter, 1994*.)

13. Interviews with energy officials, Baku, July 1994.

14. EIU, *Turkey, 2nd Quarter, 1993*, p. 24.

15. EIU, *Iraq, Country Profile, 1993/94*, p. 21; CIA, *Atlas of the Middle East* (Washington, D.C.: Government Printing Office), 1993, p. 11; and EIU, *Iraq, 1st Quarter, 1994*, p. 11.

16. Fereidun Fesharaki, et al., "OPEC and Lower Oil Prices: Impacts on Production Capacity, Export, Refining and Trade Balances," in E. Stanley Tucker (ed.) "Oil Exporting Countries: The Impact of Lower Prices," *Petroleum Economist* 56, no. 3 (March 1989), p. 79.

17. In the view of some, this interest may be short-lived if Saddam Hussein remains in Iraq. Once sanctions are removed, he may wish to exact retribution against Turkey by shifting oil exports to the south. However, this would be a political decision with economic disadvantages for Turkey, and would be unlikely to survive Saddam.

18. These assessments are based on interviews with Turks in various positions during visits to Ankara in July and August 1993. They included military officers, officials in the Foreign Office, newspaper editors, politicians, and academics. Obviously the sampling could not be exhaustive or scientific, but it attempted to probe a cross-section of opinion.

19. In a thoughtful and provocative monograph, Graham Fuller assumes that the quest "for Kurdish full autonomy may be slowed but it is not likely to be reversed" and raises the question of whether Turkey may not now represent one of the Kurds' best options. (Graham Fuller, *Iraq in the Next Decade: Will Iraq Survive Until 2002?* (Santa Monica, Calif.: RAND, 1993), pp. 14–15.) In an excellent article on Turkey's Kurdish dilemma, Henri Barkey asserts that Turkey needs to come up with a bold and imaginative solution. One would be "for Turkey to support the creation and become the guarantor of northern Iraq," an entity dependent on Turkey for support. This is based on the supposition that this would "transform Turkey's image amongst its own Kurdish population." (Henri J. Barkey, "Turkey's Kurdish Dilemma," *Survival* 35, no. 4 (Winter, 1993–94), p. 67.) For a counterargument, see Robert Olson, "Three Years On: The Kurdish Question and Geopolitical and Geostrategic Changes in the Middle East after the Gulf War," *Journal of South Asian and Middle Eastern Studies* (forthcoming). For other expositions of this topic, see Michael Gunter, "A de facto Kurdish State in Northern Iraq," *Third World Quarterly* 14, no. 2 (1993), pp. 295–319; and Mehrdad Izady, *A Concise Handbook: the Kurds* (Washington, D.C., 1992), p. 202.

20. These sentiments were expressed by a variety of Kurds in northern Iraq from university professors to ordinary villagers and town dwellers during a trip to northern Iraq in July 1993. Contrary visions of a Kurdish future in a more liberal Iraq were also sounded, especially by a leading Kurdish historian, but they were a distinct minority.

21. This conclusion is based on interviews with Turks in a variety of official positions during a trip to Ankara in July 1993.

22. This was amply borne out during a meeting of the Emergency Humanitarian Relief Program for Northern Iraq I attended in Ankara in July 1993, at which the Turkish Foreign Office representative made it clear that Turkey would not distinguish among Kurds, Shi'a, or Sunnis in delivering aid to Iraq.

23. Paul M. Pitman, ed., *Turkey, A Country Study* (Washington, D.C.: U.S. Government Printing Office, 1988), p. 357.

24. *Middle East Economic Digest,* October 21, 1994, p. 34.

5. PAHLAVAN, "TURKISH-IRANIAN RELATIONS"

1. Aabdolreza H. Mahdavi, *Tarikhe Ravabete Kharedjiye Iran* (*History of International Relations of Iran*) (Tehran: Amir Kabir Publishing House, 1985), pp. 394–395.

2. Ibid.

3. Mahdavi, *History of International Relations.*

4. In the same year a number of treaties were signed between Iran and Turkey. See *Asnade Moahedate Dodjanebeye Iran ba Sayer Dowal* (documents of bilateral agreements of Iran) (Tehran: Foreign Office of Iran, 1992), pp. 45–99.

5. Ibid., 2nd vol., pp. 127–149; *Kayhan,* July 23, 1994, p. 6; and Stanford J. Shaw and Ezel Kural Shaw, *History of the Ottoman Empire and Modern Turkey 1808–1975* (Persian translation by M. Ramezanzadeh) (Mash'had: Astane Gods Publishing House, 1991), Vol. 2, pp. 711–712.

6. Based on oral memoirs of Dr. M. Riahi, the then-cultural attaché of Iran to Turkey, in Tehran, 1990.

7. There are controversies on the nature of Turkish nationalism. Shaw and Shaw believe that Turkish nationalism tried to promote the sense of unity and solidarity among the people, although it was filled with extremism in the 1920s and 1930s. At the same time they agree that the Turkish Historical Society (Türk Tarih Kurumu) was created to assert that the Turks were the first "civilized" human beings on the earth and that the Turkish language was the first language as well. See Shaw and Shaw, *History*, p. 623. Engin Arin says that Atatürk is the father of all the Turks of the world, not only of the Turks of Turkey. See Engin Arin, *Atatürkçülük ve Moskofluk-Türkler Savasi.* (Istanbul, 1953), in E. Reza, *Turks, Pan-Turkism and Pan-Turanism* (Tehran: Ettelaate Siasi Ba Eghtesadi, 1992), no. 57–58, pp. 6–17.

8. At the very beginning the leaders of the Iranian revolution looked with mistrust at Turkey. The Iran-Iraq war ultimately compelled the Iranian leadership to resume their links with Ankara.

9. *Kayhan,* February 8, 1994, p. 3.

10. See a series of reports based on different sources on Turkey, the West, and Islamism in the daily newspaper *Kayhan*, January 31, 1994, p. 12.

11. *Zaman* is an Islamic publication in Turkey. In November 1986, the first issue of *Zaman* was published in Ankara with ten thousand copies. According to *Middle East* magazine it has a circulation of 125,000. *Kayhan*, January 31, 1994, p. 12. Some people believe that these kinds of activities enjoy the political and financial support of the Turkish government.

12. Although political pan-Turkism was not officially tolerated during the rule of Mustafa Kemal, it survived in the cultural and scientific circles and gained prominence during the Second World War. Negotiations between German and Turkish authorities during 1941–44 showed that important Turkish personalities were trying to attract Germans to support them. Turkey was interested in the creation of a state consisting of "Turks" across Azerbaijan, Turkestan, Turkmenistan, and the Volga. Iranian Azerbaijan was also mentioned during the discussions. It seems that Germans were willing to make use of Turkish experience in the occupied territories. Charles W. Hostler, *Turkism and the Soviets* (London: George Allen and Unwin, 1975), pp. 171–176. Quoted in K. Bayat, *Va Rishehaye Tarikhiye an. Negahe* (Tehran, 1991), no. 4, p. 71. In an interview with the BBC on July 12, 1992, Demirel suggested that Turkey was already an empire.

In the past, some Turkish publications envisaged the desired limits of the Turkic world and nation. See, for instance, the pan-Turkish map from Mediterranean to Central Asia on the cover of the pan-Turkish *Bozkurt* (*Gray Wolf*) periodical, July 1941, no. 11. The journal had as its motto the following: "The Turkish race is above all races," reprinted in *Pan-Turkism and the Question of Azerbaijan*, a publication of the Armenian Popular Movement, Beirut, 1992, p. 57; and a map purported to have been originally published by European Confederation of Turkish Intellectuals entitled, "Turkey in the XXI Century" includes Baku, Tabriz, Mosul, and Kerkuk. Reprinted in *Elefterotypia* (Athens), July 31, 1992.

13. Tekin Alp, in "The Restoration of Turkish History," provides a detailed rendition of the ideas advanced by Turkish scholars in support of the thesis that it was the Turks who civilized mankind. See T. Alp in Elie Kedouri (ed.), *Nationalism in Asia and Africa* (New York and Cleveland: Meridian Books, 1970), pp. 207–224.

14. Albert Hourani, *A History of the Arab Peoples* (Faber and Faber, 1990), pp. 308–310; and Ziya Gökalp, "The Idea of Nationalism: Three Currents of Thought," in Kedouri (ed.), *Nationalism*, p. 190.

15. A number of exiled Iranians went to Palestinian camps for military training prior to the Islamic Revolution. In 1979 the Islamic youth in Iran tried to imitate Palestinian fighters by wearing kefiyahs.

16. General Waters, deputy chief commander of NATO, at a Moscow press conference told reporters that NATO's presence in Central Asia is to be secured by a struggle against fundamentalism and by resistance to Iranian encroachment and influence in that region. *Kayhan*, February 26, 1994.

17. Elisabeth Picard, "Relations Between Iran and its Turkish Neighbour: From Ideological to Geopolitical Constraints," in Derek Hopwood, Habib Ishow, and Thomas Koszinowski (eds.) *Iraq: Power and Society* (Reading: Ithaca Press, 1993), pp. 348–349.

18. Turkey is a member of both the Council of Europe and NATO and is seeking full membership in the European Union.

19. General Dogan Güres, "Turkey's Defence Policy: The Role of the Armed Forces and Strategy, Concepts and Capabilities" (Persian translation), *Journal of Defence Policy* Tehran (Winter 1993–94), pp. 131–146.

20. Ibid.

21. *Kayhan*, February 1, 1994, p. 19.

22. Ibid., and *Kayhan*, February 5, 1994, p. 3.

23. *Kayhan*, October 13, 1992, p. 7.

24. *Kayhan*, March 10, 1994, p. 20.

25. *Kayhan*, January 9, 1994, p. 16.

26. *Kayhan*, January 31, 1994, p. 12.

27. *Kayhan*, February 6, 1994, p. 14.

28. *Kayhan*, February 22, 1994, p. 7.

29. Feroz Ahmad, *The Making of Modern Turkey* (London and New York: Routledge, 1993), p. 48; and Nader Entessar, *Kurdish Ethnonationalism* (Boulder & London: Lynne Rienner Publishers, 1992), pp. 51–53.

30. Entessar, *Kurdish Ethnonationalism*, p. 99.

31. Ibid.

32. Ibid.

33. David McDowall, *The Kurds: A Nation Denied* (London: Minority Rights Group, 1992). p. 78.

34. Ibid., p. 73.

35. Ibid., p. 79.

36. One of the governmental organizations published an important and costly Kurdish dictionary. See Hazhar, *Kurdish-Persian Dictionary* (Tehran: Soroush Press, 1991).

37. McDowall, *The Kurds*, p. 79.

38. Entessar, *Kurdish Ethnonationalism*, chapters 2, 3, and 4, pp. 11–112.

39. Ibid., p. 100.

40. Ibid.

41. For the first time by Anglo-Indian agent Conolly. G. L. Bondarevesky, "Lest We Forget," *Central Asia and the Caucasus in World Affairs*, December 1, 1992, p. 1.

42. Alp, "The Restoration," pp. 215–218.

43. President Turgut Özal of Turkey, before his death on April 17, 1993, "made an extensive tour of the Turkic-speaking Central Asian republics and Azerbaijan with a large delegation of Turkish businessmen. While disclaiming hegemonic ambitions, Özal's visit followed a similar one made by General Gures, the Turkish chief of staff, in March and shows the degree of Turkey's interest in Central Asia." In this trip, cultural, along with economic, affinity was frequently invoked. *Central Asia Newsfile* (London: School of Oriental and African Studies, 1993), no. 6, p. 4.

44. Alan Cowell, "Turkey Loses its Allure as a Patron in Central Asian Nations," the *New York Times*, August 4, 1993.

45. Ibid.

46. Tira Shubert, *Central Asia and the Caucasus in World Affairs*, 1992, pp. 4–5.

47. Ibid., pp. 10–11. Developments in 1995 make it very unlikely that this project will be finished.

48. *Kayhan*, July 14, 1994, p. 16.

49. Cowell, "Turkey Loses Its Allure."

50. There are many works that deal with this issue to be seen in this regard. Studies of elites show the significant share of Iranian Azeris in Iranian power structure. See Zahra Shadji, *Political Elite of Iran* (in Persian) (Tehran: I. Sokhan Publication, 1993).

51. Cowell, "Turkey Loses Its Allure."

52. Ibid.

53. *Kayhan*, June 29, 1994, p. 3.

54. *Kayhan*, March 27, 1994, p. 3.

55. *Kayhan*, July 21, 1994, p. 18.

56. *Kayhan*, June 21, 1994, p. 7.

57. Leon Petrosian said although public opinion in Iran is generally in favor of Azerbaijan, the Iranian government has been serious in playing a constructive role to achieve peace in Nagorno-Karabakh. *Salaam*, February 24, 1994.

58. According to *Ettelaat*, a Tehran daily, American President Bill Clinton is sympathetic to Armenian demands and also to the presence of Russian forces in the region. August 20, 1994, supplement, p. 1.

59. A. Sheykh Attar, *Roots of Political Behavior in Central Asia and Caucasus* (in Persian) (Tehran: Publishing House of the Foreign Ministry, 1992), pp. 61–64.

60. Soroush Erfani, "Iran, ECO and Central Asia" (in Persian), *The Journal of Central Asia and Caucasus Review*. Published by the Center for Research of Central Asia and Caucasus Research, Tehran, Vol. 2 (Spring 1994), pp. 343–344.

61. The idea for creating this organization came from the late Turkish president Turgut Özal in 1989. It initially consisted of Bulgaria, Romania, the USSR, and Turkey; but in 1992 a meeting in Turkey attended by Turkey, Russia, Greece, Republic of Azerbaijan, Armenia, Albania, Bulgaria, Romania, Ukraine, Georgia, and Moldova showed that this organization was not limited to the littoral countries of the Black Sea. It was also overlapped with ECO. *The Journal of Central Asia and Caucasus Review*, pp. 377–378.

62. Ibid.

63. *Kayhan*, February 24, 1994, p. 3.

64. A joint committee consisting of Iran and Turkmenistan for the realization of this project was joined by observers from Turkey, Russia, and Kazakstan. The committee is headed by the president of Turkmenistan, Saparmurad Niyazov, and energy ministers of the respective countries. *Kayhan*, August 22, 1994.

65. *Kayhan*, August 21, 1994, p. 3.

66. *Kayhan*, June 15, 1994, p. 3.

67. *Kayhan*, July 26, 1994, p. 3.

68. Ibid.

6. ERALP, "FACING THE CHALLENGE"

1. The author would like to express his gratitude for the assistance provided him during the preparation of this paper by the Turkish Foreign Ministry, the journalists Nazlan Ertan and Adnan Caglayan, and Lowell A. Bezanis. In the gathering of source materials, special thanks to Julide Mollaoglu and Zeynep Didem Yilbas.

2. See Atila Eralp, "Turkey in the Changing Post–War World Order: Strategies of Development and Westernization," in Caglar Keyder, Saad Ibrahim, and Ayse Öncü (eds.) *Transformation of States and Societies in Egypt and Turkey* (Cairo: Cairo University Press, 1994) for a fuller treatment of the subject.

3. Albert Wohlstetter, "Meeting the Threat in the Persian Gulf." *Survey* 25, no. 2, p. 184.

4. Halis Akder, "Turkey's Export Expansion in the Middle East, 1980–1985," *Middle East Journal* 41, no. 4 (Autumn 1987), pp. 553–567.

5. Ali Karaosmanoglu, "Turkey's Security and the Middle East," *Foreign Affairs* 62, no. 1 (Fall 1983), p. 165.

6. Birol Yesilada, "Turkish Foreign Policy Toward the Middle East," in Atila Eralp, Muharrem Tunay, and Birol Yesilada (eds.) *The Political and Socioeconomic Transformation of Turkey* (Westport, Conn.: Praeger Publishers, 1993), pp. 169–192.

7. Nilufer Göle, "Engineers and Technicist Ideology" (Paper presented to the International Conference on Turkey and the West: Encounters, Images and Praxis, Ebenhausen, November 11–13, 1990).

8. Süha Bölükbası, "Turkey Copes with Revolutionary Iran," *Journal of South Asian and Middle Eastern Studies* 13, no. 1&2 (Fall/Winter 1989), pp. 94–109.

9. Ibid., p. 100.

10. In October 1984, Ankara and Baghdad signed an agreement allowing for automatic hot pursuit incursions. On the impact of the Iran-Iraq war on Turkey, see Henri J. Barkey, "The Silent Victor: Turkey's Role in the Gulf War," in Efraim Karsh (ed.) *The Iran-Iraq War: Impact and Implications* (London: Macmillan, 1989).

11. Bölükbası, "Turkey Copes with Revolutionary Iran," p. 104.

12. Said Amin Arjomand, "A Victory for the Pragmatists: The Islamic Fundamentalist Reaction in Iran," in James Piscatori (ed.) *Islamic Fundamentalisms and the Gulf Crisis* (Chicago: The American Academy of Arts and Sciences), pp. 52–69; and R.K. Ramazani, "Iran's Export of the Revolution: Its Politics, Ends and Means," *Journal of South Asian and Middle Eastern Studies* 13, no. 1&2 (Fall/Winter 1989), pp. 69–93.

13. Atila Eralp, "Turkey in the Changing Post–War World Order."

14. Andrew Mango, "Turkish Policy in the Middle East," in Clement Dodd (ed.) *Turkish Foreign Policy: New Prospects* (Cambridgeshire: The Eothen Press, 1992), pp. 55–69; and Philip Robins, *Turkey and the Middle East* (London: The Royal Institute of International Affairs, 1991).

15. Ibid.; and Graham E. Fuller, *The "Center of the Universe": The Geopolitics of Iran* (Boulder: Westview Press).

16. See Graham E. Fuller and Ian O. Lesser (with Paul B. Henze and J. F. Brown), *Turkey's New Geopolitics: From the Balkans to Western China* (Boulder: Westview Press, 1993) for a fuller account of Turkey's new regional orientations.

17. Bernard Lewis, "Rethinking the Middle East," *Foreign Affairs* 71, no. 4 (Fall 1992), pp. 99–119; and Graham E. Fuller, "The Emergence of Central Asia," *Foreign Policy* no. 78 (Spring 1990), pp. 49–67.

18. Jim Nichol, Carol Migdalovitz, and Kenneth Katzman, "Central Asia and Azerbaijan: Regional Rivalries and Implications for the United States," CRS Report for Congress, December 4, 1992 (92–930 F); and Carol Migdalovitz, "Turkey: Ally in a Troubled Region," CRS Report for Congress, September 14, 1993 (93–835 F).

19. I have benefited immensely from the work of Lowell A. Bezanis on the Turkish model and its implications for Turkey. See Lowell A. Bezanis, "Menace, Myth or Self-Fulfilling Prophecy? Reflections on the Islamic Threat and Forces Opposed to Theocratic Rule in Former Soviet Central Asia" (Unpublished manuscript, September 1993).

20. Fuller, "The Geopolitics of Iran;" and Nichol, Migdalovitz, and Katzman, "Central Asia and Azerbaijan."

21. *Cumhuriyet*, February 5, 6, 7, and 8, 1993; and *Turkish Probe*, February 23, 1993.

22. See James Rupert, "Dateline Tashkent: Post-Soviet Central Asia," *Foreign Policy* no. 87 (Summer 1992), pp. 175–195; Leon T. Hadar, "What Green Peril," *Foreign Affairs* 72, no. 2. (Spring 1993), pp. 27–42; and Rajan Menon and Henri J. Barkey, "The Transformation of Central Asia: Implications for Regional and International Security," *Survival* 34, no. 4 (Winter 1992–1993), pp. 68-89.

7. MUSLIH, "SYRIA AND TURKEY"

1. Yüksel Söylemez, "Turkey: Western or Moslem?" *Turkish Review* 6, no. 29 (Autumn 1992), p. 48.

2. Philip S. Khoury, *Syria and the French Mandate—The Politics of Arab Nationalism, 1920–1945* (Princeton: Princeton University Press, 1987), p. 495.

3. Muta' al-Safadi, *jil al-qadar* (*The Generation of Fate*) (Damascus, 1960); and Patrick Seale, *Asad, The Struggle for the Middle East* (Berkeley: University of California Press, 1988), pp. 27–35.

4. George E. Gruen, "Turkey's Relations with Israel and its Arab Neighbors," *Middle East Review* 17, no. 3 (Spring 1985), p. 40.

5. Kemal Karpat, *Turkey's Foreign Policy in Transition, 1950–1974* (Leiden: E.J. Brill, 1975); and Amikam Nachmani, *Israel, Turkey and Greece: Uneasy Relations in the East Mediterranean* (London: Frank Cass, 1987), pp. 44–45.

6. John Foster Dulles's statement, General Assembly Official Records, 12th session, 680th meeting, p. 21.

7. Samuel Segev, *The Iranian Triangle* (New York: The Free Press, 1988), pp. 33–37.

8. Patrick Seale, *The Struggle for Syria, A Study of Post-War Arab Politics 1945–1958* (New Haven: Yale University Press, 1986), p. 306.

9. Karpat, *Turkey's Foreign Policy,* pp. 125–130.

10. Michael B. Bishku, "Turkey and its Middle Eastern Neighbors since 1945," *Journal of South Asian and Middle Eastern Studies* XV, no. 3 (Spring 1992), p. 65.

11. *Forward* (Damascus), no. 95 (November–December 1993), p. 30.

12. Seale, *Asad, The Struggle for the Middle East,* pp. 351–359.

13. Dankwart A. Rustow, *Turkey, America's Forgotten Ally* (New York: Council on Foreign Relations Press, 1989), pp. 93–103.

14. Halis Akder, "Turkey's Export Expansion in the Middle East, 1980–1985," *The Middle East Journal* 41, no. 4 (Autumn 1987), pp. 554–557.

15. Süha Bölükbası, "Turkey Challenges Iraq and Syria: The Euphrates Dispute," *Journal of South Asian and Middle Eastern Studies* XVI, no. 4 (Summer 1993), pp. 12–14.

16. Ted Robert Gurr, *Minorities at Risk, A Global View of Ethnopolitical Conflicts* (Washington, D.C., United States Institute of Peace, 1993), pp. 228–230. On Turkey's Kurdish problem see Henri J. Barkey, "Turkey's Kurdish Dilemma," *Survival* 35, no. 4 (Winter 1993–94); and Philip Robins, "The Overlord State: Turkish Policy and the Kurdish Issue," *International Affairs* 69, no. 4 (1993).

17. *MEED, Middle East Economic Digest* 36, no. 31 (August 7, 1992), p. 6.

18. Ibid.

19. Economist Intelligence Unit, *Syria: Country Profile, 1993/1994* (London: The Economist Intelligence Unit, 1994), pp. 30–31.

20. Copy of letter in author's possession.

21. For details on the Iraqi-Syrian dispute, see Eberhard Kienle, *Ba'th v. Ba'th: The Conflict between Syria and Iraq 1968–1989* (London: I.B. Tauris, 1990).

22. George E. Gruen, "Recent Negotiations over the Euphrates and Tigris Waters" (Background paper prepared for the International Symposium on Water Resources in the Middle East: Policy and Institutional Aspects, University of Illinois, Urbana-Champaign, October 24–27, 1993).

8. JOUEJATI, "WATER POLITICS AS HIGH POLITICS"

1. Gün Kut, "Burning Waters: The Hydropolitics of the Euphrates And Tigris" in *New Perspectives on Turkey* 9 (Fall 1993), p. 6.

2. Philip Robins, *The Christian Science Monitor,* March 12, 1990, p. 18.

3. Turkey's permanent diversion of the Qweiq River, despite Article 12 of the French-Turkish Treaty of 1921 (in which Turkey has to supply Aleppo), is one case in point. See Ambassador Mohamed Munib Al Rifai, "International

Law and the Waters of the Euphrates and the Tigris" (Paper presented at the 30th Scientific Week, Damascus, November 3–8, 1990), p. 3.

4. See Miriam R. Lowi, *Water and Power: The Politics of a Scarce Resource in the Jordan River Basin* (Cambridge University Press, 1993), p. 55. Kolars and Mitchell estimate a river depletion as a result of GAP of about 17 bm^3 annually. See John F. Kolars and William A. Mitchell, *The Euphrates River and the Southeast Anatolia Development Project* (Carbondale: Southern Illinois University Press, 1991), pp. 266–270.

5. David Kushner, "Conflict and Accommodation in Turkish-Syrian Relations," in Moshe Ma'oz and Avner Yaniv (eds.) *Syria Under Assad* (New York: St. Martin's Press, 1986), p. 89.

6. Lowi, *Water and Power*, p. 4.

7. Edouard Saab, *La Syrie ou la Revolution dans la Rancoeur* (Paris: Julliard, 1968), p. 206.

8. Turkish Public Works and Settlements Minister Onur Kumbaracibasi in a briefing to the Turkish National News Agency, August 12, 1993. See BBC *Summary of World Broadcasts*, August 14, 1993.

9. George E. Gruen, "Recent Negotiations over the Waters of the Euphrates and Tigris," in *Proceedings of the International Symposium on Water Resources in the Middle East: Policy and Institutional Aspects*, Urbana, Illinois, October 24–27, 1993, p. 101.

10. Ibid. Quotes from United Nations, UNGAOR, 43rd Session, at 1, UN Doc. A/CN.4/L.463/Add.4 1991, *Draft Articles on the Law of the Non-Navigational Uses of International Watercourses and Commentaries Thereto, Provisionally Adopted on First Reading by the International Law Commission at Its Forty-Third Session*, Art. 2(a).

11. Philip Robins, *Turkey and the Middle East* (New York: Council on Foreign Relations Press, 1993), p. 89.

12. The ministers of irrigation of the three riparians met in November 1988 and again in June 1990.

13. Robins, *Turkey and the Middle East*, p. 92.

14. Robins, *Turkey and the Middle East*, p. 93.

15. *Mideast Mirror*, quoting *Al Hayat*, December 17, 1991.

16. Robins, *Turkey and the Middle East*, p. 94.

17. *The Middle East*, May 1993, p. 39.

18. *The Middle East*, May 1993, p. 39.

19. The *Wall Street Journal*, October 30, 1991, p. A13(E).

20. *Syria Times*, February 6, 1994.

21. Turkish Public Works Minister Kumbaracibasi, quoted in the BBC, August 14, 1993.

22. "Draining the Rivers Dry," *Geographical Magazine* 62, no. 7 (July 1990), p. 32; and Joyce R. Starr, "Water Wars," in *Foreign Policy* no. 82 (Spring 1991), p. 31. Since 1985, the World Bank and other financial institutions have been lending assistance to Turkey. Kolars and Mitchell, *The Euphrates River*, p. 32.

23. *Rose El Youssef*, October 25, 1993.

24. Reuters, July 29, 1992.

25. *Tishrin*, February 6, 1994.

26. Robins, *Turkey and the Middle East*, p. 93.

27. Robins, *Turkey and the Middle East*, p. 94.

28. See Graham E. Fuller and Ian O. Lesser, with Paul B. Henze and J. F. Brown, *Turkey's New Geopolitics: From the Balkans to Western China* (Boulder: Westview Press, 1993), pp. 54–57; and Robins, *Turkey and the Middle East*, pp. 49–53.

29. *The Independent*, November 5, 1993, p. 12; and the *Los Angeles Times*, November 5, 1993, p. A5.

30. *Al Ahram Weekly*, November 25, 1993.

31. Lowi, *Water and Power*, p. 193.

32. Lowi, *Water and Power*, p. 57.

33. A term I borrow from Miriam R. Lowi.

34. Starr, "Water Wars," p. 28.

35. *Al Hayat*, December 24, 1992.

36. Starr, "Water Wars," p. 28.

37. Robins, *Turkey and the Middle East*, p. 98.

38. Al Rifai, "International Law," p. 7; and Kut, "Burning Waters," p. 13.

39. Al Rifai, "International Law," pp. 6–7.

40. Kut, "Burning Waters," p. 15.

41. Lowi, *Water and Power*, pp. 61–67.

42. Turkish Foreign Ministry official Burhan Ant, quoted by *National Geographic*, May 1993, p. 50.

43. Peter H. Gleick, "Water, War, and Peace in the Middle East," *Environment* 36, no. 3 (April 1994), p. 35.

9. MAKOVSKY, "ISRAELI-TURKISH RELATIONS"

1. Based on information in International Monetary Fund Yearbook, *Direction of Trade Statistics* (1989), pp. 390–391. Figure for "Islamic Middle East" derived by adding totals for Algeria, Morocco, and Tunisia to that of the "Middle East," a category which excludes the western North African states, and subtracting the total for Israel. "OECD" figure derived by adding totals for Greece and Portugal to the total for "industrial countries."

2. International Monetary Fund, *Direction of Trade Statistics* (1995), pp. 423–425. Figure derived in same manner as above. According to Turkey's State Institute of Statistics, exports to the "Middle East" accounted for only 9.5% of all exports in 1995.

3. Henri J. Barkey, "Reluctant Neighbors: Reflections on Turkish-Arab Relations," *The Beirut Review* (Spring 1994), p. 10.

4. *Yediot Aharonot*, January 28, 1994, as reported in translation on the Internet.

5. George E. Gruen, "Dynamic Progress in Turkish-Israeli Relations," *Israel Affairs* 1, no. 4 (Summer 1995), p. 47.

6. See, for example, aforementioned statements by Çiller (fn. 4) and also by Foreign Minister Hikmet Çetin during his visit to Israel, as reported in *Mideast Mirror*, November 16, 1993.

7. For a history of Turkish-Israeli relations see, for example, George Gruen, "Turkey Between the Middle East and the West," in Robert Freedman (ed.) *The Middle East from the Iran-Contra Affair to the Intifada* (Syracuse, 1991), pp. 390–422; "Turkey's Relations with Israel and Its Arab Neighbors: The Impact of Basic Interests and Changing Circumstances," *Middle East Review* 17 (Spring 1985), pp. 33–43; and his unpublished doctoral dissertation, "Turkey, Israel and the Palestine Question, 1948–1960: A Study in the Diplomacy of Ambivalence," Columbia University, 1970. The early years of Turkish-Israeli relations, particularly as revealed in Israeli archival sources, are discussed in Amikam Nachmani, *Israel, Turkey and Greece: Uneasy Relations in the East Mediterranean* (London: Frank Cass, 1987).

8. The Middle East multilateral negotiations, relatively little publicized, consist of five sets of negotiations on subjects of regionwide interest: arms control and regional security, economic development, environment, refugees, and water resources. They were established as a complement to the bilateral negotiations conducted between Israel and Jordan, Lebanon, Syria, and the Palestinians. Along with Israel and the PLO, some 13 Arab states and more than two dozen non–Middle Eastern states (known as "extra-regionals"), including Turkey, participate. Among the principal reasons the multilaterals were established was to build international and regional support for the peace process. All extra-regional participants were required to have full diplomatic relations with all the Middle Eastern participants, including Israel. Full Chinese and Russian relations with Israel were also hastened by the peace process.

9. All Arab states voted against the repeal, except Bahrain, Egypt (the only Muslim state besides Turkey with which Israel then had diplomatic relations), Morocco, and Tunisia, which were absent from the voting.

10. Foreign Broadcast Information Service, *Daily Report: West Europe* (FBIS-WEU), December 13, 1995, p. 27. The Israelis did not publicize Peres's efforts on Turkey's behalf. Initially kept secret, they were revealed by a Euro-Parliamentarian who complained in floor debate about international lobbying efforts to boost the Turkish case and cited Peres's phone calls as a prime example. The story was then reported in the Turkish press.

11. Interview in *as-Safir* (Lebanon), November 20, 1995.

12. Quoted in Gruen, "Dynamic Progress," p. 60.

13. For full elaboration of Peres's views, see Shimon Peres with Arye Naor, *The New Middle East* (New York, 1993).

14. Turkey participates in the multilateral negotiations not as a Middle Eastern state, but as an extra-regional state like the United States, the Europeans, Russia, Japan, and other non–Middle Eastern states. Its geographic status as a state bordering the Arab world, however, makes it something more than merely an interested outsider.

15. Speech by Prime Minister Tansu Çiller to the Middle East/North Africa Economic Summit, October 31, 1994. Text supplied by the Turkish Embassy, Washington, D.C.

16. Now the Organization for Security and Cooperation in Europe (OSCE).

17. See, for example, Lale Sariibrahimoglu, "OGIK için Turkiye Israil-Ürdün Isbirligi," *Cumhuriyet*, October 29, 1994.

18. For Turkish views on water, see Ali Ihsan Bagis, "The Euphrates and Tigris Watercourse Systems: Conflict or Cooperation? The Turkish View with Special Reference to the Southeastern Anatolia Project," *Turkish Review of Middle East Studies* 7 (1993), pp. 215–237.

19. See, for example, "Israil'den Çiller'e sert tepki," *Cumhuriyet*, November 7, 1994; "Küdüs'te Çiller krizi," *Milliyet*, November 7, 1994; "and Küdüs'te Çiller soku," *Hurriyet*, November 7, 1994. Also see Foreign Broadcast Information Service, *Daily Report: Near East and South Asia* (FBIS-NES), November 7, 1994, p. 36; and *Mideast Mirror*, November 7, 1994, p. 3.

20. In fact, the TIP was never formed, apparently because Israel and the PLO could not agree on its functions.

21. Çetin was actually scheduled to visit Israel in July 1993 but suspended his plans at the last moment due to Israel's military campaign in southern Lebanon. The fact that the trip was originally scheduled for July shows that bilateral ties were improving before the DOP was signed in September. However, the warmth of the visit, Çetin's publicly proclaimed vision of close ties, and the signing of a Memorandum of Understanding would not have been possible before the DOP.

22. See, for example, Foreign Broadcast Information Service, *Daily Report: Near East and South Asia* (FBIS-NES), April 18, 1995, p. 51.

23. Stanford Shaw, *The Jews of the Ottoman Empire and the Turkish Republic* (New York, 1991), p. 259.

24. On one Jewish holiday weekend in 1994, 62 chartered flights, carrying some 30,000 Israeli tourists, arrived in the Mediterranean resort town Antalya in one day. Turks were keenly aware of the Israeli "invasion," which received considerable media coverage in Turkey.

25. Statistics on tourism supplied by the Israeli Embassy, Ankara, Turkey.

26. "National Press Club Afternoon Newsmaker with Israeli Prime Minister Shimon Peres," December 12, 1995, Federal News Service transcript, p. 5.

27. *Yediot Aharonot*, January 28, 1994, as reported in translation on the Internet.

28. See reference to Çetin's effort to elicit "firm Israeli commitment against the PKK," *Mideast Mirror*, November 16, 1993, p. 8.

29. During Çetin's visit to Israel, an unnamed Israeli official was quoted as saying, "We are not interested in making enemies. The PKK has never hurt us. We also don't have any interest in antagonizing Syria," *Mideast Mirror*, November 16, 1993, p. 8.

30. *Haaretz*, December 26, 1995, p. A1, A2, as translated in FBIS-WEU, December 26, 1995, pp. 26–27.

31. "Erbakan: Çiller Israil'in figürani," *Cumhuriyet*, November 7, 1994.

32. Voice of Israel Radio, December 25, 1995, as translated in FBIS-WEU, December 26, 1995.

11. ROBINS, "AVOIDING THE QUESTION"

1. For a brief discussion of Turkish foreign policy principles prior to the Gulf crisis, see Philip Robins, *Turkey and the Middle East* (London: Pinter, 1991), p. 65.

2. For a further discussion of Turkey and the newly independent republics of Central Asia, see Philip Robins, "The Middle East and Central Asia," in Peter Ferdinand (ed.) *The New Central Asia and its Neighbours* (London: RIIA/Pinter, 1994).

3. Then still formally the European Community.

4. See "A Report on EU-Turkey Relations" (EC Representative, Ankara), October 1994.

5. Quoted from Boutros Boutros-Ghali's report on the UN Peacekeeping Force in Cyprus (UNFICYP), *Turkish Daily News*, June 11, 1994.

6. For more details on Turkey's diplomatic involvement in the Bosnian issue, see Philip Robins, "Coping with Chaos: Turkey and the Bosnian Crisis," in *Mediterranean Politics*, no. 1 (London: Pinter, 1994), p. 104.

7. See unpublished, undated paper of the Turkish Foreign Ministry, "Views of the Republic of Turkey on the question of equitable representation on and increase in the membership of the Security Council" (General Assembly resolution 47/62).

8. Turkey has been unsuccessful in its push for full membership, but has been given associate membership with an enhanced status. For the latter, see *Turkish Daily News*, May 10 and 11, 1994.

9. For a discussion of Turkey's attitude towards the Partnership for Peace, see Sami Kohen in *Milliyet*, January 7, 1994.

10. For an up-to-date and comprehensive list of the current organizational structure of the Turkish Foreign Ministry, see Kemal Girgin, "Türkiye'nin Disisleri Teskilati" (Turkey's foreign affairs organization), in Faruk Sönmezoglu (ed.) *Türk Dis Politikasinin Analizi* (Turkish foreign policy analysis) (Istanbul: Der Yayinlari, 1994), pp. 180–190.

11. For the formalization of this arrangement (and its detail) into law, see *Resmi Gazete* (Official Gazette) Law No. 4009, July 6, 1994.

12. Indicative of Russian priorities is the fact that when Foreign Minister Kozyrev first visited Central Asia in April 1992, U.S. Secretary of State James Baker had already been to the region three times. Russian embassies in the region were established only after those of Turkey, Iran, China, and the United States.

13. Turkey currently imports 5 billion cubic meters of natural gas from Russia per year, and is prepared to increase this by a further 4.5 billion m^3 pa. See *BBC Summary of World Broadcasts, Eastern Europe*, August 4, 1994.

14. In Saudi Arabia, the Wahhabis dislike this description and refer to themselves as *muwahhidun* (unitarians). See Patrick Bannerman, *Islam in Perspective* (London: Routledge/RIIA, 1988), p. 261.

15. *Turkish Daily News*, January 24, 1993.

16. Writers on both Saudi Arabia and Turkey have repeatedly made the accusation of Saudi assistance for political Islam in Turkey. See, for example, Said K. Aburish, *The Rise, Corruption and Coming Fall of the House of Saud* (London: Bloomsbury, 1994), p. 144; and Emin Çölasan, "Para ve Refah" ("Money and Welfare," referring to the Welfare Party), *Hurriyet*, May 13, 1994, reprinted in Turhan Dilligil, *Erbakancilik ve Erbakan* (Erbakanism and Erbakan) (Ankara, 1994), p. 295.

17. *Turkish Daily News*, March 31, 1994.

18. Most recently this allegation was reiterated by a senior figure in the Iranian opposition group, the Mojahedin-e Khalq, and rejected by Tehran. See *Iranian News Agency*, IRNA, quoted in BBC/SWB/EE, August 16, 1994.

19. Writing during the visit to Iran by President Demirel, one influential commentator, Mehmet Ali Birand, noted that Turkey and Iran have stopped trying to persuade one another to adopt the other side's mentality or system. Instead, they now acknowledge the differences and are beginning to shape their policies accordingly. See *Sabah*, July 27, 1994.

20. For a discussion of the July 1987 visit to Syria by then-Turkish prime minister Turgut Özal, the resulting security protocol, and its only temporary, partial implementation, see Süha Bölükbasi, "Turkey's policies challenged by Iraq and Syria: the Euphrates dispute and the Kurdish problem," unpublished paper.

21. For example, in June 1994 the Turkish government rejected the request of 16 MKO members for political asylum and deported them to Iraq. See *Turkish Daily News*, June 12, 1994.

22. Reuters report printed in *Turkish Daily News*, July 28, 1994.

23. This is the official British assessment of Iran's weapons of mass destruction program. Interview conducted with official source, November 1, 1994.

24. For a detailed background discussion of the problem, see Gün Kut, "Burning Waters: The Hydropolitics of the Euphrates and Tigris," in *New Perspectives on Turkey* 9 (Fall 1993).

25. For a discussion of the issue, see Robins, *Turkey and the Middle East*, p. 90.

26. Mehmet Ali Birand, writing in *Sabah* December 17, and reprinted in *Turkish Daily News,* December 18, 1993.

27. *Turkish Daily News*, July 29, 1994.

28. *Turkish Daily News*, March 4, 1994.

29. *Turkish Daily News*, December 29, 1993.

30. This resolution ties the end of the oil embargo against Iraq to the eradication of its weapons of mass destruction program.

31. There have been two recent examples. First, Turkey offered to be part of the Temporary International Presence in Hebron, which was established after the massacre of 29 Palestinians in February 1994. In the end, this offer was not taken up. See *Turkish Daily News*, May 5, 1994. Second, the PLO leader Yasser Arafat, during a visit to Ankara in September 1994, asked that Turkey contribute to an international peace force for Gaza. This request was accepted by the Turkish prime minister Tansu Çiller. See TRT TV broadcast September 16, reprinted in *BBC/SWB/EE* September 19, 1994.

12. FULLER, "ALTERNATIVE TURKISH ROLES IN THE FUTURE MIDDLE EAST"

1. A variation on this theme would bring the "Oghuz" or Western Turkic language group of Turks together, including the Turks of Turkey, Azerbaijan (including Iranian Azerbaijan), and Turkmenistan. Turkmenistan at present feels little closeness to the other Central Asian states.

2. Considerable debate revolves around the famous Atatürk aphorism, "*Ne mutlu Türküm diyene*" (literally, "How happy it is for one who says 'I am a Turk'"). While to some this is an unabashed expression of exclusivist Turkish pride, others point to the careful wording to suggest that anyone of any ethnic origin as a citizen of Turkey can say "I am a Turk," just as any American can say the same about being American. The grammatical form of the Turkish expression will always remain richly ambiguous.

CONTRIBUTORS

Henri J. Barkey is associate professor of international relations at Lehigh University.

Mehmet Ali Birand is a journalist for *Sabah*, a widely read Turkish daily, and editor and producer of *32nd Day*, a television news show that focuses on Turkish domestic and international issues.

Patricia Carley is a program officer in the Research and Studies Program at the United States Institute of Peace.

Selim Deringil is associate professor of history at Bogazici University, Istanbul.

Atila Eralp is chairman of the department of international relations at the Middle East Technical University in Ankara.

Graham E. Fuller is senior political analyst at the RAND corporation and a former U. S. foreign service officer in Turkey, Saudi Arabia, Lebanon, North Yemen, and Afghanistan.

Murhaf Jouejati is a specialist on Syrian affairs and a doctoral candidate in international relations at the University of Utah.

Alan Makovsky is senior research associate at the Washington Institute for Near East Policy, working on Arab-Israeli and Turkish issues.

Phebe Marr is senior fellow at the Institute for National Strategic Studies at the National Defense University.

Muhammad Muslih is associate professor of political science and director of the department of international relations at C. W. Post College, Long Island University.

Tschanguiz H. Pahlavan is a lecturer at Tehran University.

Philip Robins is senior fellow at St Antony's College and university lecturer in the politics of the Middle East at Oxford.

United States Institute of Peace

The United States Institute of Peace is an independent, nonpartisan federal institution created by Congress to promote research, education, and training on the peaceful resolution of international conflicts. Established in 1984, the Institute meets its congressional mandate through an array of programs, including research grants, fellowships, professional training programs, conferences and workshops, library services, publications, and other educational activities. The Institute's Board of Directors is appointed by the President of the United States and confirmed by the Senate.

Chairman of the Board: Chester A. Crocker
Vice Chairman: Max M. Kampelman
President: Richard H. Solomon
Executive Vice President: Harriet Hentges